Life Interrupted

Life Interrupted

Living the unimaginable, Huntington's disease patients and caregivers share their truth of strength, courage, and perseverance as they travel the rocky road of what has been called the worst disease known to mankind.

Edited by Sharon McClellan Thomason
Published by Help 4 HD International, Inc.

ISBN: 1511858257
ISBN 13: 9781511858250

Dedicated to all of our loved ones who have already lost their battle
with Huntington's disease and Juvenile Huntington's disease . . .

Fly, Angels, Fly

Huntington's Disease
By Ingrid Ward

I exist now within my own world
Time flows differently for me
I know daily torment, confusion, anger
Frustration within my mind and body

I can feel every part of my body
winding down, but I seem to have
no will or control to stop it
No one would understand the
despair I feel minute by minute

Different people speak with me
or at me, but I do not understand them
most of the time, nor can they understand me
I am never left alone now, constantly watched
much like a small child would be
that cannot care for itself

I take my pills; they make me sleepy
Only with sleep can I escape the
daily torment and unending rage
at my mind betraying me,
my body following

I don't remember my life very much anymore
They show me pictures, but I do not know
who is in them; they tell me I have a family,
but they are not here with me
A hospital room is now my home
Doctors, nurses, medical people
surround me daily

My world is shrinking more and more
I do not understand why
The doctors tell me I have Huntington's disease
I cannot remember what that is, or what it means
I want to go home, but I don't know where that is anymore

Minute by minute I exist, in my own tortured world
I am surrounded by people all day, all night,
but am very much alone now
Whatever this Huntington's disease is,
it is like a dark force closing in on me,
taking me away, I think forever
Wherever it takes me, it has to be
better than where I am now.......

About Ingrid Ward

Wife of Larry S. Minks and proud pet parent of Mimi, a gorgeous black rescue kitty, Ingrid Ward was born November 23, 1960, in Portland, Oregon. Larry developed symptoms of HD at age 48. Ingrid and Larry were best mates for 34 years until HD took him away. Ingrid loves photography and writing poetry and hopes to someday help many others who are in her situation. This is a way to honor her beloved Larry and to carry on his legacy. Given a choice, Ingrid says she would marry him all over again, even knowing that he would become afflicted with HD.

Table of Contents

Foreword

Life Interrupted
By Sharon McClellan Thomason

When Katie Jackson and Melissa Biliardi approached me with the idea for this book, I was so excited about the opportunity to share the truth of Huntington's disease with the world. After all, "Help4HD envisions a world where everyone knows what Huntington's disease and Juvenile Huntington's disease is; a world in which compassion is a normal response to the devastation that this horrific disease bestows on everyone. This can only be accomplished through positive education and advocacy efforts." What better opportunity to educate the world than by sharing the stories of people who have been affected by this horrific disease?

I just didn't know how hard it would be. Not "hard" as in time and effort, but emotionally hard. After editing each chapter, I felt completely drained, as if I had lived the story with the writer. The stories within these pages are raw and true. They are poignant and powerful. They are the stories of the folks who are bleeding in the trenches, living each day as best we can, hoping against hope that there will be an end to the suffering that is Huntington's. They are the stories of people who have Huntington's, and they are the stories of people who love and care for those with Huntington's. They are the stories of folks who never knew about this disease until it reared its ugly head, and they are the stories of folks who have lived with it for multiple generations.

Our book opens with a writer who shares the story of her three-year search for her birth family, only to discover that her birth family carries the gene for Huntington's. You will read the stories of women who have lost their children and who fear for future generations. You will read the stories of folks who have lost or are caring for their spouses, and some who are now caring for their children. You will read the stories of people who have lost their parents to Huntington's and had to look the dragon squarely in the face as they decided whether or not to test for the disease themselves. You will read the stories of folks who have turned their pain into advocacy, starting foundations, speaking at conferences, raising money for research. You will read about the physical, cognitive, and psychiatric effects of Huntington's, a disease that has been called "the worst disease known to mankind."

It is estimated that in the United States, one in 10,000 people (30,000 people) suffer from Huntington's, with another 250,000 at risk. Huntington's is a genetic neuropsychiatric disease, and each child of an affected parent has a 50/50 chance of inheriting the disease. Because of something called "anticipation," the onset of the disease frequently occurs earlier in each subsequent generation, especially with paternal transmission. It's an equal opportunity disease, affecting males and females, all ages, and all races. The disease kills the brain cells progressively over a period of 10-25 years, slowly robbing the individual of all abilities controlled by the brain. It is always fatal.

Those of us who live with this disease suspect that the prevalence is actually quite higher than reported. Some of the latest estimates are one in 7,000 in the U.S. In Scotland, there has been a 55 percent increase in cases of HD over the past three years. Many people have been misdiagnosed, and there has been a stigma attached to the disease that has kept families from talking about the illness. After all, it's often described as being like having ALS (Lou Gehrig's Disease), Parkinson's, Alzheimer's, and schizophrenia, *all at the same time.* Most doctors still will not diagnose the disease until *chorea,* the dance-like movements often associated with the disease, appears, and yet some people *never develop chorea.* There is still such a deplorable lack of knowledge about this disease, even within the medical community. It is a travesty, and we hope this book will help to change some of that.

Huntington's is a monster. It is a thief. It steals the dreams and interrupts the lives of those who fall victim to this genetic anomaly. Once someone hears that devastating diagnosis, the whole family travels a rocky road, straight into the storm, and there is no turning back.

Some names in the book have been changed to protect people who have or are at risk for Huntington's disease. Although the Affordable Care Act allows people with pre-existing conditions to get health insurance, and although we now have GINA (the Genetic Information Nondiscrimination Act), people with JHD and HD still fear discrimination—in the workplace, in care facilities, and in society at large. There is also fear of the stigma still attached to having Huntington's disease.

The people who have so courageously shared their stories within these pages are warriors, plain and simple. They fight the disease, they fight the stigma, they fight the medical establishment, they fight Social Security and other government programs, and they fight to advocate for themselves, for their loved ones, and for the HD community. They are fierce, and they are strong, though they will be the first to tell you that they are not really strong, that they are just doing what they have to do. One writer told me that writing her chapter was "healing" for her after years of grieving the tragic loss of her two children. Another shared with me that she broke down sobbing in the midst of writing her chapter and had to put it aside for a while before she could come back to it.

Two of our writers are from Mexico, where, in some rural areas, Huntington's is still looked at as a type of curse imposed by witchcraft. They face many of the same problems we face in the United States—lack of knowledge, lack of care facilities, lack of resources. We are fortunate to have their stories. For this, I owe Daniel Medina a debt of gratitude. Daniel is the International Affairs Director for Help 4 HD, and he spent a great deal of time helping me get the stories, even translating one of them from Spanish into English.

We are privileged to have an Afterword written by Jimmy Pollard. Jimmy is one of those rare souls who has put himself at the forefront of this battle although no one in his family has ever had or been at risk for Huntington's. He travels worldwide, meeting and working with JHD/HD families, gives presentations on the disease, and has written books about understanding and caring for the people with the disease. His love and compassion shine through. He's just that kind of guy, and I'm proud to call him my friend.

We are also so fortunate to have had our front and back covers designed by Randy Foster, husband of one of our writers. He took our ideas and created so professionally something that reflects exactly the mood we were after—and never lost patience with us when we changed our minds about the design!

I am also very grateful to my family—my mother, my cousin Elizabeth, and my son—who have been so supportive of me throughout the writing and editing process. They've put up with my absence, my distraction, and my obsession. They've listened to me talk endlessly about this project. They've even fed me when I wouldn't stop to fix supper!

At the end of each chapter, the writer includes a favorite researcher or organization to whom donations may be made. Please consider making a contribution to any of these as we join together to fight for a CURE! A list of all researchers, foundations, and clinics supported by Help 4 HD International, Inc. can be found at http://research4hd.org/index.html.

I am so humbled that the writers of these chapters trusted me to tell their stories of strength, perseverance, and courage in the best way possible. The stories are told in their voices, through their eyes. I was just privileged to edit them.

Sharon McClellan Thomason

About Lisa Davenport

Lisa Davenport was born in Fargo, North Dakota. She was adopted by a transient military family, moving almost every three years until her father retired in Connecticut. She grew up in a blended family with one adopted Panamanian sister and one brother born to her parents. After graduating high school, she joined the Army, serving 14 years, and received numerous commendations and medals for her achievements while serving her country. In the Army, she was hurt and retired to stay home to care for her four children. While doing so, she started searching for her biological family. Years after beginning her search, she found them and learned that they carried the fatal gene for Huntington's disease. She has authored three books and is currently working on her fourth book. She lives in North Carolina with her pack of four dogs and a cat.

CHAPTER 1

Through the Eyes of a Love Child
By Lisa Davenport

Something so deep inside me had been disturbing me for the last three years. It was like I was experiencing not only my own pain, but I could also feel a spirit presence of internal conflict from someone else that was haunting my own serenity. Somehow, I knew this presence was my birth mother and that she was fighting her own battles in life. This internal conflict kept tugging at me. I felt that it was my birth mother's own struggle, and I sensed that I was running out of time to find her. I dropped everything and everybody from my life. I knew I would have to work day and night on finding my birth mom myself.

It had been three years since I'd first contacted the adoption agency in Fargo, North Dakota. In those three years I would call them monthly for updates on their search for my birth mother. According to North Dakota adoption laws, I had to initiate my search through the agency that placed me for adoption and pay the agency $75 for non-disclosing information, which just gave me information about my nationality, birth weight, but nothing containing any information that would lead me to be able to know who my birth parents were. If I wanted the agency that placed me for adoption to search for my birth mother, I would then have to pay the adoption agency an additional $400 to initiate the search.

I paid what was required to initiate a search, and when I received absolutely no answer from the adoption agency, I hired private investigators. During that time I also would conduct my own search, send numerous letters for the adoption agency to forward, and suggest several different avenues to help both the private investigators and adoption agency. Neither agency was able to find any of my birth family. I knew that the feeling of impending doom would not go away till I found out what was happening to my birth mother, so I stopped assisting the two agencies I had hired and worked full time, day and night, taking a break only to sleep a couple of hours.

I remember like it was yesterday when I received my two pages of non-disclosing information from the adoption agency. When I received the envelope from the adoption agency, I remember looking at the postmark and being in awe that this envelope had come from the place where I was born. I carried the envelope like it was a thin piece of delicate, fine crystal that would shatter if not handled with care. Then the way I opened it, you would have thought that my birth mother was going to jump right out of it. I was trembling, for this was the first time I had ever known one single piece of history about myself. The letter from adoption agency was my non-disclosing information. It stated:

September 8, 2009
Dear Lisa,

Your birth mother was 17 years of age at the time of your birth. She stood 5 feet 3 inches tall, had dark-brown hair and a medium complexion. Your mother was of Norwegian, French, Native American and Black descent. The worker described her as a very pretty girl with a pleasant smile. She displayed a great deal of sensitivity and warmth for those with whom she came in contact. Your birth mother was in her junior year of high school. She had been working on her junior year credits through correspondence, but it is believed that she would re-enter school in the fall as a junior and fulfill her requirements at that time. Her ability was average to above average. During her freshman and sophomore years she was active in pep club, FHA activities and enjoyed sewing. Your birth mother indicated an interest in the nursing field and her desire to work in a hospital as a nurse's aide or as a nurse.

Your maternal birth grandfather was about 35 years of age at the time of your birth. He was of Norwegian descent and a member of the Baptist faith. He stood 6 feet tall and weighed 150 pounds. He had light brown hair, blue eyes, and a light complexion. Your birth mother was uncertain, but thought he had completed the eighth grade level of education. He had been employed as a mechanic. His health was good.

Your maternal birth grandmother was 36 years of age. She was of French, Native American and Black descent and of the Catholic faith. She stood 5 feet 4 inches tall and weighed approximately 150 pounds. She had black hair, brown eyes, and a medium complexion. She completed the eighth grade level of education and had worked as a waitress and a housekeeper where she also took care of a child. At the time of your birth she was working as a nurse's aide. She was in good health. Your grandparents were divorced.

Your birth mother was the oldest of four children in the family. A sister was 14 years of age and a freshman in high school at a boarding school. She was an average student in grade school, but was below average in high school. She stood 5 feet 8 inches tall and weighed 128 pounds. She had brown eyes, dark brown hair and a medium complexion. Another sister was age 7 and in second grade. She was tall and slender for her age with black hair, brown eyes and medium complexion. Your birth mother's youngest sister was age 3. She was tall for her age, had medium brown hair, brown eyes, and a light complexion. Your birth mother felt she was very intelligent for her age and talked grown-up. All siblings were in good health.

Your alleged birth father was 23 years of age. He was of Norwegian descent and a member of the Lutheran faith. He stood 5 feet 11 inches *tall, weighed 150 pounds, had dark brown hair, green eyes and a medium complexion. He was a high school graduate, attended two years of college, where he studied electronics, and one year of business school. At the time of your birth, he was helping his father farm. He was in good health.*

It went on to tell me about myself at birth and about my adoption. This two-page letter was like a gift from God himself. When I received it, I thought this would be the only information I would ever know about my family. I said to my husband, Brian, "I must have my father's green eyes, and I am the same height as my birth mom, and I have the medium complexion like everyone in my birth family. Brian, did you read the part about how she had a hard time making a decision to place me up for adoption and did you see how my mom referred to me as her child? She must have loved me." I then said out loud, "Mom, when I hold onto this letter, it is like a little girl holding onto her mother's hand for the first time."

Then I wrote on the envelope how old my mom, dad, each aunt, and grandparent would be on this day in 2009: my mother, 61; father, 67; aunt #1, 59; aunt #2, 51; aunt #3, 47; grandfather, 79; and my grandmother would be 80 years old. The information was not much to go on, but I was not going to give up, and had a bull dog tenacious attitude when I wanted to accomplish something.

I sat down and wrote in my journal: "My heart is filled with sorrow for the birth mother I never may know. After searching so long through the eyes of all suspected mothers and the endless waves of riding my own emotions, the anticipation and sorrow of yet another tomorrow without my mother, connected by some internal spirit force, I am amazed, that for someone unknown, I could feel so much. Maybe not today or tomorrow, but our paths will cross, and I will be able to meet you in not only spirit and soul, the mother who had to let go."

I had read about twenty books on adoption, adoption search and adoption reunion. I formulated my own search plan and made a search workbook in order to keep a log of everything I was doing. I kept copies of every letter I wrote and phone logs with details of every conversation I had. I created flow charts to keep track of my progress and also to see if any leads I dug up matched anything else on my charts.

If there was a clue under a rock, I was going to find it. I started by looking at old newspapers for every birth in Fargo in February 1965; then I would spend some time looking through high school yearbooks, trying to see if any girls showed up missing from their junior year at high school, the year my mother would have given birth to me. I even tried to look at college records of anyone that might have the same credentials and description as my birth father. I found that the hospital I was born in had been converted into a drug and alcohol rehab, and the doctor who'd delivered me was deceased and buried, along with all his records. Every avenue I checked had a road block, and every call I made, I learned not to say the "A" word. Anytime I mentioned I was an adoptee, I was told they could not disclose anything.

I sent off for my birth certificate from the North Dakota Department of Vital Statistics in hopes that they may just make a mistake and send me the right birth certificate. I even tried to get a copy of my birth certificate sent to me under my birth name, Dawn Marie, and then tried again with Dawn Mary. Each time, I would receive just an amended copy with my adopted name. I knew from my non-disclosing information that I was Native American, so I even contacted the Bureau of Indian Affairs of the United States Department of Interior to try to claim my right of inheritance for tribal affiliation protected by my birth right as a Native American. I talked to every bureaucrat at the Indian Bureau of Affairs, all the way down to the regional Indian Affairs for the Great Plains Region, and got nowhere.

I bounced right back to the drawing board. I looked at my baby book for clues and re-interviewed my adoptive mom, trying to jar her memory for something she may have forgotten. My mother told me that she and my father had hired a lawyer, and that he'd had to publish in the local paper an ad terminating my birth mother's parental rights. That led me right back to looking at old newspapers, and I even tried to look at old court dockets to find clues to a name.

I drafted a letter to the Social Security Department's Location Services Department in Baltimore, Maryland. (They will send a letter to the party being sought, explaining that someone is trying to locate them and that they are under no obligation to respond to the letter.) I looked through old micro-fiche newspapers for legal notices for Petitions to Adopt. I knew, because I'd become well-versed in North Dakota adoption laws, that they had to come out a month or two prior to the final order of my adoption. There was nothing to be found, though, and if I did not pinch myself occasionally, I would feel like I had never been born because of all the dead end paper trails.

I wrote a letter for my adoptive mom to have her request my full transcript from the adoption agency—the entire agency file they had on my adoption, not just the two pieces of non-disclosing information they'd sent me. While I waited for that file, I wrote a letter to the North Dakota Department of Motor Vehicles. I knew that some DMVs offered forwarding service to assist in contacting individuals. If I could just get a single name, I would be able to track everyone down. In the meantime, I also drafted a letter for the adoption agency to place in my record on a whim that my birth family might just be trying to locate me. I signed a waiver of confidentiality, so if my birth family was to try to contact me, that would be in my adoption file.

I knew that most adoptees' amended birth certificates had the same number as the original birth certificate, so I cross referenced my amended birth certificate number with all the North Dakota birth indexes from 1965. I then located all the local Fargo churches and called all the church secretaries and asked them to look at the church ledgers for the week I was born and to give me the names of the babies that were baptized. I could not tell them I was adopted. I would tell them that I was doing genealogical research.

I knew I was getting nowhere fast, but I felt, in my gut, like I was just so close to something. Every day I felt my birth mother's pain. I knew that I could not give up, no matter how frustrating this process was; after all, this process was all part of my journey. This was not a game for me; this was becoming way more personal. I would not only be doing my own search effort; now I was also involved in several adoption groups, advocating for adoptee and birth family rights. I started to do public speaking to bring awareness of the injustice of being denied your own original birth certificate, something to which even a convicted felon has rights.

Through joining different adoption groups and advocating for adoption reform, I met a lady named Candi who worked as an intermediary for adoption reunions out of Colorado. Candi and I shared a passion for changing the procedure for adoptions and reunions. I told Candi about all my efforts to search and all about the adoption agency's lack of effort. I told her that the lady at the adoption agency was also going to a conference that Candi planned to attend. The conference was to be geared towards adoption reunion and the Indian Child Welfare Act, two key elements in my search. Candi met with the Fargo adoption agency lady and lit a fire under her ass. By the end of the conference, I had my first lead in three years.

On April 12, 2010, I received another letter in response to a ten-page letter I had written to the adoption agency. Finally, with a lot of direction, the adoption agency had started to look for other family members. I had suggested to them that they look for male relatives because female relatives change their names and are more difficult to find. They wrote to me and said they were able to locate one brother but were unable to find a phone number for him. When they looked for my grandfather, as I had suggested they do, they found out that he was deceased. Bingo! That was the lead I needed to send me sniffing like a bloodhound in the right direction.

Something as simple as obtaining a copy of an obituary was screwed up by the adoption agency and would slow me down again while waiting for them to send off for the right obituary. Their lack of efficiency was very frustrating to me. I knew that if they could only get hold of the right obituary, I would be able to conduct an interrogation of the adoption agency, which would lead me to find more clues to fit the pieces of this family puzzle together.

At a certain point, I realized I could be as sweet as pie with the lady from the adoption agency, whom I secretly called The Rock, and that would not get me any closer to finding my birth mom. From the gut feeling I had, I knew game time was over. I was running out of time. I had to apply pressure like never before to find my birth mother. Candi had lit the fire under the adoption agency, but I was about to pour gasoline on their fire. I had waited long enough for The Rock to obtain my grandfather's obituary. I had finally made contact with a social worker, Jodi, who worked in Washington for the Bureau of Indian Affairs. Jodi worked primarily with the Indian Child Welfare Act of 1978, and was very helpful in explaining to me my rights. She made it very clear that because I was born before 1978, the Indian Child Welfare Act did not apply to my circumstances, but she would fill my ear with enough ammunition to fire right back at the adoption agency.

My next call would be not to The Rock, but to an attorney who specialized in the United States Constitution and also the Freedom of Information Act and the Privacy Act of 1974. I spent an hour talking to him, picking his brain and taking notes like a court reporter. After my conversation with this attorney, I spent another week familiarizing myself with not only the U.S. Constitutional law, but also with the Freedom of Information and Privacy laws. Like most people, I had no idea how to use these laws for my own purpose. Just as I'd done in my earlier years of searching, when I felt like I was studying to take the bar to become a lawyer, once again I was hitting the law library to prepare for my final hurrah with the adoption agency.

I called the adoption agency the first week of November 2011, this time asking to speak to the director. By the time I was done educating the director on the laws of the land, I felt that the director herself would apply enough pressure to light a tower of inferno under The Rock's butt.

Within a week, I received a letter from the adoption agency, stating that they had finally received my grandfather's obituary, but it had only listed the first names of my mother and her sisters. But what The Rock gave me in the letter was enough to put some more pieces of the puzzle together. From the information I had received three years earlier, I knew that my grandfather was 35 years old when I was born. The letter said he had died in 1999, in a nursing home. After doing the math, I figured I would be looking for a man who died at 69 years of age in 1999, somewhere in North Dakota. The obituary also said he enjoyed hunting and fishing and had a love for dogs. He worked as a farm hand and a mechanic and also had worked in the mines. He had six daughters and four sons.

By law, they could not send me the obituary, but this was enough information to go on. I was sure if I started looking at the major metro newspapers for the obituaries in 1999, I could find his name and find everyone else from there. I was back to the drawing board, looking at obituary after obituary. I continued my assault of letters to The Rock and found out that I had an uncle and a nephew who had been incarcerated. I asked The Rock one day, "Oh, by the way, you said the North Dakota prison, right?" I was playing dumb because she had never said that, but she replied, "Yes." One more piece to my puzzle. By confirming that at least three family members had lived in North Dakota, I knew I would more than likely find my mother there.

I wrote letters for The Rock to send to every tribe I could locate in North Dakota. After much correspondence back and forth, one of the ladies from the conference in Colorado received one of my letters and called the adoption agency and told them they had an address for my birth mom.

My contact at the adoption agency sent out a certified letter to the address provided by the tribal leader for my birth mother. It was the first week of February 2012, and I had waited patiently long enough. In my gut, I felt that I had run out of time, even though my birth mom would only be 62 if I would find her today. I did not know what this horrible gut feeling was. I thought maybe it was my own insecurities of possibly being rejected a second time if I found her. All the "what ifs" would haunt me till the adoption agency received the confirmation of receipt of the letter they'd sent.

On February 23, 2012, the adoption agency wrote the following letter:

Hi, a bit of discouraging news—just received the letter back and the post office says address unknown. So I am going to contact a priest in that town or someone who can drive there and see if this is a valid address. In the meantime, since I now have a married name (or at least I hope it is still her married name), I used one of our search programs and got two phone numbers for her BUT both have been disconnected when I called. There was an address, though, in another town, so I am going to write there while I wait for the other address to be verified. We will keep at this.

Yes, I thought; I would keep this up, even though I was emotionally trashed from the ups and downs of this journey.

My birthday had been on the 13th of February, and I had so hoped that I would be gifted with a phone call saying, "We found your birth mom." It had been four days since the priest was supposed to stroll by the unverifiable address. I had taken a couple of days off to recoup from finding out that the receipt for the certified letter had been returned without a signature. It was the end of February, but for Wilmington, North Carolina, where I live, that meant spring and warmer weather.

Through my long hours of searching for my birth family, I still kept up with all my house chores and hiking with my dog Buddy. Being outside hiking was the only way for me to find internal peace. I was heading out the door for some much needed solace when the phone rang. My heart stopped beating, and I froze. The caller ID showed the name of the adoption agency. They never called me. I was the one always calling them and initiating all the correspondence with them. I knew what that phone call was before I even answered it.

"Lisa, this is Sherry from the adoption agency. Are you alone, or is there someone with you?" I knew something awful was coming next, so I called to Brian, "The adoption agency is on the phone, Brian. Come here now!"

"Sherry, what is it?" I said.

Sherry then said to me, "Lisa, the priest confirmed your mom's address, and it was a nursing home." From her tone, I knew something else was to follow. The case worker then said to me, "Lisa, the priest went in and asked to see your mother, and the nurses informed him that she had passed away, and, are you sitting down?" By that time my knees had buckled, and I was, in fact, sitting at that point, and sobbing. "Lisa, there's more that I need to tell you. Your mother died of a genetic neurological brain disease called Huntington's. You really need to look into this medical problem," said Sherry.

I then said through my sobs, "I don't care why she died; I was looking for her, not her medical history. I wanted to give her a hug and tell her I loved her. I don't care about some disease she had."

Sherry then said, "Lisa, I can see how upsetting this is. Please, when you calm down and find the time, look into this Huntington's disease."

I hung up the phone from the last conversation I would ever have with the adoption agency.

Any other person might have thrown in the towel and conceded that the search was in fact through, but not me. I had a burning desire to just find anyone that might have known my mother. I wanted someone to just describe her to me, or if I could find someone who knew her, maybe they would even have a picture of her. My birth mother was deceased, but because my adoption was closed, the adoption agency would not disclose any information about any other relative. While talking with the adoption agency for the last time, I did write down my mother's name, and hoped that would be enough for me to find someone that might have known her. Only one day had passed when I received the following letter from the adoption agency:

> *Dear Lisa,*
>
> *This is a follow-up to our phone conversation of today. Again, I was sorry to have to report to you that your birth mother had passed away. Her name was Dina Marie Travers. In some places I saw Dina spelled with one n and in other places it was spelled with two ns. She was born in Bottineau, NC, on 1-18-1948. She was in Trinity Lutheran Nursing home in Minot, ND, when she died on 11-27-2010. As I mentioned, she had Huntington's disease and dementia at the time of her death. She had been in the nursing home since 2006. She was a member of the Turtle Mountain Band of Chippewa Indians. I am enclosing your footprint card from the hospital and also your Certificate of Baptism. I have written the funeral home to see if I can get any information from them, and I have also written for a copy of the death certificate. I will be back in touch when I hear from them.*

I read the letter out loud again to Brian and said, "Maybe I should look up Huntington's disease on the internet." As we both sat in the living room, I looked it up on the internet and read out loud,

Huntington's disease is an inherited brain disorder that results in the progressive loss of both mental faculties and physical control. Symptoms usually appear between the ages of 30 to 50, and worsen over a 10 to 25 year period. Ultimately, the weakened individual succumbs to pneumonia, heart failure or other complications. Everyone has the HD gene, but it is those individuals that inherit the expansion of the gene who will develop HD and perhaps pass it on to each of their children. Presently there is no cure. Research has yet to find a means of slowing the deadly progression of Huntington's disease. Symptoms include personality changes, mood swings, depression, forgetfulness, impaired judgment, unsteady gait, involuntary movements, slurred speech and difficulty swallowing.

Brian and I looked at each other, and I said, "Holy shit!" We both agreed that there was no way I had this genetic disease, and I said to Brian, "Did I read that right? Did it say no cure and that each kid has a possibility of having this passed on to them?"

Brian said, "Read it again."

I reread it out loud to Brian, and then I read it again to myself and said to Brian, "I am calling my mom!" My mom is a nurse by trade, but I think she knows more about the medical field than most doctors.

"Mom, you aren't going to believe this! My birth mom died of Huntington's, and I think I just read that it is passed on through genetics. What do you know about this?"

My mom was dead silent for a moment, lost for words, which my mother never is, and then finally she said, "Now, if you had told me about this when you first got out of the Army and moved to Texas, I would have said I believed it, but not now; you are so much better now. I don't think you have it. Besides, I think you would have shown signs of this at your age. Did the adoption agency know about this?"

I answered my mom with the only answer I had, "Yes, they told me about it." After much discussion with my mom and Brian, we all came to the same determination: I must not have this incurable genetic brain disease. I put that thought on the back burner to simmer while I cooked up some more leads to find anyone that might have known my mom.

The next four days I burned the candle at both ends, trying to research my mother and every person that shared the many places she had lived. I compiled a huge list with names that kept showing up in places she had lived. I made lists of people who shared some of her addresses, and then I found her marriage certificate on the internet. The case worker intimated that my mother had no more children, but there were two names that kept coming up with my birth mom's: the Devens family and Lucy Lene.

I was able to locate Lucy Lene and suspected that she was my mom's oldest sister, but every time I tried to call her, I would get a disconnected number or wrong number and address. I even called quite a few Lenes who had no idea who she was, so I put her and her name on hold and tried to work the marriage certificate angle to see if I could find my birth mom's groom, Tim Travers. I didn't think this would be a good lead because Tim was 36 years plus my mother's age when they married, which would mean the chances of finding a 93-year-old man were not very promising. It was very difficult to find women, though, because of their name changes, so I gave it a shot and tried to locate Tim Travers.

It only took one night of research to locate his last address. I went back to my birth mom's previous addresses for the last fifteen years of her life and went through all the names of everyone living during that time in the same buildings. My birth mom had lived in several apartments, so cross referencing people was not an easy task.

Occasionally, I would write down names that kept popping up, like the Devens family and a lady named Sally. Through studying the charts I had made and data bases I had created of possible relatives, I surmised that my mother had spent time moving between California, North Dakota, eventually married in Arizona, and had finally landed in Utah. It seemed that she was always in transit, moving from place to place.

As soon as I narrowed her location down to just the states she'd lived in, it made it easier for me to just call directory assistance for each state on my list. I started with California and North Dakota, because my birth mom had lived mostly in those two states, and I figured I might just find her ex-husband, Tim, there. I did not expect to find Tim living, so I had prepared a statement for a potential relative that just might have known Tim Travers and my birth mother.

California and North Dakota had no listings for any Tim Travers, so I moved on to Arizona and Utah. Arizona had no Tim Travers in their directory. I was starting to lose a little faith in finding a live, 93-year-old man, or even finding someone who may have known Tim or my birth mother.

Utah was the last state I called, and when I dialed directory assistance, I did so halfheartedly, anticipating another, "No, Miss, I have no listing for Tim Travers." It was getting late, and my frustration level was at its peak, but I figured I would make this last call before retiring from my search for the night.

The phone buzzed in my ear, like I was actually calling someone from directory assistance from back in the old days, when you would get a living, breathing person, not just some computerized recording. "Hello, this is Utah, the operator; how may I direct your call?" said an older lady on the other end of the phone. I was so shocked that a live person had answered that I stumbled with my words.

After regaining my composure, I was able to say, "Tim Travers' phone number, please," and that was all I would say. The operator rattled off a number, and I scribbled it down and hung up. In my haste to hang up, I had forgotten to listen to whether she was giving me the number for Tim Travers, or a Travers in Utah. I was beyond exhausted and would just call the number tomorrow.

My sleep had been seriously disrupted by all the ups and downs of my search, and tonight was no different. I had learned how to function with sleep deprivation in the Army and had used it to my benefit while bringing up my children, and also had applied it to my searching. I was now sleeping only two hours a night and could not stop thinking about how to find my next clue. As I lay there in my bed, I role played different scenarios of the conversation I would have when I called Travers' number.

After much tossing and turning, I got up at first sign of daylight. I wrote a couple of scripts for calling this unknown Travers. I concentrated more on writing a script for the scenario of reaching a relative of Tim's on the phone, and not so much on talking to my birth mother's ex-husband.

It was already 8:00 a.m. I was ready to make my call to Travers and did so, forgetting that there was in fact a three-hour time zone difference between North Carolina and Utah. Too late, the phone was ringing, and a man picked up and said, "Hello, can I help you?" This person that I had reached sounded very military like, and was obviously not upset by the fact someone had just called him at o-dark-thirty!

"My name is Lisa Davenport, and I am looking for Tim Travers or anyone that may have known him," I said.

The gentleman on the other end of the phone was quick and sharp in his reply and said, "Known him? I am Tim Travers. What can I do for you?" I was not so quick with my response, and almost fell out of my chair with the realization that I had found the right Tim Travers, very much alive and sharp as a whistle.

All scripts were out the window now, and I would wing it from here on out. I said, "Tim, I understand that you were married to my mother, Dina Marie Travers. My mother Dina had placed me up for adoption in 1965, and I have been trying to locate anyone that might be able to tell me something about her."

Tim then said quickly, "I have a meeting in town today; you can call me back between the hours of 3:00 and 6:00 p.m. I will not answer after that because I retire for the day. I am on my way now, and do not like to be late. Good day," and hung up the phone.

Not only was Tim alive at 93, but he was really with it. My mind was running wild with anticipation of all the things Tim would tell me about my birth mother. I thought that surely he must still have some pictures of her!

Like a reporter trying to dig up a bestselling story for her newspaper, I started writing all the questions I thought Tim just might have the answers to. Maybe Tim and my mother had had children together, and maybe I would have a half-sister. I thought maybe Tim would know how to reach any living relatives of my birth mom. As my mind drifted to all the possibilities that might exist with this call, I fell asleep in my office chair, as I had not had slept peacefully in quite a while. I knew from looking Tim up on the internet that he was a World War II decorated veteran. When he directed me the times to call him, I knew he meant business. I knew that I was not to call a minute early or a minute late.

As I drifted back awake from my sleep, I jumped, like I used to when the alarm would go off and I thought I was late for first formation in the Army. "Holy Crap!" I said out loud. I had slept in my chair till 2:15 p.m., and I had to call Tim now if I was not going to be late.

"Hello, Tim, this is Lisa Davenport calling again. I am Dina's daughter, the one that called earlier today. Tim, I never got to meet my mother before she passed away, and I was hoping you had some old photos of her and maybe you could share something about what she was like."

Tim replied, "Yes, I received a call from her mother that she had died. I never got to call her mother back to relay my condolences. I lost the number and have forgotten her name. The answering machine message has long been erased."

I then told Tim, trying to build some form of rapport with him, "Tim, I have not located any of Dina's family, but if I do, I will certainly pass it on that you would like to call them, if that is what you would like."

"Yes, indeed," Tim replied.

I asked him if he had any photos of my mom, and he said no. Then I asked him what she was like.

Tim said, "Dina was a good cook, kept a clean house, and was good at gardening. She loved animals and brought many of them home from the Kanab rescue she volunteered at. I have to hang up now; you can call me back tomorrow before 9:00 a.m. and not after 10:00 a.m. I have several appointments to attend to," and he hung up.

I felt that Tim was not being forthcoming about something, so I decided to do a police record check on my own birth mother, something I knew how to do from all the training on background checks I'd received during my years in the Army. What I would find on her police record would send most curious people running. Curiosity killed the cat, but this cat, being me, was not fazed by what I found. It was obvious to me, from her police record, that my birth mother had a problem with alcohol. She had been arrested several times for DWI and driving under a suspended license. There were charges of petty theft and writing bad checks, which I thought might be to support her alcohol habit. My birth mother even spent a year in jail for an alcohol-related incident that involved one too many arrests for DWI and driving with no insurance, without a license or registration.

Now I had done my homework and knew why Tim Travers was holding back on his knowledge of what my birth mom was like. During my next call, I would be sure to bring up the fact that I knew my mother had had a problem with drinking, and just maybe Tim would feel more at ease with sharing with me.

I would not be intimidated by my mother's alcohol abuse, because I had grown up with a father and brother that were also alcoholics. I had also married three times, and all three of my husbands had had some form of substance abuse problem. I loved my father, brother, and Brian, but I did not like their actions and behaviors while under the influence of their substances of choice. I also knew that, like diabetes, alcoholism was a disease, and that most people who abused substances were in fact self-medicating to cover some of life's past hurt.

If there was anything I felt towards my birth mother and her life circumstances, it was compassion. I knew, from feeling my mother's pain off and on throughout my life, she'd had a rough life. That is why I'd felt the urgent need to stop at nothing, to find her, to give her a hug and profess my unconditional love for her.

It was time to make my call to Tim, who'd married Dina in 1984. I was hoping Tim would have more time to discuss her. I knew that I would have to be more direct in my questions to him. He wasn't one that was into talking about feelings; he was one to just stick to the facts. So the facts and direct questioning was the protocol I stuck with.

"Hello, Tim, this is Lisa again, calling during the time you stated. Tim, I know my mother had a difficult life and that she drank too much some times," and before I could finish, Tim interjected with, "I should have never had liquor in the bar at home. I had no idea she was an alcoholic."

"Tim, it certainly was not your fault that my mother drank," and once again Tim interrupted, saying, "I probably should not have left her alone all the time while I went to the town meetings."

I said, "Tim, it was not your fault, and she would have drunk no matter what you did; alcoholics just do that. Tim, did you happen to remember the name of Dina's mother?"

"No," Tim said.

What Tim would tell me next would open the flood gates to my search, without Tim even knowing what he had said.

"Tim, did you and my mother have any children together?"

Tim said, "No," and then paused for a moment, like he was digging back to the depths of time in his old, but sharp mind, and then he said,

"There was a child. When we moved to Utah, your mother and I decided we had better get married, because the child would have to go to Mormon school."

I tried to maintain my composure and not assault him with an onslaught of questions. I asked, "Was this child a boy or girl?"

Tim replied, not offering me any more information than what he said next, "It was a girl."

Calmly, I asked Tim, "Was it my mother's daughter?"

Tim replied, "The child was young, and I cannot remember the relationship and whether or not it was her child."

That was all Tim remembered. After I hung up, I drafted a thank you note and added a picture of myself, in hopes that looking at a picture of me would rattle some more information from him. Even though I was not sure that the girl Tim spoke about was a sister, or even related to me, any clue at this point was a good clue. The possibility of having a sister made me all the more determined to work even harder to find answers.

It was still early in the day. As mandated by Tim, our conversation time was over by 10:00 a.m. This would give me a whole day to work on finding this mystery child that Tim spoke of. I knew that my birth mother's maiden name was Beckman, so I wanted to search for a while on the internet to see if I could find any of her siblings first, before embarking on a search for some mystery child that I was not even sure was related to me.

I was pretty sure Lucy Lene was my mom's sister, but she disappeared off the grid, like most women in my search had, so I started my search with the men in the Beckman family. I knew from the adoption agency that I had an uncle and a nephew that were in jail. I knew that jail records were public records, so I figured I would start there.

Brian was awake by now and working on his computer in his office, which is attached to my office. For the next few hours, I would find a relative through my search on the computer and I would shout through the wall to Brian, "Brian, I found another one! Oh, wait. They're dead." I found that every relative I was able to locate was also listed on the Social Security death index. This was spookier and more unnerving to me than the fact that I had relatives in jail. I finally said to Brian, "I have to take a break from this. Every time I get excited about finding someone, they come with a death certificate."

I switched gears and was back on the road to finding the mystery child. While compiling my information on charts of people that shared the same address as my birth mother, I recalled the two names that kept showing up. Yolanda Devens and Sally Devens were the only female names that might belong to the mystery child. Both of them had lived in California around the same time my mother did, at the same address. I searched for Yolanda first, but found that she was much too old to be my younger sibling.

I thought Yolanda was probably Sally's mother. It was a long shot, but I searched for the last female on my chart, Sally Devens. I screamed to Brian through the wall, "Brian, I found my sister! Sally is my sister! It says right here on her birth certificate that her mother is Dina Marie Devens!"

After we both calmed down, I noticed that there was one more record available to open online. I clicked my mouse to open the file, my heart dropped, and my head crashed down on my desk. I looked up at my husband and said, "What the hell is going on here? Everyone is dead!" The file I had opened with a click of my mouse was Sally Devens' death certificate. She was born in 1972, only 31 years old at the time of her death in 2003.

I needed to go for a very long walk to clear my head. How could I have come this far, only to find that most of my relations came with a death certificate? I was really starting to believe that I would find no one that knew anything about my birth mother. As I was walking and clearing my mind of all the gloom and doom, I recalled that one of the letters from the adoption agency mentioned that my birth mom had lived at the Trinity Lutheran Nursing Home in Minot, North Dakota. I double timed it back to my house so I could call that nursing home.

"Hello, my name is Lisa," I said to the person who answered. "I am Dina Marie Travers's daughter. She was a patient in your facility and died while I was away serving my country in the Army. Can you please tell me who handled her funeral arrangements?"

"Let me pull up her file for you. Can you please hold a minute?"

I thought I'd pulled this off without telling too much of a white lie.

"Hello, Lisa, all I have listed is a lady named Debra Scott, and that is the only information I can release to you."

"Thank you very much. Have a nice day," I said, and I hung up the phone.

I said out loud, "What the heck? Now I have a Beckman, Travers, Devens, and now a Scott."

Each time I found a branch of my family tree, it would snap in half, never branching out anywhere. My patience was running on empty, and I was on the verge of waving my white flag of surrender and defeat.

I could not stop thinking of my little sister, Sally, and how young she was, and then out loud, I said, "Sally was too young to be that little girl in Utah, with Tim and my birth mom!" I grabbed my calculator and did the math. Sally was definitely too young to be the girl Tim Travers had spoken about. I yelled to Brian, "Brian, I have another sister!"

"That's nice. Is she living?" Brian said.

"I don't even know her name," I replied, "but I know I have one because Sally was too dang young to be in Utah with Tim and my birth mom."

"Let me know when you find a live one," Brian said.

It had only been three days since finding out my birth mother's name and that she had passed away, but my gut feeling told me to drive on, that I was just about to find someone who knew my mother.

I remembered that Debra Scott was the one the nursing home had listed as the person handling my mother's funeral. I thought maybe she was an administrator, or maybe she was related to my birth mom, too. Either way, she would probably know something about my mom. So just like I found Tim Travers, I would go through the process of elimination to try to come up with one state in which to locate Debra Scott. I knew the first states I would try would be Utah, Arizona, North Dakota, and then California.

Utah had absolutely no Debra Scotts in the entire state, so that was easy; then Arizona had 273 D. Scotts and Debra Scotts in different variations. None that I called would be the Debra Scott I was looking for. After calling the 273 Scotts in Arizona, I moved on to North Dakota. Luckily, there were just a few hundred calls to weed through, none of which was the Debra Scott I was looking for. There was only California left to call to track down the real Debra Scott. I saved the hardest for last, having made literally thousands of calls up to this point.

It was extremely late, and I had been at this for four days straight without sleep. I said to my husband, "This is stupid. I am going to make this last call, and we are going to bed. I don't care if it is only 9:00 p.m." I dialed the number and got an answering machine, so I left the following message: "Hello, my name is Lisa Davenport. You don't know me, but I think you handled my mother's funeral, and we may even be sisters." I hung up and walked like a dog with my tail between my legs and went to bed to sulk. I was through, and I didn't want to make another call.

Brian and I were lying in bed just looking at each other like we had both been to hell and back, when the phone rang once. Just as I was getting up to answer it, the caller hung up. Then the phone rang again, and again they hung up. This was really pissing me off, and I was in no mood for crank calls, so when the phone rang again, I jumped up and said, "What the fuck!" I never use that kind of language, so my reaction caught me off guard, and I knew I must be beyond exhausted from all the searching.

Whoever it was, they were now leaving a long, drawn-out message on my answering machine, so I jumped up to give them a piece of my mind before they hung up again. I ran to the living room, picked up the phone, and said, "Who is this?"

I was walking back into my bedroom when the lady said to me, "Hello, my name is Lisa, and I am your sister."

I was totally confused now because I was not looking for a Lisa; I was looking for a Debra. I said, "No, you must be mistaken. I think my sister's name is Debra, not Lisa. That's my name."

Then, before I could say any more, the lady said, "Debra is my sister, and we both are your sisters."

After a brief pause, I said, "You both are my sisters?"

And then Lisa said, "Debra is my sister, and we all are sisters; we all have the same mom!"

Before I started jumping on my bed like a joyful child, I asked Lisa, "What about Sally Devens? Is she your sister, too?"

Then Lisa said, "Debra, Sally, and I are all your sisters. Our mom gave you up for adoption."

All my hard work had paid off, and I was actually talking to my sister! I screamed to Brian with excitement, "Brian, I have two sisters, and they are both living! This is my sister Lisa on the phone, and she is Debra's sister, my sister, too, and Sally was also my sister!" By now, I was jumping on the bed, breaking the sound barrier and the laws of gravity with my excitement.

I was in total shock that I was talking to my sister and that she and Debra might be able to tell me more about my birth mom, our mom. In just four days after receiving my mother's name, I was able to locate all my sisters and quite a few deceased relatives. I was happy that I had managed to do this, but I also was pissed and had some unfinished business to attend to with the adoption agency and their neglect in not finding my birth family.

I talked to Lisa for four hours and then talked to Debra till the following morning. Both of them said that after my call to Debra, they looked me up on the adoption registries, and both of them pulled me up on Facebook. Debra and Lisa kept telling me over and over how I looked like my mother.

Lisa posted a picture of my mother on Facebook, and for the first time ever, I looked at my birth mother.

Debra and Lisa shared with me the names of other family members and birthdates and, most importantly, addresses and phone numbers. I wrote down everything they were telling me. With all the thousands of calls I'd made, I was afraid that each time I would get through to someone; it might be my only opportunity to talk to them. I felt after my lengthy conversation with each newly found sister that we all were full of questions and curiosity, all trying to catch each other up to the present after a lifetime apart.

On March 3, 2012, I wrote the adoption agency one last time, telling them I'd found my birth family and adding, "I hope someday that there will be some method of accountability for birth families and agencies to have a reporting system in place for medical conditions such as Huntington's disease. The current adoption system is very broken, and I plan on doing everything in my power to advocate for legislation to be passed to stop this kind of negligence conducted by your adoption agency."

For the next few months Debra, Lisa and I would talk on the phone with each other a couple of times a week. Debra and Lisa both lived in California, and I was still living in North Carolina. I wanted to jump on a plane the very next day to meet them, but I knew that I would have to give them both time to digest everything, and also I wanted to get to know them as they wanted to also get to know me.

They both told me stories of Sally, my sister that had died, and each sister's recollection of her was quite different. Lisa and Debra were not only different in personalities; they also had different perceptions, and they viewed differently how things had happened in our family.

There was one thing that was the same with Lisa and Debra: neither had too much to say about our mother or her family in North Dakota that I had yet to call. I know families are complicated, even under the best of circumstances, but this was too strange for me to grasp, their lack of knowledge of the entire side of my mother's family tree.

Through Lisa I would learn the names of my maternal grandmother and three aunts. I also would learn that she did not know if my 84-year-old grandmother was alive or not, and neither one had current addresses or phone numbers for our mother's side of the family.

Debra was divorced and had only one son, Mitch. Debra told me about her life as a single parent and also about her work. She had just retired the day I called, because she also, like Sally, had inherited the genetic disease Huntington's. Debra was ecstatic about the forming of a new relationship and being replaced as the oldest sister, for I now held the title of oldest sibling.

Lisa would share her story of how she took care of Sally during her first years of marriage to her husband, Alex. I could tell by the inflection in her voice that it was traumatic to undertake such a task, and even harder for her to watch her younger sister die. Lisa and Alex had tried several times to have children, always ending with miscarriages. They ended up adopting two Indian babies, one named Danny and one named Roger. Danny and Roger both were six at the time I found them. Lisa was a very busy mom with a hectic schedule. Lisa shared with me that she, too, had also just retired from nursing because of having Huntington's disease.

During my conversation, I would learn that my mother had married Vic Devens, Debra, Lisa and Sally's father, after she had placed me up for adoption. He was in the Air Force when he and our mother met in North Dakota. Debra would tell me that Yolanda Devens was, "Our evil step-monster." Another piece to the puzzle fell into place. Vic and our mother had divorced, and he had married Yolanda. It's a wonder with all these name changes, marriages, and divorces, that I was able to find anyone at all.

In between all my calls to my California sisters, I was able to track my mother's mom, my grandma Martha Olsen. Martha had just relocated from Minot, North Dakota, to Bismarck, North Dakota, so finding her was not too difficult. Lisa, my sister, had Martha's last known address and phone number. I used that to locate Martha's new address and phone number and decided I would initiate my first call to my mother's side of the family.

I dialed the phone number for the Martha Olsen I thought was my grandmother. Every time I had to make contact with a newly found family member, it was extremely anxiety evoking, to say the least. I was not only anxious about the possibilities of forming a new relationship, but also I had to anticipate the reality of possibly being rejected by the family member. With every call I made, I felt rushed to explain in a tactful manner who I was and the purpose of my call. I would take scrupulous notes, for fear of not getting another opportunity to talk to the person again.

A very old sounding man picked up, and I said, "Can I please speak with Martha Olsen?" The older man wasted no time screaming for Martha and also into the phone receiver, making me pull the phone away from my ear. When I put my ear back to the phone, I heard an older lady say, "Ed, there is no one here on the phone," and before she could hang up on me, I yelled back into the receiver, "Martha, I am here! Don't hang up!"

"Hello, who is this?" Martha said.

"Martha, I am Lisa Davenport, and I am looking for Dina Marie Travers's mother," I said real fast. Martha said, "Dina is gone; she passed away."

I said, "I know, Martha. I am looking for you. You are Dina's mother, right?"

"Why, yes, I am. Who is this now?" Martha said, sounding confused.

"Martha, I was given your name by Debra and Lisa," I said. "They both are my sisters, and you are my grandmother," and before I could finish, Martha said, "Lisa, I have not talked to you in years. How are your boys Danny and Roger, and how is Alex doing?"

It was obvious that my grandmother was very sharp for her age, but she had confused me with Lisa Haynes, my sister, so I had to reiterate that I was another daughter of Dina's named Lisa, too.

"Grandma Martha, I have been looking for you a very long time. I am the baby girl that your daughter Dina gave up for adoption. My name was changed to Lisa. I have been in contact with both my sisters in California, Lisa and Debra. I am Lisa Davenport, the child my mom, Dina, gave up, and I finally found you."

There was dead silence on the phone, and I didn't know if Martha was going to hang up or not. Then Martha said, "You found us, and you know that we have black in us?"

I said, "Yes, Grandma, I know about that, and I also know that just like me, we are both a lot of things."

There was another pause, and then Grandma Martha said to me, "You know that your mother died in a nursing home from Huntington's disease?"

"Yes, Martha, I know that, too," I said.

There are always two sides to a story, but this family story had several layers of sides. From all my conversations with Debra and Lisa and now Grandma Martha, I would piece together enough from each person's stories to paint my own picture of this fragmented family.

Grandmother was delighted to share her oral history of her family tree with me, and we would spend several hours on the phone, trying to catch me up with years of family history. She would grow to trust me and share the intimate details of my mother's life and death, from her perspective. Grandma Martha also shared her pain over not being contacted by Lisa and Debra over the years. It made her feel very sad that the daughters of her daughter, Dina, had not kept in contact with her side of the family.

Grandmother said to me, "Lisa and Debra never sent Dina birthday cards, and never came to visit their mother the last seven years of her life while she was dying in the nursing home. Not only did they never visit Dina, they took the insurance money that Sally had left to her mother after dying. I could have helped Dina to manage that money, to buy her things like a TV for her room, which she never had. Vic, Sally's dad, called me to tell me about Dina's inheritance. I never heard another thing about the money until I found out, nine years later, Lisa and Debra, three months after Dina died, tried to get her death certificate, so they could now claim the insurance money from their sister Sally. I really felt bad for Dina being treated that way by her daughters and am upset at Debra and Lisa for taking Dina's money like that." She also told me they'd refused to help pay for a headstone, and that my mother was buried in an unmarked grave.

Martha would later share why she thought Lisa and Debra, my last living sisters, had become estranged from her, when she said this to me on the phone: "Lisa and Debra are mad at our family because their mother Dina passed on the horrible genetic disease Huntington's to them, plus they must not want to be around us, because we know about Sally's money that she left to Dina. Lisa, have you been tested yet?"

I said, "Yes, Grandma, I am going to be tested, and I want you to know that whatever the result is, I will not let that deter me from having a relationship with you. It is not anyone's fault that this mutated gene is passed on. I will still call you and love you either way, whatever my results show."

My old/new family had many broken branches of their own family tree, not just me. My grandmother shared her stories of growing up as a biracial, single parent woman. Her life was not easy, just as I would learn that my mother's was not, either. Debra, Lisa, and Sally, like me, had grown up without my mother as their full-time mom. After our mother divorced, she would go into a downward spiral with alcoholism and everything associated with it. Vic Devens gained full custody of all three of my sisters. Not only had Dina not been given any option but to place me for adoption, but she also lost another child, Angela Marie Devens, right after me. After giving birth to a second daughter, the baby died a week later. Then to top everything off, my mother would have to relinquish her next three daughters to a divorce. She grew up feeling the shame of being biracial and also of being a victim of child molestation.

During one of my calls to Lisa, she educated me on everything that she knew about Huntington's disease and asked if I'd given any thought to getting tested for Huntington's disease. I told her, "Yes, I have been doing a lot of my own research on this, and it is a very tough decision to make, only because I don't think I'm exhibiting any of the symptoms I've read about and that we've discussed. I think I've decided to go ahead and be tested. I have four kids, and if there is a chance that I have Huntington's, they might have it, too, and pass it on to my grandchildren. I want my four children to have the information I did not have. I didn't know my medical history and still to this day can't access it because of my adoption being a closed adoption. If I do have it, at least with that knowledge, my children can make their own personal decision on whether to be tested or have children."

My appointment at the veterans' clinic in Wilmington was the very next day. As I sat waiting for the medical technician to draw my blood, I saw him pick up the phone and then heard him say to the person on the other end, "I have a female, 47-year-old veteran that needs to have genetic testing done for Huntington's disease. I've never heard of this, and I don't see any protocol on how to test for it."

One hour later, the medical technician finally drew my blood and told me, "This has to be sent to a Virginia lab for genetic testing; we should get your test results back in no longer than two weeks."

I got home just in time to answer a call from Debra. I mentioned that I'd just had my blood drawn at the VA and that I should know in two weeks if I'd inherited Huntington's disease from our mother. Debra was quite shocked by this and said, "They did not counsel you or have you see a genetic counselor? They are just going to hand you your results, just like that? Doesn't the VA know it's the law that you have to be counseled by a genetic counselor before they will even administer the test?"

I explained to Debra that the veterans' clinics tend to march to their own drums, and the VA did not even know what Huntington's disease was, much less how to test for it.

The next time I spoke with my grandmother, I felt I had built enough rapport with her to ask her the burning question I had been holding back: "Grandma Martha, do you know who my father was and what his name was?"

She replied, "Yes, I remember his family coming over to beg me not to have him arrested for statutory rape. His parents came over and begged me because he was married and had two small children to support. I don't remember his name, but Lucy might. I was not going to have him arrested. I just wanted the problem to go away. I sent Dina away to give up her baby." My grandmother's words cut right into me, without her intending to do so.

I asked my grandmother next about my three aunts I had yet to talk to. "Grandma Martha, can I have the phone numbers for Lucy, Sandra, and Rhonda?" These were my mother's sisters. Grandma Martha said she would give them to me and that she was going to my Aunt Lucy's ex-husband Brad's funeral the next day, so she would tell everyone about me.

An hour after the funeral, I heard the phone ringing off the hook. I jumped up and looked at the caller ID, and it was my grandmother's cell phone number. I slowly picked it up and said, "Hello."

An unfamiliar voice said, "Hi, we just came back from the funeral in a car that I bought for Ed and my mother, and he won't let me drive it. If he does let me drive, he bitches at me about my driving. Ed can't even figure out how to use his cell phone, much less drive and talk at the same time! Grandma Martha tried to have me give my George up for adoption, too, just like your mother Dina did you, and she also tried to get Rhonda to give up John, but your mother was the only one that went through with it. Oh, I am your Aunt Sandra."

I had talked to my first aunt! My grandmother explained that since my Aunt Lucy was in the middle of a move and dealing with her ex-husband's estate, it would be better to call her after things had settled down for her.

My grandmother did not offer me my Aunt Rhonda's number, and I had learned through my process of searching to be patient. My grandmother would give me my Aunt Rhonda's number when she was ready to.

It had only been two months since finding everyone, and I felt that I was ready to meet all of my birth family. I'd wanted to fly out to see my two sisters in California the week I found Debra and Lisa, but I knew to just be patient. I was still developing my phone relationship with my grandmother and had yet to talk to my Aunt Lucy and Aunt Rhonda, so I decided to go to California first. Debra, Lisa, and I had already discussed me flying out to see them. All of us wanted to meet; it was just a matter of timing. We were all retired, so the only thing we had to plan around was Lisa's sons' schedules. I was also still waiting to hear back from the VA about my genetic test results.

I planned to fly into the San Diego airport and stay at my sister Lisa's home for a week. Debra lives in Los Angeles, and she was going to be staying a week at Lisa's house while I was there. Then Debra and I would drive from San Diego to Los Angeles. I would stay a week with just her, and I would fly back home from there. I knew what Debra and Lisa looked like from checking their pictures out on Facebook. Debra and Lisa also knew what I looked like from my picture on Facebook, too.

The day before my flight, while I was packing, I received a call midafternoon from the VA to come in to see them. I dropped what I was doing, drove to the Wilmington VA clinic to see what they wanted. The next day, when I pulled out my itinerary to look at it, the paper that I'd received from the VA doctor the previous afternoon was right there in it.

I was overwhelmed with joy and excitement from the anticipation of finally meeting my sisters, but I also had a dark cloud that followed me as I flew through the sky to meet Debra and Lisa. There was no time to tell my husband, Brian, what my paper from the VA read. I was certainly not going to tell him about it as I was boarding a plane to California. I knew how I felt reading it, and I was definitely not going to dump my test results in his lap and kiss him and run. I tried to focus my thoughts on the joy of finally meeting my sisters and put the paperwork from the VA away, deep in my purse, in hopes that it would just disappear. The closer to California the plane got, the more nervous I was.

I looked into my mirror one last time as my plane descended into the San Diego airport. My plane had arrived right on time, with no delays. I don't like to be late, and I was a bundle of nerves from the overwhelming excitement. It had been such a long, hard journey finding them, and this moment flooded me with all the ups and downs of years of searching.

I'd promised Brian that I would call him as soon as I arrived, but before I called him, I walked up and down the airport, not seeing either of my sisters. I decided I should call them first. I called Lisa's cell phone first, and there was no answer, so I called Debra's cell phone. Again, there was no answer.

I had brought plenty of money with me, just in case my meeting with my sisters turned out to be disastrous. If that happened, I would just get a hotel and see the sights of California. While I gave my sisters time to show up, I picked up my luggage and called my husband. "Hi, Brian, I arrived on time, but Debra and Lisa are nowhere to be found, and I can't reach them on their cell phones, either."

"They may just be caught in traffic. I wonder why they didn't pick up their cell phones when you called," Brian replied.

"Brian, I've got to go! They are calling me right now! Love you, babe!"

I hung up and clicked over to Debra's call. She said, "We're here. We are pulling up right in front of the airport. Which side are you on?" I told her that I would go outside and find them.

I was on one side of the airport, and off in the distance I saw two ladies, both with their long hair blowing in the wind. I started to walk towards them, not knowing for sure if these two ladies were my sisters or not. As I got closer, I could see them also looking at me, not sure if I was their sister.

Their silhouettes were becoming clearer as I got nearer to them. They both were very petite in size, the same height as me, but definitely not the same body frame. I am short and much heavier, and one of them looked so pale that for a second I thought this must not be my sisters. They both were dressed very differently. One looked like she was a slightly dressed up country cowgirl, and the other one was dressed in a low cut shirt and tight jeans. Both of them were pretty in their own styles. One looked like she may have Chinese features, while the other lady bordered on looking Mexican and Indian.

The closer we got, the faster we all walked to get to each other. In no time, without any words said yet, we were all hugging each other. I had goose bumps all over and fought back my tears of joy. After embracing each other, we inspected each other up and down, just like a new mother does to her baby after giving birth. Debra was in the jeans, looking like a city girl, and Lisa was the country cowgirl I'd seen from afar.

Lisa broke the silence first by saying, "Isn't it wild crazy that we have the same name, Lisa?"

I said, "Yes, it's been hard talking with Grandmother with the same name as my sister! Debra, did you know our mother named her first three kids with the same middle name, Marie? Our mother named me Dawn Marie, then Angela Marie and then finally you Debra Marie. Crazy, isn't it?"

We all decided to go to lunch before going on to Lisa's house, and all during our drive to the restaurant we all were talking, laughing and comparing each other's fingers, noses, and bodies. As soon as we got to the restaurant and were seated, Lisa asked me, "Did you get your results back from the Veterans Clinic yet?" I had not wanted to talk about my results yet, but I handed Lisa the paperwork I'd received from the VA the day before. She didn't open it immediately.

I had thought during the waiting period for my genetic testing results that it would be horrible to have to meet my sisters and tell them that I did not have Huntington's disease. I had dealt with survivor's guilt in the military, and it was not easy. I knew that if my test results came back negative, I would endure the same survivor's guilt from these two sisters having it, and one sister, Sally, and our mother dying from Huntington's disease. In a weird, twisted way, I wanted to have Huntington's disease, so I would not have to tell my sisters any differently, yet I also did not want to have Huntington's disease, so my husband would not have to suffer watching me die. I also did not want to pass it on to my four children.

Lisa was much different than Debra, just as I had concluded from our conversations prior to meeting them. Debra's conversation was filled with the excitement of our reunion, and Lisa's was more about the rattlesnake pit bite of doom, from the family's inheritance of Huntington's. I liked them both, as different as they were. I saw personality traits of both of them in me. I could be serious and controlling, yet had a zest for life, and I could find laughter in anything. I looked at my two sisters and their personalities like a see-saw teetering back and forth, and I was balancing in between with my own personality.

The waiter had brought our meals, and Debra and I were done sharing our first sister moment in the bathroom. Like two giddy school girls talking through the bathroom stalls, we laughed and giggled about the simple fact that our sister, Lisa, never had to pee like us two. Returning to our table, Debra and I continued giggling, and Lisa gave us the look of an older sister, even though Debra and I were both older than Lisa. Lisa then said to me, "I did not think it possible that all of us would get Huntington's from our mother." Lisa looked very upset and distraught. While Debra and I had gone to the bathroom, Lisa had read my test results.

I said to both of my sisters, now looking at me with the dread of the reality of my test results, "It is what it is, and I will get through this. We all have each other, and that is what is important now. We will get through this all together." We all held each other's hand in a moment of silence; I realized that both Debra and Lisa had seen what this deadly brain disease can do by watching Sally succumb to it. I had never had to face it like my two sisters had to.

Finding my birth family was like a double-edged sword for me: on one end was the joy of finally knowing and being reunited with my family, and on the other end of the sword, piercing through my heart, was the reality that I, too, had inherited the incurable, fatal, genetic, family disease.

Brian always tells me that I don't miss a thing, and he'd even given me a Native American name of Dawn Eagle Eyes. When I walked into Lisa's home, I noticed a wall of pictures of different family members, but none of our mother or her family, either. I had hoped that by visiting I would learn more about my mother and also be able to look at some family pictures.

The first day of my visit we spent looking at our fingers and toes and only talking about our mother when we would find something in common with each other that was like our mother. All of us, including our mother, were 5 feet 2 inches, and we all wore the same size shoe. The next few days Debra, Lisa, and I would spend hiking and shopping. Our first sister moment, with all three of us, came the day while we were out shopping, and a sales clerk said to us, "Are you three sisters?" All three of us looked at each other and giggled. We proceeded to tell the sales clerk our tale of being reunited in sisterhood.

My time in San Diego was running out, so one night before going to bed, I finally asked Lisa if she had any pictures of our mother. I had only seen one, and that was on Facebook and not very clear. Lisa said to me, "I think when I was packing Sally's stuff up after she died, I saw some that Sally had. I have not even looked at those boxes since she passed away nine years ago."

Lisa brought in a few of Sally's boxes filled with her belongings, and all three of us went through our deceased sister's possessions. I would get to know my sister Sally a little more through her collections of pictures, articles and cards she had saved throughout her short life. I was overwhelmed with a feeling of loss and the sadness of never being able to meet Sally. As

I sat and looked at Debra and Lisa, I felt a twinge of pain in my heart that I had missed all the years growing up with them. Once again, I felt like an outsider looking in, as I did as a small child, watching my mom and her bond with her only natural child. I looked at my sisters, knowing I would never fill the role of sisterhood with them. That was gone and lost, and I knew I could only be a friend to them if they so desired.

As Lisa and Debra looked though some of Sally's pictures of our mother, I watched the pain in their eyes. Lisa shared that she felt bad that she'd blamed our mother's actions on alcoholism when it very well could have been her suffering from Huntington's disease.

We came upon a picture of our mother in one of the many rehabs she was in; Lisa pointed to the picture and said, "This is the last rehab my mother was in. She wrote an autobiography about her life. That was the first time I knew she had given you up for adoption. When she got out of the rehab, I told her that I had done the paperwork to send to the adoption agency to find you. In her autobiography, I could tell that giving you up destroyed her. I tore up that paperwork, because when she was at the airport to come see us, she got drunk, and I didn't want anything more to do with her."

I asked Lisa if I could see the autobiography and read it, but Lisa told me she didn't have it. "I probably threw it away," Lisa said.

My heart sank with disappointment, not only for the lack of pictures and her autobiography, but also at what I perceived as a lack of empathy for our mother. I had felt her pain all those years; did my two sisters not sense it? I could not let my mother's soul be left to be tormented any longer. If it was the last thing on earth I would do, I would carry the memory of my mother forever; her spirit would forever live on through my lips when I speak her name.

My visit at Lisa's home in San Diego was over, and Debra and I headed to her place in L.A. I would miss Lisa's little boys and Lisa, too. I had watched Danny's and Roger's little ears perk up when Lisa would talk of the kids not knowing about her Huntington's disease. I had caught the boys both looking at each other one day when Lisa spoke of letting Alex do everything with the boys so that Danny and Roger would get used to not having her around. Lisa discussed with Debra and me how, when she became too sick and a burden to her family, she would wander off and live in a cabin somewhere to die, so her family wouldn't suffer.

Debra and I took the scenic route up the coast to L.A. The road trip gave us much needed one-on-one time. Both Debra's and my kids were grown, and we both sighed with relief for the moment of peace we both were enjoying. Debra's life was much like mine, our kids grown, and we were retired and used to a quiet, less stressful life. We both expressed how hectic Lisa's life was with two young sons and battling an incurable illness. Debra had only one son named Mitch, and she was glad he was on his own, too.

When we arrived in L.A., I instantly felt the energy of the buzz of the California I had seen on TV. Debra introduced me to her boyfriend, Yazzy, and his family. We would all eat at Yazzy's family's house, and I would finally get a chance to meet Debra's son, Mitch. Debra must have done something right, because her son was a complete gentleman and a delight to be around.

During my stay, Debra took me to art museums, and we drove with her son to Santa Monica for the day. Debra was very open with her son and spoke with him honestly about her Huntington's. Mitch had gone through genetic counseling; he wanted to be tested for Huntington's. The genetic counselors thought that even though he was of legal age to have the test done, he was not quite ready to handle the knowledge if he had Huntington's. Through watching and learning from my sisters how they handled their children, I would leave California with a better view of what to do with mine.

Debra also had no pictures of extended family on her wall. I had come to California in hopes of getting a better understanding of my sisters and my birth mom, but left without much to work with. On the last day of my visit with Debra, she surprised me with a gift. Debra obviously sensed my desire to just see or hold onto something that was my mother's, so she had dug deep in her closet and presented me with an afghan my mom had knitted. Debra could tell from my reaction, with the tears forming now in both of our eyes, that this gift meant the world to me.

While flying home, I reflected on my two-week trip to meet my sisters. The experience of looking into the eyes of someone that shares my blood is one that I am still processing.

During my visit, I had told Debra and Lisa about my test results, but I had yet to tell my husband and children. Both my husband and mother were so sure I did not have Huntington's that we all had not prepared for getting positive test results. I knew that the news of me having inherited the disease would be very hard for my family. I wasn't looking forward to telling Brian and even toyed with the idea of just not sharing it with him. I was worried that it would devastate him. I knew well enough that soon enough, Huntington's disease would show its ugly self in me, when I would become more symptomatic from the disease. A conversation I'd had with my mother two years ago about me being on her heels, as far as doing the same things a woman her age was doing, made sense to me now. Also, the severe period of my depression while in Texas made it clear to me that I was, in fact, in the beginning stages of Huntington's disease all the way back to when I was in Texas, and there was not some multiple personality that had taken over me.

My own emotions were all over the map, from being angry to being sad about the fact I had this disease. It was like some sort of sick joke that after something as beautiful and special as finally being reunited with my birth family, I'd learned that I'd better create my bucket list fast, because I wasn't going to be around to enjoy the fruits of all my hard work. I was sad because I felt no control over my own destiny, but the fact that my children's and husband's lives would be affected by all this was the true travesty for me. I felt like I had a ticking bomb inside me, not knowing when it would go off, and I was sure telling Brian would send him into his own depression. I felt a sense of urgency to try to fix my own strained relationships with my children, yet I realized they would not have that same sense of urgency. I had to give them time to process everything. After explaining to them about the genetics of Huntington's disease, I realized, they might have the knowledge that I did not have, but they were also, like me, likely to be in some form of denial.

I knew I had to tell my husband. I could not deny my loved one something that would impact our entire family. I understood more about why my grandmother thought Lisa and Debra were angered at her side of the family over having inherited this disease. But I knew that I was angered about having it, not about the cause of it. Lisa and Debra may very well have been hurt by inheriting Huntington's disease and may have held some deep-seated anger towards our mother and family; I do not know. But I was not going to fall into the trap of hurt people sometimes hurting people. I was not going to continue this pattern of pain from generation to generation. I had a choice, and I would choose to break the chain of hurt and anger in my family. Instead, I would meet anger with empathy, contempt with compassion, and cruelty with kindness. I would keep my smile to stomp out grimaces and use the love in my heart as a weapon to forgive and forget, so my family's future generations could heal and break the cycle of pain. As my very wise adoptive mom had said to me over and over, "It is what it is!" I knew this was no one's fault. If I turned away from my birth mom's family because of this, I would be no better than anyone who condemned them for this disease.

As I suspected, my husband was crushed by my news. We spent many nights holding each other and sobbing about the injustices of life. I was my husband's first real love and first wife. Our last few years together, prior to finding out my test results, had been filled with lots of traveling and living the good life. I really believed he thought, with this news, that our lives were over in that instant, but I knew differently. Finding out that you or a loved one has an incurable disease with no treatment can paralyze even the strongest person. My husband was trying real hard to be strong for me, as I was for him, too. Brian would look at me for the next several months with the look of big deer eyes caught in the hunter's spotlight. I wanted him to just look at me like he used to, with his loving eyes, not the look of pain that I now saw. I knew it would take time for both of us.

I was not going to let the news of having HD kick my butt. Instead of succumbing to a seriously sucky situation, I would add Huntington's disease to one of my causes to advocate for. I started researching what was available in my town of Wilmington and found there weren't any local support groups for Huntington's. I thought it would be helpful for my husband and me to attend a support group, but we didn't want to travel 100 miles one way to do so. So I did what I do best and contacted the head-quarters for Huntington's disease organizations to see what I had to do to start the first Huntington's group in Wilmington.

After talking to several people in New York, I was on my way to starting our group. I had to take several teleconference classes. Within three months of deciding to start the group, finishing my classes and contracting with the local library for a meeting room, I held the first Wilmington, North Carolina Huntington's Chapter group meeting. Our group was a success. It was listed in the local newspaper every month and also listed with the North Carolina information help phone directory.

There was one more leg to my journey I had yet to travel. I had not been to visit all my family in North Dakota yet. I had made contact with all three of my aunts by now and felt that we were all on the road to establishing a pretty good relationship. My grandmother, while talking on the phone one day, told me she'd decided to send me a drawing of my birth mom, Dina, which she had saved. Prior to Martha telling me she was going to gift me the picture, I'd had several conversations with my Aunt Lucy, the real gatekeeper to my past. Aunt Lucy was closest in age to my birth mom. She remembered very clearly my birth mother's pregnancy with me, and she knew exactly who my father was.

As most teenage girls would do, my aunt and my mother had told my grandmother that my birth father was someone else in order to protect my birth mother's boyfriend, my father. My grandmother was 84 and had believed all this time that my father was another man. My Aunt Lucy knew different, and she said to me one day, "The drawing Grandmother is sending you was drawn by your father, of your mother when she was pregnant with you. Your father was a good artist. He had dark hair and green eyes. He passed away in his fifties from falling off a roof."

I had thought the search part of my journey was over, but with my Aunt Lucy's disclosure of who my birth father was, I was back at it again. With the help of another adoptee friend, I was able to locate my birth father's widow and my half-brother. By nightfall, I was looking right into the big, green eyes of my brother's picture on Facebook. I had big, green eyes like my father's and now like my brother's, too. I could not locate my brother Matthews's phone number, but was able to find his mother's.

In between keeping contact with all my birth family and my adopted family, and trying to book a trip to see everyone in North Dakota, plus run my new Huntington's support group, I was able to manage a call to Laura, my birth father's widow. I wanted to see if she would give me a picture of my birth father and my half-brother's phone number. Up until this point, everyone had been very receptive to being reunited. I did anticipate the call to Laura would be a little uncomfortable, but I didn't anticipate the reaction she dished out to me. After getting nowhere with Laura, I would spend numerous hours trying to somehow locate my half-brother's address or phone number, and also tried to message him through Facebook, but it was becoming clear to me that Matthew also did not want to have anything to do with me. I thought that I might be able to find my father's picture on either Laura's or Matthew's Facebook page, but nothing showed up.

I was at the point of just being happy with what I'd found out when my Aunt Lucy opened another door, leading to another direction of hope to procure a picture of my father. Aunt Lucy told me that an aunt through her previous marriage, Maggie, had married my dad's brother and would probably have lots of pictures, maybe even one of my father. I was a little timid about calling another person related to my dad's widow, but was pleasantly surprised by the nicest older woman on the other end of the phone. Maggie had also given up a baby for adoption, my Aunt Lucy had shared with me, and the baby boy, now much older, had also just found Maggie. After talking to Maggie, I knew that when she was faced with the same circumstance of an adoptee that comes looking, she was just sweet as pie.

Just like with Tim Travers, every contact I made, I was sure to follow through with a thank you letter and a picture of me, to make it more personal. When I received my own letter and package from my grandmother, I was trembling with joy; this was bigger than any gift I would ever receive. I opened it, and inside was my father's drawing of my mother while pregnant with me. To think I was holding something in my hands that my grandmother, mother and father had touched sent shivers of goose bumps all over me. I said to Brian, "If someone was to come in and lay a million bucks on our table to buy my drawing, I would tell them no way!" My grandmother also included a picture of herself and my mother's funeral notice.

The drawing of my birth mother was signed by my birth father on the front, and when I looked on the back of it, he had written: "Dina, you are a very nice girl and very pretty. This drawing I did of you does not belie the fact. Love, Byron Johnson." Underneath that my mother had written, "I love Byron Johnson." I matted this picture and hung it right away. The pieces of my family puzzle were finally coming together. I had a picture of my mother, grandmother, and now a portrait that my dad had drawn. I may not have had my birth father's picture to see what he looked like, but

I was happy with what I did have. I had not heard back from Maggie and felt that I had to respect her boundaries, also.

It was the height of the winter season in North Dakota, but Brian and I boarded a plane in February, to head there anyway. We were headed to Bismarck for the first three days, and then traveling even further north, almost to the Canadian border, to see my two aunts, Lucy and Rhonda, who lived on the Turtle Mountain Chippewa Reservation in Belcourt, North Dakota. I had come to know through our many conversations on the phone each family member's personality a little bit. My grandmother was full of stories and sharp for her age, but would lose words here and there, too. She was sweet as could be, and tried very hard not to say an ill word about anyone. She was proud of graduating from college in her fifties and of all she had accomplished as a social worker.

My Aunt Sandra was the one who I had talked to the least. She sounded frazzled by life and also by the realization that she was too young to be a caregiver for my grandmother and her second husband, Ed. She was going through a lot of transition from changing jobs, relationships, and moving in with Grandma and Ed. Aunt Sandra had two grown sons, George and Tyron, and she also missed her grandson, who lived in the other side of the state.

My Aunt Rhonda was very verbal and forthcoming. She was extremely smart, just like my birth mom had said in the information I'd received from the adoption agency. Rhonda and Sandra were the closest in age, and my birth mother and my Aunt Lucy were closest in their age, too. My Aunt Rhonda, out of all the family members, was the most traditional in her Native American ancestral beliefs.

She had a son named John and a daughter named Erin. I had spoken to Erin quite a few times and enjoyed her zest and outlook on life. John lives in Roswell, New Mexico, where I had visited so many times before locating my birth family. It was so strange: so many of the places where I located my family were places I had been or lived. Erin lives in Texas, the same state as two of my kids, Josh and Susan.

Aunt Lucy seemed to remember the most about my birth mom. She seemed to me to be the peacekeeper of the family and the caretaker kind. She also seemed to be a very private person, and one whose trust you would have to earn. Through our conversations on the phone, I could tell she was uncomfortable at first talking with me, but as time went on, she shared more and more with me. One day on the phone, Aunt Lucy broke down crying. She told me about the day my mother died. She shared with me that my birth mom loved deer, and when Lucy had looked out her window and had seen a big buck look her right in the eye and then take off running, she knew that my mother, Dina, had passed to the other side.

Aunt Lucy has two children, also, a son named Bill who lived in Minnesota and a daughter named Tanya who lived in Arizona. From finding their pictures on Facebook I was able to see that they both loved animals. Tanya looked, from her pictures, to be a loving, family-oriented mom, and Bill looked like a huge, lovable teddy bear with very kind eyes.

Our plane was now descending into our final destination, Bismarck. I did not remember anything about North Dakota. I had left with my new family shortly after my adoption. I was even more anxious and filled with butterflies in my belly from my anticipation at finally meeting the rest of my birth family. Grandma Martha and Ed had told us that they would meet us at the airport. I didn't see them anywhere, but I trusted they surely would be somewhere in the airport. I felt a little of the same panic come rushing back that I'd felt when Lisa and Debra were late picking me up. I didn't realize that our gate was on the first level, and there were two levels to this airport. Brian and I headed for the escalator to go rent our vehicle downstairs, and that's when I saw Ed standing near the bottom of the escalator. He looked just like his picture and was easy to spot. I didn't see Grandma with him, so I assumed she'd stayed behind at home. After the formalities of introducing myself and Brian to Ed, he pointed and said, "Grandma Martha is sitting over there." I wasted no time and walked toward her, leaving both Brian and Ed to follow behind.

I walked up to Martha and said, "Hello, Grandmother, we are finally here to meet you all," and before I could finish, my grandmother said, "It's Dina! I saw Dina coming down the escalator."

I wasn't sure if she was confused, so I said gently, "No, it's Lisa, Dina's daughter. I have come from North Carolina to meet you for the first time."

I don't know if she had a senior moment or not, but then she said, "Yes, I know."

We gave each other a long hug, and looked each other up and down. I could tell right away from my grandmother's eyes that she'd had a tough life and noticed she would often look away or not in my eyes. I knew right away that I'd inherited my grandmother's full figure. It was surreal to me to be in North Dakota, where my life started, and with my grandmother who had made the decision for my birth mother to give me away.

We went first out to dinner and then went on to my grandmother's, Ed's and Sandra's house. There was not as much snow on the ground as I expected, but it sure was colder than any cold I had felt. I had brought gifts for everyone, and Brian was real good about taking pictures and video of everybody. The second day there, Ed took Brian to breakfast, and that gave my grandmother and me some time alone. She had gathered two big storage boxes of pictures, and piece by piece we went through each one of the pictures, each with a story told by my grandmother. This was what I wanted, to finally see and hear all the stories behind my birth family. Slowly but surely, with each pictured matched with Grandmother's stories, I was able to piece together all my maternal birth family's puzzle.

My grandmother saw how awed I was to be looking at these photos, and she told me to take home with me any of them I wanted. I filled my treasure box with those pictures, not forgetting a face, name, or the story my grandmother had shared. To me, these were better than any treasure box filled with gold. Grandmother also had a beautiful bedspread afghan my mother had knitted, along with a smaller one and a shawl she gave to me. I could tell by the way she handled them and by the way they looked brand new that my grandmother had taken special care of them. She was proud of her daughter's work, and I knew it must have been hard for her to gift them to me.

Grandma and I would spend the next couple of days going through those big plastic containers of pictures, and at one point, I knew just how hard it was for my grandmother to be sitting there with her daughter's oldest daughter. She held one of Dina's pictures and started to tell me about it. She stopped and caught herself crying, and for the first time, my grandmother looked me straight in the eyes and said, "It wasn't easy watching your mother die. I am sorry that she did not get to meet you. I wish she could have had that hug from you."

I then said to my grandmother, "She knows I am here and that you are telling me everything about her. She can rest in peace knowing that." For a moment I was filled with guilt. I felt selfish for coming and having my grandmother relive so much, but I knew that it was just as healing for my grandmother to finally have that family branch of my birth mother there. It had only been two years since my birth mom had passed away, and I could see and feel the terrible pain that it still evoked in my grandmother. I was honored that my grandmother would take so much time and care sharing my birth mother's oral history. Even though it was not easy for her to do, she did it with grace. She knew how important it was for not only me, but for my birth mother, too.

I would only get to spend one evening with my Aunt Sandra. Brian and I met her at the Dakota Farms for coffee. She looked so different in person, much younger, very tall and thin. Aunt Sandra was definitely under a lot of stress. She worked long hours and held two jobs, one as a school teacher and another at Pier One. She was a hard worker, but I worried that she worked so much making a living that she would miss out on living.

The next leg of our trip was to Turtle Mountain Chippewa Reservation. The forecast did not look good at all, and Ed and Grandmother thought we shouldn't go. I thought if we left early enough, we could beat the snowstorm. I told Grandma and Ed that Brian and I had decided to go, and if they didn't want to, we surely would understand. They decided to go with us, and we drove our rental car two hundred miles to Belcourt, which is situated right next to the Canadian border.

We stopped in Minot because I wanted to visit my birth mother's grave. Ed remembered where it was, even though it was unmarked, and the ground was covered in two feet of snow. I had wanted to bring flowers or something, but we could not get close enough to her grave because of the snow. Ed stopped in the road in front of her grave, two steel poles marking her spot. How symbolic that was for me, to look at those two pillars of thin, cold, steel rods. It made me think of how cold hearted it was for her to be buried there, without her own two children helping to buy her a marker. This angered me, and I now understood how deeply these steel rods had run right through my mother's very heart. I had thought long and hard before coming to her grave about what I would say to her, and all I could do was fall to my knees and say how sorry for her I was. In an instant, I saw myself buried right next to my birth mother, marked only by four cold, steel poles running through my heart, from my own four children. I understood all too well now, and I knew that the knowledge I had sought out would now be a burden in my heart to carry forever.

As I stood up, I felt Brian's arm wrap around me. It was then that the warm tears flowed endlessly from my eyes. I knew that the tears shed over my mother's resting place entered her eternal soul and were more meaningful than any marker on her grave. I could not give my mother a hug, but I knew that from that moment, she felt the tears of love, and the pain that had haunted me from her unrested soul was finally lifted. My birth mother Dina's family had finally been reunited.

Brian helped me back into the car where Ed and Martha had been waiting for us. Grandmother Martha apologized for not getting out. I apologized to her for crying, and I wonder now why we felt compelled to apologize to each other. We then drove to the nearest gas station in Minot, and my cell phone rang. It was Debra. She was extremely upset because the father of her boyfriend of 17 years, Yazzy, had just passed away. I told Debra how sorry I was and that I was glad that she had called me. But I also felt I needed to tell her my own sorrow in just visiting our mother's grave.

As we neared Belcourt, we drove up a small, rolling hill, and Grandmother Martha pointed to some rolling mountains off in the distance and said, "Those are the Turtle Mountains. Aren't they beautiful?" I could tell my grandmother loved North Dakota and the reservation. Off in the distance, I could see the Queen of Peace, a bed and breakfast, on the top of the hill, and right before the hill was a row of small houses where both my aunts lived. I saw a tall, thin, woman with short, salt and pepper hair come out of the end house. I knew that must be my Aunt Lucy. I was taken aback at how tall she was. I was overcome with a child-like shyness that I have not felt since maybe age two. What had come over me, I still don't know to this day. I knew that my Aunt Lucy was the closest with my mother, and she knew the most about her. Maybe that is why I felt that way.

As soon as we were all in Lucy's house, we all started talking at once and looking closely at each other. Then I said to my Aunt Lucy, "I am really sorry I did not find my mother in time to give her the hug I have wanted to give to her, so I would like to give it to you." We both teared up.

Aunt Lucy looked at me and said, "It's haunting; it's haunting; it's like I'm looking into the eyes of my sister."

There was a knock on my Aunt Lucy's door, and in came my Aunt Rhonda. Rhonda is built nothing like Lucy; she is built more like Grandma Martha and me. She's a little taller than me, with long black hair, graying in the front, and she looks the most Indian out of all of us. She has a very pretty face and the same pretty eyes as Aunt Lucy. Aunt Rhonda and I hugged right away, and she gave me a shawl that she had made for my mother.

Aunt Rhonda told me, "I was upset when your mother passed away because she was supposed to be buried in the shawl, but it came up missing. The day you first called me to introduce yourself to me, the shawl showed up on my coffee table. I knew after talking with you that I wanted to gift it to you. I want to give this to you so you can carry it over to the other side to give to your mom when it is your time. I made this for your mom, and with each ribbon I tied to it, I said a prayer for your mother." Then my Aunt Rhonda wrapped me in the shawl to present it to me.

Aunt Lucy said, "I have something for you also," and handed me a gold heart locket with my mother's initials engraved on it. I recognized the locket immediately from one of my mother's baby pictures Grandma Martha had given me.

Grandma Martha said, "I gave that to Dina when she was just a baby."

I said to Aunt Lucy, "I can't take this. This was your sister's, and you must want it for yourself."

Lucy then said, "No, I want you to have it, and your mom would, too. Someday it would be nice to go to your daughter Susan, who is Dina's only granddaughter. I have gifts from my sister in my bedroom."

I said, "Aunt Lucy, thank you so much. I will make sure Susan will receive it someday, and Aunt Rhonda, thank you for the shawl. It will be an honor to bring it to my mother on the other side."

A few days later, as we sat around my Aunt Lucy's kitchen table sharing ham, Lucy said to me, "You look just like the Johnson kids I grew up playing with. Rhonda, don't you think she looks like a Johnson?"

Aunt Rhonda said, "Yes, she looks just like them." Up until that point everyone had said I looked like my birth mom, Dina, and also like my cousin Tanya, Aunt Lucy's daughter. I guess after sitting with me, they both also saw my dad, Byron Johnson, in my looks. I wondered if I could ever get a picture of my dad Byron, but I did not feel it was proper to broach the subject.

The next couple of days I spent hiking back and forth between my aunts' homes so I could spend time with them. There was just not enough time in one trip to cover a lifetime without them. I was glad we got snowed in and that I had an extra day with my two aunts, but when we left Belcourt, I still felt I had unfinished business. It was going to take the rest of my lifetime to play catchup with my birth family.

Brian and I caught our flight home, even though I was pretty sick. Within a week, I had a pneumonia, which kept me down long enough to process all that had happened on my trip. During that week, I looked at all the pictures my grandmother had given me and could not let go of the idea that maybe if I wrote Laura, Matthew, and Maggie one last time, they might just give me a picture of my dad. I wrote a joint letter to the three of them, telling them about meeting my birth family and learning that I'd inherited Huntington's disease from my mother. I told them about the picture my dad had drawn of my mom, and I asked one last time for a photograph of my father.

I mailed out the letters as a last ditch effort in March 2013, shortly after my return from my trip to North Dakota. Waiting for any kind of response was and is the hardest part of searching. My half-brother's letter came back by the middle of March with a return to sender yellow sticker from the post office. I knew that I would probably not hear from my birth father's widow, Laura, so I prayed that my Aunt Maggie would be kind enough to send me a picture of my father if she had one.

One day, my husband came to my office carrying a large envelope. I asked him, "What is it?"

Brian said, "It's from Maggie, and it's marked do not bend!" I jumped up out of my office chair and grabbed the envelope.

"It is from my Aunt Maggie, and I think it has photos in it," I said to Brian. I slowly opened it, and inside there was not only one picture, but several of my father and a family portrait of the entire Johnson family. My Aunt Maggie had also included my birth dad's funeral memorial, some baby pictures, and graduation pictures of my dad. I spent the rest of the day just looking at them the way I looked at all my birth mom's pictures for the first time, and all I could say and think was, "Wow, what a blessing. Now I have pictures of all my family, the picture my dad drew of my mom pregnant with me, and all the other wonderful gifts that my birth family gave me."

In the months and years since then, I've learned that Martha divorced my grandfather, Harold Beckman, because of his erratic behavior before they knew what Huntington's was. He was the man described in the information I'd received from the adoption agency as a 35-year-old man of Norwegian descent and a member of the Baptist faith, six feet tall and weighing 150 pounds, with light brown hair, blue eyes, and a light complexion. They had reported his health as "good." Martha and Harold had two daughters, my mother and her younger sister, Lucy. Lucy tested negative for Huntington's, but Harold went on to father 14 more children, and Huntington's disease spread like wildfire throughout the Turtle Mountain Reservation. A doctor I talked to said that while HD is rampant there, the people are resistant to treatment, and I've learned that they are resistant to education, too. Instead, they go to the tribal medicine woman who treats them by using smudge pots and tarot cards and sending them off into the mountains with a special diet.

When I started my search for my birth family, I thought I was looking for a person; I had no idea what I was embarking on or what I would find. The thousands of miles I flew to meet my birth family were only a small segment of my life journey to search for them and for myself. I would ultimately learn that the search for them would indeed be the start of getting to know who I am. Having Huntington's disease could have crushed me, but instead it helped me with my outlook on life. What *was* important, and what was not so much anymore, is cut with clarity, as seen with my new

Huntington's eyes. I will not sweat the small stuff in life, and will enjoy the simple things. I've learned to take my time and really smell the roses and watch the little wonders of life, like butterflies and birds singing. Through having this disease, I've had the opportunity to meet some of the nicest people that otherwise I would never have met. With the eyes of a love child with Huntington's disease, I am able to see more clearly than most, and by practicing compassion, I know I will in turn find happiness beyond my wildest dreams. I will make each moment in my life a masterpiece.

—⟡—

Please consider making a donation to Help 4 HD International, Inc., a nonprofit organization.

Donations can be made via their secure web site, www.help4hd-international.org, or by mailing a check to:

Help 4 HD International, Inc.
436 Playa Blanca Street
Santa Maria, CA 93455

You can also contact Help 4 HD International at 805-441-5618.

About Sarah Foster

Sarah Foster was born in North Carolina and graduated from UNC Chapel Hill. She is a Tar Heel basketball fan, especially when UNC plays Duke or NC State. After living in Atlanta and Tokyo, Sarah settled down in New Bern, NC. She and her husband, Randy, share five sons. Sarah uses social media to raise awareness about HD. She launched and documented the HD Pie in the Face Challenge on the heels of the ALS Ice Bucket Challenge. She uses her personal blog (meandhd.wordpress.com) to describe her HD symptoms to others and to draw attention to the needs and accomplishments of people and organizations in the HD community. Her blog Sarah's HD List (sarahshdlist.wordpress.com) provides a consolidated list of information and resources about HD. Sarah is always eager to assist and collaborate with other people in the HD community to raise awareness.

CHAPTER 2

Written Descent
By Sarah Foster

My return to writing

I was a freelance writer for part of my life. Paid to write what people wanted me to say, I developed a repertoire of writing skills. But my relationship with words was strictly professional. When I divorced the father of my two oldest boys, I switched careers to ensure financial stability of my smaller family and didn't look back, not even when my family re-expanded to include my second and final husband, two stepsons, and a new baby boy. When time allowed, I picked up a paintbrush instead of a pen as a creative outlet.

Huntington's disease got me writing again. Only today it serves as a bridge to the world instead of a means to a paycheck. Writing is my primary and preferred means of communication. It's a way to untangle and expel thoughts when they build up in my head. I can write about the experiences of HD symptoms so people I care about might be able to understand them. I've also used writing to raise awareness about HD. I reconnected with writing gradually. It was a process filled with discovery.

After my diagnosis, either some brain synapses created work-arounds or I developed 20/20 hindsight. As a result, I became able to see connections between past behavior and the beginnings of HD symptoms.

I recently took a few days to re-read some of the emails I've sent over the past several years. I began finding clues as to when things started going south. Before my diagnosis, I didn't recognize some of the emails I wrote as warnings. At the time, I didn't even see them as mistakes, much less as forms of aberrant behavior.

A hallmark symptom of HD is the angry verbal outburst. I've discovered that I do it in writing.

I know from being on the receiving end that, while spoken words fade away, their emotional damage hangs around a lot longer.

A relative (who needs to be tested) recently sent me pages of spiteful written words. I was sad to find out that this method of the angry outburst inflicts just as much pain as the spoken words. Still, if you are the recipient of abusive writing, you can simply have someone screen your emails or learn to hit the delete button. There's no screaming to forget or wall to patch up.

But if you are the regretful author, it's harder to gain any permanent distance from the missive. What you say lives on in someone else's inbox, and you can't unsend it.

During my post hoc analysis of my writing, I identified several written harbingers of HD. And as recently as last week, I have used who I write to and what I say as an emotional barometer. But a lot happened in between, so hold on tight.

―☈―

HD Foreshadowed

I am embarrassed as I describe my actions below. Even though they were manifestations of HD symptoms, people still suffered their consequences. Apologizing to people who don't understand HD is a useless formality which I will continue nonetheless. Still, I get the feeling that the unenlightened liken my apologies to blaming my imaginary friend.

Harbinger 1: Never mind

Sometime during 2009, one of my sons went to live with his father in a different city. It was difficult for me, as a mom and a teacher in his school, to accept that I could no longer keep my eye on him by looking across the hall. So I found out his school district, his teacher, and then hammered out a long, terse, uppity letter about my expectations as far as the level of communication I expected from his teachers. I hated getting letters like this from parents. But the hypocrisy was lost on me.

I sent a two-page, demanding, imperious letter which used lots of inappropriate "quotation marks" to "emphasize" what I was saying. Rereading it, I immediately pick up on the misdirected anger and frustration about losing custody of my son.

But despite what I put that poor teacher through, this is how I responded when I learned my son was accepted to an out-of district-school:

Ms. Bell,

I've discovered that my son is enrolled in Acme Middle School instead of yours.

I apologize for the error, and I thank you so much for your kind response.

Have a great school year!

I turned on a dime. Did I think my son's lack of enrollment there suddenly un-ruined that teacher's day? No, I didn't give her feelings another thought until right now. And the nasty email sent to the wrong teacher turned out to be my last attempt to communicate with anyone who has taught him since. That great big, misdirected email served as a drain spout, releasing any fervor and immediacy from my brain. I couldn't reach action after that: my last squawk as a mother hen.

So while I still maintain love and concern, I can't tap into those feelings and use them to fuel actions like checking on his progress. It is like trying to catch butterflies with my hands tied behind my back.

If one of them happens to fly into my mouth, I'm lucky.

Fortunately, with no help from me, my son is thriving. Even with written words, I can't explain how happy I am about that.

Harbinger 2: Much ado about groceries

In August of 2010, I sent this e-mail to a grocery store manager. You can tell by my description of the event that my threshold for frustration was low. My organizational skills and my ability to handle the unexpected were slipping as well. In retrospect, cognitive symptoms, as well as my weakening fine motor skills, were what really prevented me from completing the transaction. What I find most alarming about this email, aside from me making a big deal out of nothing, was how I seemed to derive pleasure from saying bad things about the store and the employees.

Today's shopping experience was the worst. As I was getting into a checkout line, I was whisked to a self-checkout without being given a choice. The checkout lady rushed me and chastised me for taking so long to take my SpecialCARD out of my wallet. (It was stuck in the slot.) She was visibly annoyed that it took me so long, and it really made me anxious. Then when I couldn't find my check card, she scolded me and said she'd have to void it all.

I told the store manager that I was going home to get cash and to leave the items. He acted like he didn't understand or care what I was talking about, and he rushed to help someone else. On the way back from my house with the cash, I called to say I was coming and was told that my order was voided. I felt like some sort of criminal.

When I finally got home with the groceries, my son found the check card right in my wallet where I usually put it. I would have been able to go right to it had this woman not tried to rush me through. She is all about speed of check-out, but I am not. I am for being treated with dignity as a customer who has, since moving to New Bern, chosen to shop at Special Grocery.

Today was to have been a very important breakfast at my household, and it was ruined because SG tried to rush me through.

And it wasn't even that busy yet. Perhaps the management does not know that this checkout lady is overeager and is upsetting customers. That is one of two scenarios which would explain why I have not, and most likely will not, receive any sort of apology from this store. The second scenario would be that they know she rushes people to the point that they are irritated and flustered, but don't care, because the hourly sales are higher when she treats us like paying cattle.

Bitchy, I know. But that's just the opening act. Let's begin with the honest-to-goodness, verifiable truth that I normally was, and am, innately kind. I never say things to people like "you ruined this event for me," even during disagreements.

Now are you ready for the show-stopper? I was working as a Special Education teacher and knew, without a doubt, that the checkout lady I attacked was functioning highly on the autism spectrum. I even threw in the Temple Grandin cattle reference to twist the knife, if only in my own mind! Helping people check out efficiently was probably one of the few work-related tasks she could do well, and she probably took pride in her work.

I had forgotten about this letter, and when I came across it, the frustration surrounding the experience came flooding back. But the tone of the letter was so surprising. The mean and haughty person who wrote that letter was only thinking of herself. She was also looking for anyone else to blame for the changes she felt.

UPDATE: The store manager did call, but by that time, I was so embarrassed and confused about the whole thing that I simply told him I had a bad day.

—◊—

The need to know

Several people have told me that I was a different person when I came back to work at school in the fall of 2009. By the third staff day, I had screwed up in every imaginable way. I stood up and chastised the speaker at the opening assembly, telling him he was playing on people's fears in order to sell his pepper spray. I forgot nearly every policy that I was taught the last year and dropped the ball so many times that the new principal came in and screamed at me, telling me that she was not going to allow me to put a blight on her school.

In previous school years, I'd already noticed my memory was worse than other people's, and to compensate, I had an elaborate system with layers of logs, lists, and binders. Every written communication was documented, along with the date. Otherwise, I'd either duplicate or forget to do those things. But now, my systems no longer provided enough support. To make matters worse, I couldn't remember things people told me long enough to write them down.

Several culminating events illustrated the far-reaching impact of my memory loss. In this particular example, I felt so badly for the student involved. My student was having difficulties and, in a good-hearted effort to help me assist the student, coworkers looked in her file to see how these difficulties were addressed in the child's plan. The room grew silent. They found that, only a few months ago, I had spent an entire Saturday writing a creative plan that was perfectly suited for this child.

But they were puzzled and concerned that I had forgotten having written it. I was concerned, too. Following individual learning plans was a big part of what I was supposed to do every day. Each student I taught had his or her own plan, but I couldn't keep track of what I was supposed to teach to whom. And no matter how many times I checked, I couldn't retain anything.

My outbox shows that around the time all of this was going down, I began pelleting my husband, Randy, with a barrage of links to lists of HD cognitive and behavioral symptoms from the far corners of Google. Too many symptoms could explain my moods and my problems at work. I decided that I needed to rule out HD as a potential problem, and then address what was really causing all these changes. I sent this email to Randy.

One of the things that convinced me to get tested, in addition to my worsening psychiatric symptoms, is the fact that my job performance is declining noticeably. Everyone can tell that my performance is declining, including the principal ... And by delaying the test, I was just digging a deeper hole. *Because of the many situations that arise from my cognitive decline, I am extremely anxious, which only causes me to make more, worse mistakes.*

I had to know. I had to test.

I'm lucky to live in North Carolina because there is a fabulous non-profit here called HD Reach that provides information, resources and support to families facing HD. I developed a great relationship with an HD Reach social worker who was very knowledgeable about HD. After explaining the testing process, the social worker introduced me to the Genetic Counselors at UNC-Chapel Hill.

The salt on the wound of needing a genetic test is the fact that the process takes forever. In my case, it would have taken three trips to the big city, with unusually long weeks in between. But I didn't even make it to the first appointment. When my friend asked for an update, I wrote this.

When I spoke to you last, I had made an appointment to come in for testing. What has since transpired I can only number in order of incredulity:

3) I coincidentally fall into a major depressive state and check myself into a psych hospital for 5 days. I postpone the genetic testing appointment until I can "collect" myself.

2) My brother calls. My estranged and wobbly mother has been suddenly, officially "diagnosed." She's at UNC-CH, after a psychotic break during which she thought that the water from her faucet was emitting toxins into her kitchen, and she kept calling the sheriff to report it.

1) My estranged mother calls. She reminds me of a conversation we had several years ago after we'd come back from seeing her (HD stricken) brother, who was for many years a prisoner of paralytic drugs. I promised her that I would never let her be over-medicated like that. That I would make sure she didn't have to wait out the rest of her life like he did.

She forces out the words, "Don't let them over-medicate me."

Then she hangs up.

Somehow, it just seemed to make sense for me to tell you all of this. That's the only thing that seems to make sense.

Question: How do I make good on my word?

My grip on reality was tenuous when I described what was going on. Looking at it now, aside from my residual irritation over my use of "inappropriate quotation marks," I see that I was completely overwhelmed. Desperate to be tested for the HD gene, I was waylaid instead in a psych ward, and in this setting, I was forced to face what I already knew was true about my mom. And I felt powerless to do anything about any of it.

Sometimes I like to work words into what I write for my own entertainment, like the word trousers. Above, you'll see I exercised my right to use the word *incredulity* and for my further amusement, used the format of Letterman's countdown lists as the template for the letter. So even though times were tough, hope was still there. I still tried to comfort myself with inside jokes.

UPDATE: I am happy to report that, due to advances in treatment rather than a result of my own actions, my mother has been taking Tetrabenazine. As you read this, she is probably sitting in her own kitchen eating ice cream. She is immortal.

My hospital stay ended, and I got back on track for testing.

My answers to the psychological questions were too honest, and I was almost turned away. But after conferences, meetings and phone calls, someone rightly decided that I would be less suicidal knowing my genetic status than continuing without an answer to guide my future action.

So, the blood went off in one direction, and I went home in another to wait. I envisioned some man out west, maybe in Utah, wearing a white, short-sleeved shirt, in a room full of blood samples, working his way to my vial and discovering my genetic future.

Since I was on Christmas vacation from work, my stress level had decreased considerably. By the time the test results came back, I had recalled all of the hypochondriasis that I'd exhibited throughout my life and was secretly calmed by the idea that I was neurotic instead of sick.

12/23/10—Found out yesterday that I am positive with a CAG repeat of 40. I am sad for my three children, and my husband says that I need to set an example for them now, so that is what I am trying to do. But it is a long journey from basket case to example.

These were hollow, hopeless times, and my words reflected that. Everything around me fell away and then apart, like used up sections of a launched rocket. I spent many of the following months either in a fetal position or visiting a mental health professional.

—⁓—

The journey from basket case

Talking about somebody else

When I emerged from the catatonic state, I used writing to report my facts in a detached tone, as if I were describing someone else. I told my story leading up to, but not really accepting, the results. Notice that a lot of my sentences are I statements, probably because I was trying to wrap my head around this new reality which, despite my reluctance, I needed to claim to be able to move forward.

The degree of depression that I have experienced has been debilitating. I have been suicidal, nearly catatonic with crying, and I have had these symptoms daily for over a year.

I seem to reverse or not retain the times that things happen. I manage to still do this even if the info is written on a calendar. Just now, I realized that two of my sons are coming before Christmas and leaving Christmas Day instead of the other half of the holiday break. I have misunderstandings like this about everything I do. It happened at work, and it is happening at home with more frequency.

I take antidepressants and anti-anxiety medication. I go to therapy every week and focus on ways to improve my adaptive behavior skills, like making lists and schedules to get things done. The treatment doesn't really treat the disease, just the symptoms. And the therapy doesn't stick, meaning that I never make any lasting progress. I have to continue working on the same goals; otherwise, I will regress. Despite my best efforts, progress isn't permanent, and I know that it is going to get much, much worse, nightmarishly so, and there is nothing that I can do to stop it. I carry an overwhelming sense of fear, shame, and despair about my disease which no pill or therapy has been able to relieve.

I have good days and bad ones. The difference these days is that there are some good days or sections of good days splattered throughout where there were none a month ago.

I keep to myself more. I have a sense of apathy that prevents me from seeking out social situations. So I don't have a lot of friends locally. I feel that people don't really want to be around me. However, my old friends have been very supportive of me.

My husband runs the household, including finances, in addition to working full time. He spends a lot of time encouraging me and supporting me. I feel like I have ruined my husband's life because he is doomed to be the caregiver of someone that will ultimately bear no resemblance to the woman he married.

I am starting to have trouble with balance and gait, so I have to be careful with stairs and getting dressed. Other people carry things up and down stairs for me because once I fell and sprained my ankle.

I have three sons who are at risk, and I fear for their futures.

Wading through denial

I also wrote in an attempt to reclaim some control over my life, dismissing what the doctor told me.

Regarding my problems with memory, organization, confusion, and prioritizing tasks ... I discussed my problems with my neurologist, and he says he believes that this is the way the HD is currently expressing itself in my brain, and that my problems were a result of the disease.

I think that my inability to perform at work is more of a function of the depression than mental decline, although that is not what the neurologist said.

But he did not base that on anything.

Of course, as soon as I said that, someone suggested that I have a neuropsychological evaluation, but I stood firm.

I think that if I had a neuropsychological evaluation that it would reveal even functioning. That is my hunch.

The people who were helping me navigate the disability process convinced me that taking the evaluation would be useful, even if only to establish a baseline of performance.

So I took the damn test, and I was really surprised at how many times I simply could not answer questions. Mostly because I didn't remember what the test administrator said. I began to accept that some damage had already been done.

> *When I was first told I'd be undergoing neuropsychiatric testing, I said that I was pretty sure I would display even performance in all areas. But having taken the test, I think they may have pinpointed some areas where I am having real trouble, and am hopeful this will be reflected in the report. I had extreme difficulties with tasks … related to auditory memory and visual recognition.*

Landing in acceptance

Sure enough, the neuropsychological evaluation results reflected my poor performance.

> *In the first sentence, it reports that I have problems with many issues. There is a 23-point discrepancy between my FSIQ and processing speed due to memory impairment.*

I begin to write to describe my current level of functioning and apprehensions.

> *I am no longer working, and disability as an income is in my future. I am starting to have to wear shoes with backs to contain my unexpectedly moving feet. It is difficult to go through the steps of preparing a meal.*

And I had to race against time to tell my sons I had HD before they found out on their own.

The worst part of the whole experience so far is anticipation of telling my children about the disease. The geneticists and counselors say to inform children fully, simply, and as soon as possible. "I have a brain disease called Huntington's which will make it harder for me to walk and talk. It is genetic. Your grandmother has it. You have a 50% chance of getting it." This is a conversation that I plan to have with them later in the summer, when we can spend some quality time together afterwards.

Working with a family therapist, I created a plan for telling the boys and had a dress-rehearsal before the big day. I used a dry-erase board and drew a family tree of stick figures and mutated each of them by putting the letters H and D on them, all the way until I got to myself. I gave them the reassurance that they would never have to worry about it affecting them in their lifetime because a cure would be found by then. Then I labelled my stick figure with HD.

I have read about at least one person in the US who has HD in his family who became a neuroscientist. He works hard to find a cure for the disease because he, too, is gene positive for HD. On my sons' behalf, I like to envision that lots of people with his kind of incentive are working hard right this minute.

Jumping into description
In hopes of shining brighter than the distorting fluorescent lights of bureaucracy, my writing purpose changed abruptly from informing to describing.

The Social Security disability process is only now expanding its procedural knowledge to match the current scientific and medical realities of HD. A wonderful, anonymous group of people supported every step of my disability process. They were covering all the bases and thought that if the people at Social Security could just understand HD's full effects beyond chorea, the agency certainly would approve my application. Towards that end, a team member asked me if I could describe what my absolute worst day ever with HD is like. So I answered them with this email.

Having Huntington's disease is like waking up in a nightmare that, each day, becomes more horrific. The person I used to be is gone forever, and in her place is a stranger who has and will continue to regress cognitively, functionally, and physically. The person I used to be was involved and active in the upbringing of her children. But now, two of my sons choose to live with their father, largely out of their desires for more structure and less parental apathy. The person I used to be had a life filled with friends, work, and hobbies. Now, I don't recognize most of the people I meet, even after several introductions, nor can I remember anything that they have told me which has not been written down. My verbal comprehension deficits impact my ability to converse, follow directions, and keep appointments. The person I used to be felt hopeful about contributing to the human experience. Now, I feel as if I have been stripped of my creative soul, and that life from now on has to be merely about trying to meet my basic functional needs, and even this is an increasing struggle. It is becoming increasingly difficult to wake up, do housework, care for the kids and pets, and it's impossible to manage money. The person I used to be experienced joy and creative inspiration. Today, I am unable to summon the initiative to do anything, and my best mood is apathy. I struggle constantly with anxiety, stemming from shame of my inability to function as a mother, wife, and person, and with debilitating depression that often leads me to feel hopeless and suicidal. Without a cure, I will not have a "better tomorrow." Today, unfortunately, is as good as it gets, and each day propels me further into the nightmare of HD.

The person who read this email was moved by it and shared it with other members of my team. She called me and told me I had succeeded and said that the whole office was either in tears or close to it. Another person, who didn't know about the specific nature of my assignment, freaked out (bless his heart) and sent me a plea to live on. He lovingly assured me that I wasn't gone forever, that I mattered and would live on through my children. Despite the truth that my description reflected how I felt most days, I lied to reassure him because I think he was trying to talk me off a ledge. To set everyone's mind at ease, I wrote a soothing response that I wished was the truth:

> *Your letter is a gem which I have printed out and put in the top drawer of my nightstand so I can refer to it when needed. Thank you. Your positive perspective on things … is inspiring. Be assured that what you read was in answer to the question, "How has HD negatively impacted your life?" I am at the point now in the acceptance process that when my dear friends ask me how I am doing, the answer would read nothing like the passage you read. Instead, I would tell them about the things I am trying to do, what I am able to do, and that I want to do. I'd describe how wonderfully my boys are growing up. I'd remind them that I have the world's most loving husband who accepts me for who I am and stands by me at every turn.*
>
> *So, while despair always looms, I am learning to beat it back, in no small part because of the support I have received along the way from people like you and Jean Doe.*
>
> *I am grateful for the existence of the The Anonymous Organization and for the people in it. It really lives up to its name.*

They were really relieved to hear that. They were so happy that it actually rubbed off on me, and I felt happier, too.

I learned two things from that experience. First, I have come to be able describe my own experience with HD in a way that draws some sort of response. Second, by writing the reality I wanted, I was able to move toward it. My assurances to them ultimately manifested. I learned that I could exist in either of the worlds I described. And a lot of times I had the power to choose which one. That made the choice easy.

Perseverating on dwellings

Before the HD, before the recession, Randy and I invested all of our money into a business which lasted 18 nail-biting months, when it should've closed after one week. We were in the process of lifting ourselves out of financial ruin, and New Bern was our fresh start, our happy ending. I emailed Randy:

> *I have lived in 23 places since leaving my parents' home for college. I was fortunate, as were you, to have a stable growing-up place when I was young. But it has not been the case since I grew up, and every time I have had to move, it breaks my heart a little bit. I so want to work towards settling, even if that means signing a ten-year lease instead of buying. I want to plant a tree somewhere and be able to pick its fruit. I want to stay in one place long enough to make friends because I never learned how. I want us all to live happily ever after. If that means that we need to live in an apartment long enough to save money and make a long term plan, I'm all for that. The only thing that makes it easier now is you, because you are like my home. I love you very much, and I always will.*

Within a week of writing an email about going to live in an apartment in order to save and settle down, our home found me.

While driving through Ghent, an early New Bern suburb, entranced by the lovely shade trees, I just happened to look up and see the house. It captured my heart before I parked the car. It had a for sale sign in front of it! Aesthetics or architecture of a house had never impressed me until that moment. Its wrap-around porch was supported by Greek Ionic columns. I walked up the porch steps. The porch ceiling had been painted light pink! I later found out that the pink was inspired by the blooming rosemary bushes.

I called the realtor and, since the house was vacant, walked around back. The house is situated on a corner lot with a good-for-climbing magnolia tree and two good-for-meeting-people pomegranate trees. When I walked behind the magnolia tree to see where the jagged lot line extended, I felt like a child who discovered the secret garden. An old, stone fireplace stood there waiting, along with four columns, some of which had collapsed.

Built in 1917, the house has over 500 windows, the small ones. The ones in front have beveled edges, and the original front door frames a large pane of beveled glass. After a year of hell, something was now enchanting the hell out of me. The house has an updated kitchen, original, refinished hardwood floors, and room for all five boys to visit. I wanted, needed, and stalked it. I perseverated because it felt close to being happy.

I showed Randy the house, and he loved it, too, but he pointed out that we weren't yet ready to buy. Without missing a beat, I began negotiating a lease-purchase agreement with the realtor. The angelic owners were sympathetic to our series of hard knocks, open to our ideas, and trusting enough to give us a chance. It was a win-win: the real estate market was nonexistent, and we needed time to rebuild our credit.

I worked the numbers to show Randy how it could work. Gun-shy from our last leap of faith, he balked. I pushed back too hard, and he said that he couldn't allow us make this mistake. I ended up in the emergency room that night for evaluation of suicidal ideation. I was absolutely out of my mind. Later, I met people who said that I talked to them that night and had cried and told them how much I loved my husband and wanted the house. I didn't remember the people or the conversations, but I believe that they occurred.

After my extreme reaction to his objections and to resolve the stalemate, Randy challenged me: "If you can make it happen. I'll back you up."

I levitated.

Making things happen

Over the next three years, everybody told me at one point or another that there was no way my plan would work. Doctors, therapists, friends, family—everyone who had a stake in my sanity told me that I needed to prepare myself for the possibility of failure.

But every day for three years, no matter what else was going on in my life or in the world or on Facebook, I was also very obsessed about buying the house, which by now we had moved into with this intention.

Getting this far along with the house gave me a taste of confidence, so I decided to ride it in an effort to apply that confidence to resolving my identity. I tweeted as a person with HD on Twitter and began to search around, reaching towards anyone else with HD. The first person who threw me a line was a fellow named Matt Ward from Nottingham. I later found out Matt posted a very popular video diary documenting his journey with HD. Matt and Marie Ward's honesty inspired me to be public about my condition. Any positive things I've done since then can be traced directly to the influence of the Ward family.

Next, I joined Facebook HD support groups, but hid my HD status on my Facebook page. In time, it became increasingly difficult to live two lives without having them overlap. It felt like I was cheating on myself. One less stressor would be in my life if I simply told people I had HD. I'd already had tearful telephone conversations with my best friends in the days following the test results. But that's where my revelations ended.

When I spoke my truth to my Facebook friends I felt so much lighter afterwards. I gave them the facts about HD, then added:

Oftentimes, the person may be mistaken for someone who is drunk. If you know me well, you can see the irony in that. ...

Why am I telling you this now? First of all, I don't know how much longer I will be the "me" that you and I know, and I want my words to be as authentically mine as possible. Second, I am trying my hardest to live every day fully (some days are better than others), and the lie of omitting the truth looms large and spawns its own distractions. Third, I'm hoping that you'll keep your eyes and ears open for other people with the same condition who might like to correspond via phone or e-mail. Oh, yeah, and if you hear they've found a cure, let me know.

Let me close by saying that I am glad that I am alive. I get to be here and watch my kids grow up and experience life. ... I appreciate each of you and thank you for being my friend.

One thing remained to complete my reintegration. My husband is the editor of the local paper. He writes a Sunday column and often talks about our family's experiences, with the exception of HD. So he printed this, at my request, in the Sunday space that usually contains his column.

Every week in this space, Randy tells you a little bit about our family. Pretty little stories about houses and boys and bats.

But he hasn't told you about me, because I asked him not to say anything. I've struggled with a secret for a year.

I have Huntington's disease. It's a neurodegenerative disease that is progressive and incurable. It is genetic, so I've watched many of my relatives die slow deaths. First, they lose control of their behavior and thinking; then their speech is slurred, and their movements become uncontrollable. Many of my ancestors have spent their final years wallowing in nursing home beds, ripping off sheets between doses of paralytic drugs.

I only had a 50% chance of inheriting the disease, so I lived like hell and was determined that I would ultimately learn that the odds were in my favor. But then I started having noticeable symptoms. My work was affected, to the point that I had to go on disability. Many of my coworkers commented that I seemed like a different person. So I was tested, and the odds screwed me.

I am now living my golden years. In the words of Jack Nicholson, this is as good as it gets. Every day will bring me closer to my grandmother's, my uncle's, and now my mother's fate.

I have counselors and people that I talk to that encourage me to Carpe Diem: Seize the day, and I try to, for the kids' sake and for Randy's sake. But sometimes I just think that the situation just sucks.

I was feeling that way last night when we were at the Fireman's Blue Jean Ball, and a nice lady came up to Randy and told him how much she appreciated his columns every week. How much she enjoyed hearing about the family, about me and Mark, and she thanked him for being honest and putting everything out there.

How he can accentuate the positive, week after week, when he is essentially my caregiver is beyond my comprehension. He wakes me and points me in the right direction each day, which often involves pep talks and what to wear. He reminds me of things over and over and then has to do them himself anyway. He catches me when I stumble and tells me that it is probably just the shoes I am wearing. He always seems to know what I need, and his job is not easy. This is his pretty little life now, thanks to me.

Yet every week, he manages to come up with a sunny collection of anecdotes to share with New Bern. Carpe Diem.

There is a reason that he thanks you for letting him in your homes each week. I think it gives him respite and a sense of normalcy. So I wanted to use this space to thank all of Randy's fans for their support of him. (Reprinted with permission from the New Bern Sun Journal.)

Reaching out

A journalist named Ben Casey read this column and immediately reached out to Randy and me, saying he was moved to do something to raise awareness for HD. Before we knew it, he had planned the first Paddle for HD. I decided the proceeds should go to HD Reach.

This organization has helped me greatly from the very beginning. From deciding whether or not to test, to dealing with the agony of the diagnosis, to obtaining help with disability and subsequently finding knowledgeable providers in the area, every step of the way, they have been there for me. And I'd like it if we could help them help others. If the event goes above and beyond raising awareness and raises any money, HD Reach would be a worthy recipient. Perhaps we could have some info at the event describing what they do for North Carolinians with HD. I could take care of that. What do you think?

I am so camera shy that I've always joked that "I don't appear on film." But I let my mug be posted all over town for the paddling event. Paddle for HD turned out to be a beautiful experience, and we aim to hold it every year.

Revealing myself

Crowdfunding for our down payment on GoFundMe stripped away any residue of shame I felt about appearing figuratively naked in front of lots of people. Showing people the truth about my weight and my health was a big deal. But sharing about my financial mishap removed the last layer of embarrassment. Everybody knew everything about me. So, free from shameful secrets, I issued this plea.

Aside from a cure, the thing that would make me happiest of all would be the security of a forever home. We have the opportunity to buy the house we have been living in for three years. It seems ready-made for a disabled person. There is an accessible bathroom, room for a wheelchair ramp, and a downstairs room I can move into when my disability demands it. It is bright with lots of windows.

Plus, I feel that I belong in this house, and can barely fathom the possibility of packing up and moving elsewhere.

In the beginning, the crowdfunding updates I wrote were statistical reports of views, shares, and donations because I figured that's what people wanted to know about.

44.94% to our goal, and we, the lender, the real estate agent, and the seller are poised to pounce on the deal when the funding goal is reached. We are THAT close, and it is exciting! Have a great day!

But then someone advised me that I would reach more people if I were more genuine about my daily experiences and gave them little updates. At first, I had no idea what to write about myself. I spent a long time trying to create an emotional snapshot for people. And ended up simply writing about the unusually winter-like week and how I loved it. Because it was real and true.

Getting iced in. Enjoying the silence and the tapping of sleet. No snowmen for Mark yet, but he and his friends enjoyed sliding around on the sidewalks.

Anticipation! Eight-year-old Mark anticipates the first flake of snow, so he can claim it, and I am not far behind in my enthusiasm. When I first found out I had HD, I thought I had nothing to look forward to, that my life was over. But I've since learned to appreciate things much more than I did before. There is so much in life to enjoy, to relish, to look forward to. And today, it is definitely SNOW!!!!

I was so happy this morning to wake up to snow! Even though it is melting pretty quickly, it is beautiful, and I am glad that I love it. People with Huntington's disease slowly lose interest in things they used to enjoy, and become apathetic. So today I am grateful that I can still enjoy the snow!

Mark is already out there in the snow. I am going to have some chai and just listen to the silence of the snow for a while. I hope that, if you're also in the land of few snows, you are enjoying this one today.

No school tomorrow and no need to go anywhere to get anything, and I'm perfectly content. Hope you are enjoying your conditions, wherever they are.

I am getting used to the quiet of the snow, and I feel relaxed and peaceful. Mark has set off to begin his day of playing in the snow. I am going to have some tea, then make a double batch of brownies for when he comes back with his friends.

The brownies are cooling in the kitchen, and Mark is waiting for a taste... I have the sense that everything is just as it should be at this very moment. Snow must have a sedating effect on me!

I also posted affirmations and statements of gratitude. As I wrote the feelings, they became as real as the snow.

Good morning! I am grateful for another day of good health. Today I choose to act as if I don't have HD, and the world is open wide as a result.

Today, I am just going to focus on being me, without the HD. If I let it, HD can become a specter that overshadows everything I do. That's why being rooted in the moment is so important for me; I am just me right now, going about my day. And that is very satisfying!

Good morning! Let me describe to you the embodiment of generosity.... The woman who owns this house! She has delayed her retirement in order to continue renting to us until we can obtain a mortgage. The proceeds of the sale of the house would supplement her retirement, yet she has chosen to continue working until we can qualify as buyers. If anybody who reads this is close to retirement, I'm sure you can understand what an enormous gift she has given us. Thanks again to all of the donors and everyone who has been sharing my link on their Facebook wall. It is making a huge difference for my family, and I will always be grateful!

Crowdfunding was not my proudest moment, but it led to my later efforts to raise awareness for HD. While I could never really shake the embarrassment of asking for money, I honestly laid out what I needed and why it was important to me. And people surprised me with their support. They donated, and they spread the word. Whole families that I grew up with who are now scattered across the country donated. People who had been touched by HD donated.

... The deeper I get into this campaign, the more I appreciate how innately kind people are. They want to help any way they can. Donations, messages, prayers, and good wishes have come from people around the world.... From folks I grew up with and worked with. But also from people I have never met, but have in common HD. It is ironic how a disease so vile can produce such solidarity among people around the world. In fact, the very first donation came from an HD family in Nottingham, England (Matt Ward). We are a tight knit, supportive group. This experience will certainly encourage me to look for big ways that I can share this sort of kindness with others.

What amazed me as much as people's financial generosity was people's willingness to share my story. And if it was possible for me to let that many people know about HD once, the experience could be replicated.

I just looked and saw that we have reached 2000 shares/tweets! And 3,550 people have visited this site. That is a lot of people who perhaps didn't know anything about Huntington's disease that do now! Besides the house, THAT will be the (perhaps more far-reaching) legacy of this campaign. I am terribly camera-shy, especially at my current weight, but it has been worth discarding that fear and coming forward so all of you can know about this reality that thousands of other people endure, many still in silence. So if you have been sharing and tweeting, you have been doing something big to help HD come out of the shadows. Thank you. And thanks for all the generous donors. Our dream will come true because of many small donations. Have a great day!

For an unexpected finish, a friend of mine who runs a huge Facebook Travel page told his followers that he provided them information about travel at no cost, but if they wanted to repay him, they could help me. Donors from that site included people who were able to travel to that country several times a year. Also, many natives of that country with a more modest means followed his directive as well. One woman said she would go without eating meat for a week so she could donate $15 to my cause. And she did. I would like to one day send her an Omaha steak.

Then the Travel page group cheered me on to victory and wanted to hear all about what happened later. People want to be really, really good to each other, and, given the chance, they will be. I don't think I realized that until the crowdfunding experience. I told my Travel page friend that I would name a room in the house after him.

"OK," he said, "Just as long as it's not the bathroom."

Then, finally,

The fundraiser is OVER. YOU DID IT! YOU GAVE US A HOME!!! We are starting the process of buying the house on Monday! Thank you from the bottom of my heart. You can expect a thank-you video in a few days, but I wanted to let everyone know, so the donations and sharing could stop, and you could have your internet back!!! Thank you again and again... Love, Sarah

Crowdfunding gave us the down payment, and after three and a half years of logistical efforts and a few false starts, during which I bit my nails up to the elbows, on Friday, March 13, 2015, we closed on this house. As I set out towards my intention of buying our home, I developed a tenacity I soon learned was perseveration. I realized that I could choose to perseverate about good things or bad things, so while I was waiting to buy the house, I tried to think of the next good thing.

I had already bared my soul and exposed my physical largeness. There was nothing left to lose except weight, maybe. On the heels of the ALS Ice Bucket Challenge, I went to the grocery store. I bought whipped cream and paper plates. I made the first HD Pie in the Face Challenge video and then shared it everywhere on social media. Keeping the challenge going and trying to promote it was not always easy or healthy.

Around the same time, I started a personal blog. People seemed to enjoy and identify with my descriptions of what life with HD was like during the GoFundMe campaign. It was also good to feel understood and to be loved anyway. So the next time my friends suggested I start my own blog, I did (www.meandhd@wordpress.com). I write there to describe, to report, and to write snapshots of emotional moments.

The sum of all the previous exposure desensitized my shyness and enabled me to share things about myself on my blog that I never even understood until I wrote them.

During the HD Pie in the Face Challenge, it was only when I started trying to get the attention of celebrities on Twitter that HD got in the way. Otherwise, I was channeling my ability to perseverate with good results.

But I became obsessed with getting James Franco's attention, which now I realize was such a waste of time. I wasn't mean to James Franco, but I realized that I was stalker-ish because although my intentions were pure, I could not stop trying to elicit a response from him. My husband and therapist and friends had to carry me through that. But I will always maintain that if I were presented with the choice of taking a Pie in the Face for HD awareness or making the movie, "The Interview," my choice would have been a better one.

I actually did insult John Cusack on Twitter because, ironically, I was disappointed that he directed all his attention to trolls and not people that needed help, like, say, the HD community. So I compared him unfavorably to the Grinch, and I consciously, with malice aforethought, put an @ before his name right before I pressed tweet. Then and there, I became a troll! Well, of course, THAT got his attention, and he rightly demanded to know what he ever did to me.

Let me tell you that the social media equivalent of having HD is having John Cusack fans pissed off at you. I spent the whole night crying. My husband won't let me go to Cusack's Twitter page anymore, which has helped me to settle down and let it go. I have no further interest in his films, either.

It was the pressure, I thought, of wanting to keep the momentum up for the HD Pie in the Face Challenge that was causing my symptoms to increase, thus sending me swimming upstream. I had never been a celebrity hunter before. However, I became fixated on the idea that finding a celebrity to take a pic in the face for Huntington's disease would be the only way the challenge would go viral. And maybe I was right, and that's why it didn't. I am happy that it was a success among the HD communities around the world. But I learned that relying on sanity was more productive than following tangential obsessions, so I don't allow myself to celebrity seek anymore. They'll have to come find me. LOL!

Recently, I searched for Huntington's disease on GoFundMe and got more results than I expected. Not in a position to give financially but wanting to help, I wondered how I could aggregate all these HD families in need and put them in another visible spot. That was the seed for sarahshdlist.wordpress.com. Next, I remembered a comprehensive list of HD-related books, TV, and movie titles that I kept finding and losing on a Facebook support page, so I added that so I would be able to go right to it.

Pretty soon, I was working round the clock, adding everything I could think of to unveil it as a present for Pi Day, March 14, 2015. So now I'm a temporary curator of one collection of information and resources about HD. Eventually, I will give the keys to that collection to someone else—whenever my time is up.

—∽—

How HD is poisoning my inkwell

I alluded to what is going on in my life now, so I'll just spill it. I have had uncontrollable, impulsive behavior which has manifested itself in the form of long, pleading, over-informing, or angrily composed emails sent to several people and organizations.

I am having these micro-aggressions that are borne of frustration, the lack of emotional regulation, and the absence of someone around to talk me out of pressing the send button. I cringe as I go into the sent folder to retrieve some samples.

Let me preface these samples with my cry for help which came afterward.

Need stronger meds to stop impulsive behavior

Dear Doctor, I am including Randy because he has had to deal with my behaviors.

Instead of saying mean or insensitive things in person or over the phone, I have been using email and Facebook messages impulsively and in ways that have hurt other people.

After the first two times I did it, I made a plan with Randy to review any emotionally charged email to make sure it passed the sanity check.

Only problem is, the third time, Randy and one of his employees were my victims. I said the worst possible thing I could have said on the worst possible day because I couldn't stop thinking about it and wanted them to understand.

After I do this stuff, I can look back and realize that it was damaging and socially inappropriate. But there is no taking it back once it is done. I cannot stop myself from doing it again and am praying there is something I can take to help me fight these compulsions so I will not act on them.

I am not behaving like the person I want to be or believe I am. I cannot put my husband or child through this. I would rather be zombie than to be an insensitive, impulsive troublemaker.

I hope you can call something into my 24-hour pharmacy. As soon as it is filled, I will go down there and get it and start taking it.

HD is remarkable in that you can act perfectly normal one minute, then totally reactive, impulsive and, um, mean the next.

I sent a long, mean letter to my youngest child's teacher. That might not seem too bad to you, but I knew he was a first-year teacher but still told him he wasn't doing his job well and was letting my son slip through the cracks. I demanded to meet with him and the principal and cc'd the principal. My husband attended the meeting without me because I was too ashamed to go.

Here is the end of a two page diatribe I sent to every email address I could find at this unfortunate radio station. I am lucky that my husband knew the station manager, who happens to be a fine person, as I'm sure his coworkers are. This is after I tried one time to use their event calendar. It just didn't show up. Nobody rejected it. The email I sent them would have been more appropriate if it was my fourth or fifth letter, or if anyone had told me that my information had been rejected. But I led with it.

I request:

If you rejected the event because you have never heard of HD, please rescind your rejection. Please don't discriminate because HD is an invisible disease.

If you didn't post it because you thought I was running a scam, it should be crystal clear by now that my statements are honest, and my intentions are charitable, and the information I submitted, I considered to be correct, and I request that you approve it.

If the event was rejected due to a procedural error or lack of information on my part, please contact me with specific instructions about how to get this event on your calendar.

If the event is not showing up due to a technical error that can be and will be remedied easily, please let me know. If this is the case, all of the blather above can serve to just give you an idea of the daily frustrations that people with Huntington's disease engage in. Nothing is easy.

Thank you if you've made it this far.

The station manager not only understood that HD made me write the angry email. He solved my calendar problem, too.

The next email is by far the worst one I have written, and I hope it will never be duplicated. I am too disgusted to share the words I used, but I will describe the situation.

In February of 2015, I sent an email to a mid-level manager at a company in response to a minor procedural change she had requested regarding our transaction. Ironically, the subject line read: Boundaries. In the body of the email, I humiliated, insulted, accused, threatened, and insinuated. I was sarcastic, pompous, and even bombastic. I cc'd that person's boss as well as a friendly acquaintance who had the misfortune of being in the periphery of the situation.

I didn't care about the feelings of the email's primary recipient, but was desperate to save my potential friendship with the other woman. But even my apology to her seems dangerously out of control.

> *You are blameless in a situation where someone else needs to reexamine the authority that they assume to have over other people. I am sorry you have been made a party to this, and I will go all the way to the head of the company to defend you if you catch one iota of flack or negative response about this from anyone; just privately let me know. I know exactly what I'll explain to them. I hope you have a fine weekend.*

I never apologized for my awful letter to that manager, because although my behavior was atrocious, I felt that I had said what I thought everyone else wanted to say, but was afraid to say it. In other instances, I have felt like I was speaking for a group, when it turned out I was the only one who held the opinion. I decided I definitely needed help.

I felt horrible for putting my potential friend in such an awful position. I will probably never hear back from her because that was not the first of such letters she had seen. Soon after we met, I explained all about my illness to her, and she seemed to understand and accept me for who I was. She clearly acted differently towards me after the first letter. After reading the second letter, she must have known that I was out of control and retreated for her own safety. I don't blame her, but I would give anything to be able to press undo and not have sent those stupid emails.

These angry outbursts have begun to taint my one form of expression. Even in the paragraph above that I just wrote, I am still more concerned about my friendship with the woman than about the fact that people were hurt. I thought that writing would be a way around upsetting other people, instead of just a mouth substitute, because there is that pause of self-reflection beforehand that angry verbal interactions lack. But HD has broken the mirror and is taking control.

Almost anything can set off a micro-aggression. It can be small things, like my son playfully jumping out to scare me, or my husband going to the new burrito joint without me. Just a little spark and the gas ignites, and my brain burns into hot oil that will have to cool and congeal, or it will never be fit for lucid thought again.

The angry letter experience led me to a total emotional breakdown, and intervention and new meds are helping me get better. During a micro-aggression, when I was angry at HD for using me to hurt my family, I wrote this blog entry. I'll start winding things down by sharing it. I make sure I state that I am speaking strictly for myself!

How to feed this person with HD and avoid getting bitten.
Please do not tell me that maybe HD is the best thing that could have happened to me and that it has given me direction. I would've preferred living aimlessly rather than spending decades going through and putting people through hell.

Please do not commiserate with me by comparing your age-related symptoms to my HD symptoms. It is like me commiserating with someone with cancer by showing them my hang nails.

Please do not assume that my HD experiences are not real. If you need proof that you are wrong, just ask the people I unintentionally hurt each day.

Please don't think members of my family can handle by themselves the repercussions of the mother's brain functions switching off. Can you imagine how YOU would be affected if that actually happened to you? Think of all you would lose: sanity, memory, motor control—and how that would express itself through your body every day and night. Imagine forcing your children and loved ones to live in that mess.

Please do not tell me that tomorrow will be better because I have no assurances that it will be. That has not been the trend.

Please do not tell me that you admire what I'm doing because what I am actually doing is destroying the lives of my family and friends.

Please do not tell me to let you know if there's anything you can do unless you want a list.

Please do not think that I am the same person I was when we met or even yesterday.

Please do not think I can get away from HD or decide when or how my brain damage will manifest. If I had that ability, I would use it to cure Huntington's disease.

Please do not feed me with false hope because it always leaves a bitter aftertaste.

Please do not tell me I am doing better because that will never be true. My brain will not regenerate. I will always be getting worse.

If you want to help me, start by offering emotional support and respite to my burned-out family. They didn't sign up for this. There was no way they could've imagined how awful it would be. I am destroying their lives against my will. Something can be done for them. Their spirits need special care.

If you want to help me, press the share button instead of the like button for HD awareness Facebook posts. Not necessarily this one, but that is a point I want to get across. It's the same way as in real life.

In real life, you can like me, but then turn around and do your Relay for Life and your bucket challenge and all these popular things for diseases that everyone already knows about. Your liking me won't do me a damn bit of good. It is only through sharing your generosity of spirit towards me and my family or through taking a moment of your time to let other people know about HD and what they can do to help end it that you can help.

> *So feed this friend with HD by drawing attention to the disease so people will help support a cure.*
> *Just don't take it personally if I bite you.*
> *(If you do, please refer to my feeding instructions again.)*

Just as poison pen letters remain to leave an impression, anytime I write a blog entry or update the HD List or think of some silly way to raise awareness and persuade people to participate, I leave behind written tracks. I fear that if I don't leave visible tracks that when I am gone, I will truly be gone. Nothing tangible would exist to express who I was or to describe my experience. My children would not know my experience as fully as I would like.

The choice is either write or succumb to HD. If I am not propelling myself forward into something with my words, I fear I will be overtaken by HD. Writing is (now arguably) my way to stay one jump ahead from total insanity. Recent events have been terrifying because they have shown me a glimpse of what can lie ahead if medicines and interventions no longer keep me sane enough to write.

I write this between intervals of HD hitting me hard, like waves. I perseverate on really bad things to the point of hyperventilating and crying and freaking out. Then my psychiatrist talks to me and to Randy, and things seem okay until the next wave.

The bottom line is that I realize this is no longer foreshadowing. This is the real thing. HD is destroying my brain right now, and I am fearful of how I will feel five minutes from now. Generating written words to speak my truth and describe my experiences is my only comfort, and I must write as much as I can until I can't.

There's sadness here, too. I feel more relaxed writing than I do interacting with other people, and I tend to do what I like. So a lot of people just read emails from me now. We don't converse or get together anymore because I don't have any interest in it. I just want to be left alone so I can do what I need to do. In the long run, this will give them a better shot at knowing anything about me.

I don't know if this is the new normal, if I will need to resign myself to being out of control of my feelings, but I hope that it is something that can be slowed down, stopped, or reversed.

The very, very bottom line is that every syllable I have written has been for my husband and my children so they will know who I was and what I went through. I struggle to be able to leave these records for them, even as the promise of a cure glimmers on the horizon. I would be happy if my words served as artifacts describing a disease wiped out long ago.

But the very, very, very bottom line is that Randy, Noah, Ezra, and Mark, I love you dearly, and while I cannot express that very well verbally, I can write it now, and you can have a record of it.

You are the best parts of my life.

—⁂—

Please consider making a donation to HD Reach, a nonprofit organization.

Donations can be made via their secure web site, Network for Good, http://hdreach.org, or by mailing a check to:

HD Reach
1004 Dresser Ct., Suite 107
Raleigh, NC 27609-7325

You can also contact HD Reach at **919-803-8128.**

About Ben Lamoreau

Ben Lamoreau was born on May 12, 1977, in Brunswick, Maine, to what he says are two of the best parents he could ask for. They were married in January of 1977 and had three kids. Ben is the oldest. His brother passed away in 2001, and he has one sister, who is the baby. Ben has two kids, a boy and a girl, and two stepdaughters. He also has three companion dogs, Mitzy, Dusty, and Miley. Ben currently lives in Maine, where he is a carpenter's helper, and his hobbies include, but are not limited to, arts and crafts, photography, sports, and wood working.

CHAPTER 3

∼≫∽

Just Listen
by Ben Lamoreau

Sometimes in a relationship, there a few things we all would change. Let me start from the beginning of a wonderful relationship I had the privilege to be in. It was a Saturday morning on July 14 of 2007. I had dated a few nice women, but the relationships just didn't work out for one reason or another. Back then, the big media hubbub was Myspace. As I was scrolling through Myspace early that morning, I got a message from a very beautiful girl. She had the most beautiful green eyes I had ever seen.

Her name was Lisa. We chatted for a bit. After a while, she asked if we could meet. I said, "Yes I'd love to."

She then wrote, "There's only one thing. Have you ever heard of a disease called Huntington's chorea?"

My reply was like most people. "Nope, never have."

Lisa said, "Okay, I will send you some info. If it doesn't scare you off, write me back."

I'm not that selfish, so I already knew I was going to at least meet her, but I read it anyway. It seemed pretty scary. It mentioned that over time, people with HD develop balance issues and fall a lot, have behavioral changes, and sometimes have symptoms like bipolar disorder, to name a few things.

But again, I was not selfish, so I wrote her back, and as nervous as I was, we met that afternoon at my apartment. My first thought upon laying eyes on her was that she was beautiful, yeah, but in a different kind of way.

Can't really explain it, but WOW. She had a free-flow attitude that I had never seen in any girl I had dated. She had eyebrow rings and tattoos. That was new to me.

We took a short walk down to the river by my house, had a great dinner at a local restaurant, and went back to my place to hang out. We talked into the night about different things like our shared love of our children. We watched the movie "Armageddon" that she hadn't seen yet. At three o'clock in the morning, she got sick from a bad migraine and puked in a bowl. She asked me to make her a cup of coffee. She always marveled at the fact that I made her coffee at 3:00 a.m. on our first date.

After that night, I knew we would spend eternity together. The chemistry we had was magical. I always wanted to find someone I could "take care of," and I know God put us together. As most people with Huntington's disease will do, over the next several weeks she would try to push me away. I think it was more of a "scared" thing. She was scared by how fast things were moving.

In February of 2007, Lisa had participated in a pre-symptomatic study group for HD patients down at Massachusetts General Hospital. On her MRI in February, they had found a spot on the right side of her head. They waited six months, and in August of that year, Lisa and I went down for another MRI. The spot had turned to a mass. When we got to the car, we cried together. I held her for an hour before she called her parents. She always joked that she must have killed a pope in her past life. How else to explain not one but two terminal illnesses?

The doctor recommended that we see a specialist at Massachusetts General and gave us a few minutes together. Lisa gave me every opportunity to get out of the relationship. She would tell me that I should go be with someone healthy, and I would tell her a million times, "No, I'm not leaving."

So at the end of August, we went down to see the neurosurgeon at MGH. After consulting with him, we decided to schedule cranium surgery for September 14, 2007. They would cut her skull out, just forward and above her ear, take out the mass, put her skull back in, and screw it in with a plate made of titanium. It was scary for us both. As we knew, things can go wrong with any surgery, but working on the brain, it seemed that so much more could go wrong.

The surgery took six hours. Her father was there as well, and he and I walked around Boston. We were down there for a total of four days, and the doctors told us they'd gotten it all. I got five hours of sleep in those four days. I was so "helpful" that when I went to change her sheets on the hospital bed, the nurses would get upset with me and tell me that was their job.

About a month before Lisa and I met, I won tickets to a Trace Adkins concert. I was getting excited to be going to my first concert. Well, I met Lisa, and she had just finalized her divorce and had booked a cruise for two. We had met in July, and a few weeks later she invited me on this cruise. It happened to be the same time the concert. We went at the end of August, beginning of September. We went to the Caribbean and had a blast. We swam with dolphins and sting rays, tubed down a river in Jamaica. Although she was sick most of the time, she made the most of it.

We were so happy, but in the ensuing next few appointments at MGH, we found out that the surgeons had only gotten 90 percent of the mass, an astrocytoma. It was shaped like a star, hence the name astrocytoma, and they could not get the tentacle parts of it. At that point, it was only a stage one tumor (tumors are ranked stage one to stage four, with four being the worst). Lisa and I were devastated because we thought they'd gotten it all. We talked about chemo and radiation, but the more times you have radiation, the less well it works, and we decided to wait until it would work best, when there was blood flow to the tumor. The doctor refused to do chemo or radiation, though, because there was no research on whether it would make her symptomatic from the HD.

Not long after her surgery, we were going to the local McDonald's with her two girls and my two kids. They all were within three years of each other. We didn't know the McDonald's was closed for repairs, so we ended up heading back to the truck. As we were walking back to our truck, another truck was leaving, and the driver honked his horn. Lisa thought he was honking at us, so she raised her middle finger to him. He pulled up beside her, and they started yelling at each other.

I was putting the kids in the truck, but I heard him say, "You're just a baldheaded dyke," as he pulled away.

No one talks to my lady like that. I took off after him on foot. Luckily, he only went about 200 feet to the Shaw's nearby. He saw me come in and decided to grab his baby out of the backseat. When I got up to him, I was yelling at him that she had just had brain surgery, and that was why she had the bald head. His jaw just hit the ground. The kids were all crying for me to get into the truck, so I did.

Her fault or not, no one yelled at my baby girl, but he was inconsiderate and rude. I hope he learned his lesson that day.

As the years went on, and the more doctors and ER visits we had, I learned a lot about my Lisa. I found out she had a history of Post-Traumatic Stress Disorder. She had been sexually assaulted when she was 11 and 12, and she would have nightmares and flashbacks. All I could do was hold her. After her diagnosis of HD, before I came into her life, Lisa had tried to commit suicide three times, something that is very common in patients with HD, by cutting and by overdosing on meds. She was a veteran, having served in the Navy for a brief time before shattering her ankle in boot camp. She loved art, hiking, biking, going to the gym, and she loved her girls and was so proud of them.

We were very factual people who would hear a term from a doctor and go home and Google it, so we learned a lot of information. The only problem was that because Lisa had a brain tumor in addition to Huntington's disease, some of the symptoms ran together, like behavioral problems. We didn't know for sure if they were caused by the brain tumor or by Huntington's, or maybe by both.

We learned that symptoms of Huntington's disease can vary from person to person, and onset can vary in age from 1 to 99. HD is passed down from generation to generation, with each child having a fifty-fifty chance of inheriting the fatal gene. Lisa had found out she had HD before we met; therefore, she knew her girls had the chance to get it as well. When the oldest turned 12, we told them about HD. Their reaction wasn't what we thought it might have been; they really had no reaction.

People who have Huntington's disease sometimes look to be drunk and stumbling. The last two years of her life, Lisa was constantly losing balance and falling down often, looking like she was drunk. It was upsetting, and I was concerned for Lisa's safety. I was so worried she would take a hard fall one of those times.

Lisa's mom was in a nursing home with Huntington's disease. As we visited her over the years, one time she would be happy to see us, and the next time, she would scowl. Lisa had been estranged from her mom for a long time, not seeing her for twenty years. Just after her second daughter was born, Lisa had gotten in touch with her mom. Her mom was showing signs of HD at the time. That's when Lisa found out she had a fifty-fifty chance of getting HD and got tested. She always thought her grandfather had had HD, but she wasn't sure.

Lisa hated to go see her mom sometimes because of the scowling and sometimes because it reminded her of her future with HD. I would try to convince her to go see her mom because I didn't want her have the "what ifs" after she passed. Lisa got to hold her mom the whole night before her mom passed the next morning.

On May 12, 2010, in the morning, Lisa came into our bedroom and jumped on me and asked me if I wanted to get married that day. That day, May 12, is my birthday, too. So that day we went up to the town hall and got married. Yeah, maybe it wasn't a big, elaborate wedding, but it was a great day for me.

In December of 2010, Lisa had a hysterectomy. She had a "lesion" on her cervix that the doctor was concerned could turn cancerous. Her list of surgeries is long: ankle eight times, knee four times, appendix, gall bladder, ear tubes many times, nose surgery a few times. I used to joke and tell her that the only thing she hadn't had work on was her elbow. Sometime in 2011, she had a feeding tube put in because she wasn't eating much at all. When she did eat, she would throw it up. When she was on the table getting cut open for the feeding tube, they made the first incision, and she felt it. She screamed in pain until they gave her more medicine to knock her out.

We were together 24/7. Just when she would start feeling better, and we would discuss me getting a job, something would happen. She would have a seizure or take a bad fall that would set her back to being almost completely bedridden. Some months were better than others. Some months, it would be a once weekly trip to the ER. Sometimes with falls she would hit her head or twist her ankle just right. She was diagnosed with pre-osteoporosis, which makes the bones weak, so any kind of fall could have broken any number of bones. Most times, though, we went to the ER because she could no longer handle her headaches.

From February 2011 until she passed away, Lisa and I lived in a lakefront house at the end of a dirt road. It was kind of like camping all year round. It was beautiful. We took many trips to the ocean when she was up for it, and she loved going to Mexicali Blues and Goodwill to browse.

Lisa was the most selfless person I knew and had a heart of gold to match. She was always helping other people and always forgiving the bad in people. At one point, we had two other couples living with us. But that's the way we both were, always giving out advice and being the "wise" ones. I learned a lot from my doll face.

We always talked about what would happen to me after she passed. Her biggest thing that she always made sure to tell me was that it was ok for me to move on, but she is someone from whom it will never be easy to move on.

Lisa's mom passed away in August 2013. I think she was in her 60s, and I think she started showed signs when she was 35. It may sound funny, but the one thing we were thankful for was the brain tumor because we knew that would take Lisa before Huntington's would. She wrote about her fear of being a vegetable, not being able to talk or move, but being able to understand everything that is being said and done, and said HD is a cruel, dark disease. As some people know, Huntington's disease is sometimes known as the devil's disease.

From the time I met Lisa, she always had constant headaches. I think it was because of the brain tumor. Over the years, they got worse, to the point where a migraine was a good day. Eventually, she only had about an hour's worth of good time a day. Most of her days were spent lying down in bed or on the couch with an ice pack on her head.

Lisa was a realist. She really didn't believe in miracles. Yes, she prayed and believed in God, but it was more about how she felt. It was more of a gut feeling. She started telling me that she only had about a year left to live. I would argue with her in the beginning, but she would never change her mind, so I never argued with her again, but to myself I always thought she had five to ten years left to live.

Lisa was born September 4, 1975, and passed away in her sleep by my side on June 22, 2014. She was only 38 years old. Lisa would go days without sleep, then sleep for the next three days. That weekend, we had her girls over. She slept most all that Saturday, which was common. I ran to town to get some lunch for the girls and me. While I was in the drive-through at Kentucky Fried Chicken, Lisa called me, asking if I could get some enemas because she was on pain meds, and pain meds tend to harden the stool. I went to Walgreens and got some for her and went back home. I went into the bedroom and told her I was back and got her the enemas.

She barely opened her eyes but did say, "Thank you." Again, everything seemed normal.

At about 12:30 that night, I went to bed. Lisa was snoring. Looking back now, it was a little deeper than normal, but I didn't think anything of it then. I fell asleep and woke up around 3:00 a.m. Lisa wasn't snoring, so I put my hand in front of her mouth and felt no air, so I shook her very hard while saying "Lisa!" loudly.

I checked for a pulse but couldn't find one. I then called 911. The operator told me Lisa needed to be on the floor, so the quickest way I could do that was to grab her by the ankles and pull her off the bed. Mind you, our mattresses were sitting on the floor, so it wasn't a big drop, but I can still picture the way her head was flopping. The girl from 911 told me to start chest compressions until rescue got there. When the paramedics got there, they took over.

A short while later, I got two text messages from her girls. The youngest, who was 13, had a friend over, and they were sleeping outside on the trampoline. She texted me to ask what was going on. The oldest (15), knowing her mom went to the hospital a lot, texted me, "Beny, if you need to take her to the hospital, I will stay here with the young girls." I didn't text either back right then because I didn't have an answer at that point. It seemed like hours passed from the time I woke up at 3:00 and the time they pronounced her dead, but it was only about 35 minutes.

After they gave me the official word, I went into "rock" mode because of the girls. I went out and got the young girls and brought them all upstairs and told them what had happened. They both cried, and the older one asked for a few moments alone. I went downstairs and called her dad and stepmom, then my parents. I had a lot of people come visit me the next day and for days afterwards. We had a great celebration of life service for her. Lots of people came. Some days, I still think she is just a phone call away. When is she gonna call me? I also have the "what ifs," like what if I had gone to bed later or woken earlier or recognized her labored snoring?

At the end of August, I found a bunch of notes Lisa had written to me, notes meant for me to read only after she was gone. One said, "I know you know I had to go but I feel your love—every second—of any day. I can't wait to surf. I'll have my balance, and it will be calm. I am so sorry that you feel like you are going through this alone. There was no single second in our time together that I would give up."

Another one told me she hoped I'd seek counseling for my grief because that was the only way she'd gotten through HD. She said, "I truly believe God gave me HD so I had the knowhow to deal with cancer and all."

Starting over without your "wobby" sucks. The only way I used to be able to fall asleep was by contact with her. I'm sleeping better but not great now. Some days I just want to be with her so badly. Sometimes, when I'm driving, I subconsciously reach for her leg, and it's not there. I still breathe each day, but I breathe one less breath each day. She was my air, my everything. If I could dream of her all night, I'd never wake up. I'm glad she doesn't feel any pain anymore, but just to be with her one more tomorrow would be the best thing ever. One step at a time, I'm trying to build a new life without my Lisa.

I decided to start a scholarship in Lisa's name so that she will never be forgotten. It will be going to the Dance Studio of Maine in Gorham. She loved watching her girls dance in our home. They have been dancing since we first met and even before that. The first year, there will be two scholarships, and they will go to Lisa's girls, but starting next year, it will go to a "hard-luck" person, maybe someone who couldn't afford dance lessons or who lost her mom or dad. I would love to make it bigger and turn it into an adult Make-a-Wish.

People say she was lucky to have me. I always say I'm lucky to have had her. My Lisa taught me patience and a whole 'nother way to parent better. I was a "yeller," yet she taught me that we need to talk to one another. She also taught me that "if it isn't gonna matter in five minutes, don't worry about it." She taught me what true love is. She taught me so much in the seven years we had here together. She was strong beyond strength.

There isn't much I would change about my relationship with Lisa. She may not have been perfect, but she was perfect for me. Besides the fact that she was so sick, the only thing I would change is that I wish I had listened to her at the end when she said she only had a year left to live. I would have pushed her to do more instead of just lying down. We would have made so many more memories.

—⁓—

Please consider making a donation to The Wilderness Kids, a non-profit organization that provides a family relief fund for families affected by HD and JHD.

Donations can be made via their secure web site, http://www.help4hdinternational.org/WildernessKids.html, or by mailing a check to:

Help 4 HD International, Inc.
436 Playa Blanca Street
Santa Maria, CA 93455

In the "memo" section of your check, please specify "Wilderness Kids Drawing."

You can also contact the Wilderness Kids at:
6 Ginger Lane
Saco, ME 04072
Email: WildernessKidsFirewood@gmail.com
Cell: 207-229-8240

You can also find the Wilderness Kids on Facebook as "Wilderness Kids Firewood—Help4HD Relief Fund."

About Jeannie Grundborg

Jeannie Grundborg was born in Massachusetts in October, 1943. She attended Burdett College, then went to Bainbridge Island, Washington, to visit her aunt in 1962. There, she met and married Bernard Thompson. They had a daughter, Melissa, born in 1967, and a son, Brett, born in 1969. They moved to Kirkland, Washington. After her husband's diagnosis of HD, Jeannie returned to college to better her career as a medical business manager. After moving to Newport Beach, California, she again went back to college, UC Fullerton for Human Resources Management. Jeannie was a charter member of the Orange County Chapter, HDSA, and did fundraisers for galas and walks at UC Irvine. Her first husband passed away at the age of 39. Her son passed away at age 33, and her daughter passed away at age 39. Jeannie, now retired, lives with her husband, Bob, in southwest Florida. Together, they are looking forward to helping others in the area of service work and spreading the word to everyone about HD.

CHAPTER 4

※

Three Stolen Futures
By Jeannie Grundborg

I want to start my story with the following speech Detective Tina Drain gives to Seattle Police officers after working on my case. I will be forever grateful to her.

"People often ask why I would want to work in Missing Persons.

"I want to tell you about Jeannie Zetz [Grundborg]. Jeannie lives in southern California and has two adult children, Melissa and Brett Thompson. Both suffered from Huntington's disease, a terminal, degenerative disease that is a combination of ALS, Parkinson's and Alzheimer's. Jeannie's husband died of Huntington's some years ago.

"In April of 2003, Jeannie went to her local police department to report her son, Brett, missing. He had moved to Seattle a few months earlier and suddenly stopped contacting his mother. Even though Brett was 33 years old and becoming increasingly ill, he always called his mother.

"The agency refused to take a report. After all, wasn't he an adult and free to make his own choices? Jeannie would not leave the police department until a report was taken. The report was appropriately referred to Seattle. Three months later, we learned the fate of Brett Thompson. He had been strangled to death by his roommate, Brian Robertson. Brian killed Brett, placed his body inside a large recycling container, and wheeled it into a remote location at Carkeek Park. He

then dug a hole and threw Brett's body into it. We dug Brett out of the ground on the fourth of July. He had been dead four months.

"Jeannie came to Seattle for the trial over a year later. I was with Jeannie numerous times as she sat in the court day after day, listening to how her son spent the last hours of his life. I stood by her while she placed her hand on the dusty, dirty recycling container her son had been dumped into. At her request, I took Jeannie to the gravesite of her son, a remote place that required walking and sometimes stumbling over brush and branches and through nettles. I waited while she stood quietly over the gaping hole in the ground at Carkeek Park and then turned to me and said, "This is a pretty place, isn't it?" During court recesses, I watched her as she would call and check up on her daughter, Melissa, who was in a nursing home, in the final stages of her ravaging disease. And I was with Jeannie when the jury convicted Brian Robertson of First Degree Murder. I didn't teach Jeannie a thing. I was humbled by her. Rarely have I seen such a reservoir of dignity, strength, and grace from an individual, especially one who has endured so much. Jeannie Zetz is why I work in Missing Persons."

My story begins.

My Aunt Muriel invited me to go to the Seattle World's Fair and stay at her home on Bainbridge Island, WA. Surprisingly, she had set up a blind date to take me there.

It was a warm, sunny June day in 1962 when down the driveway came a white Jaguar XKE convertible. The dust was flying, so it was difficult to see the driver clearly. Out stepped a tall, handsome blonde who resembled Troy Donahue. I couldn't believe what I saw. Never did I see in Saugus, MA, a man who was so clean cut and had such pizzazz! This man was going to take me to the Seattle World's Fair. His tanned face was shockingly handsome. He was coming down the long gravel driveway on Bainbridge Island. That was my first view of Bernard Thompson.

Bainbridge Island is where my Aunt Muriel had moved after she married Howard Springer, a well-known naval architect. Howdy, as he was called, had built a large home overlooking the Seattle skyline on more than a couple of waterfront acres at the north end of the island. Auntie Mike, as she was nicknamed, divorced Howdy, sold that house and built a two-story salt box home closer to the beach. Bernard, along with a few neighbors, helped with the construction. It was called The Gray House. With gray board and batten siding, gray field stone fireplace, large black and white tile floor with furnishings in shades of blue, green and purple, including the bathrooms, the home was very pretty and sunnier than any house I had ever been in. The home was not ostentatious by any means, yet was very comfortable, and I was happy there. Auntie Mike had Mason jars full of Indian beads she collected on her beach. They lined the shelf in her kitchen window. This relaxed life style was nothing I could have imagined as I was growing up in Saugus.

Bernie, as Bernard was called, had just finished building a wooden B-2 runabout for West Port Madison Bay. He loved the water and boats. His father went to sea as a purser for almost a year at a time. His grandfather was a salmon fisherman who kept his fishing boat at the dock in front of his house. They lived down the road from Auntie Mike. Everyone knew each other, and it was common for people to stop by.

My first date with Bernie was a day at the Seattle World's Fair. We walked all day, visiting many different exhibits. We stopped at a pearl diver booth near the Space Needle. Inside every oyster was a pearl, different sizes, shapes, or colors. My prize was an oval shaped pearl. Bernie wanted me to pick out a gold ring setting for my souvenir. I was thrilled.

The rest of the summer we were inseparable. On weekends, we jumped from the dock and swam in the bay. Other times, we went out in Bernie's boat to a lagoon near the sandbar facing Seattle and swam in the shallow, clear, warm water. Another time, we were invited to the Seattle Seafair Hydroplane Race on Lake Washington by a naval architect who lived across West Port Madison Bay. Bernie had gone to high school with his son.

Bernie took the Jaguar out on the back roads of Bainbridge to see how fast it would go and took me with him. The last time I could look at the speedometer, it read 120 miles per hour. I covered my eyes with my scarf. It didn't take long to know I never wanted to go back home to Saugus and Burdett College. I no longer had a future there. By November, I was wearing an engagement ring. My future was with Bernie. I returned to Saugus for a month's visit to tie up loose ends, withdraw from college and say goodbye to my family and girlfriends.

The following September, Bernie and I were married in St. Barnabas Episcopal Church, a beautiful stone church on Bainbridge Island. After a honeymoon trip to San Francisco, we set up our apartment in Seattle with all the wedding gifts from the many Thompson friends and business associates. We received an entire set of platinum band crystal and platinum band china. My grandmother gave us her complete set of Damask Rose silverware. We did not want for anything. Life couldn't get any better for us. We were on top of cloud nine and very much in love. Cloud nine wouldn't last very long.

I got a job in Seattle at Leavitt Brothers as the account receivable manager. The four brothers who owned the store purchased designer clothes from across the country. They were stored until the next season, then sold in their store. I was their model for knit suits, which were popular at that time.

Life with Bernie was very unusual as he kept having accidents. I was told by Bernie's father, Wilbur, that he was accident prone, which was attributed to him growing tall very quickly at a young age. He'd also had a serious fall while in the Coast Guard Reserve and had been hospitalized with injuries. Riding with him scared me so much my knuckles turned white. He had to meet the ships that his company represented when they were coming into Puget Sound. One time, I was riding with him from

Seattle to Bellingham, and I was frightened. Several times he drove up onto the center median at 70 miles per hour. His parents said I was "too nervous."

This was Huntington's disease, only I didn't know it.

Bernie fell off the ladder at our home in Kirkland several times, causing many scrapes and open gashes. He was working with a band saw in the garage one day and walked away and left it turned on. Our son, Brett, five years old and curious, touched the blade and sliced his finger down to the bone and needed x-rays and stitches at Evergreen Hospital. That was the first of many trips to emergency rooms for Bernie and the children.

On our vacation trip to see Bernie's relatives in Victoria, British Columbia, he wanted to take our children outside to play. Minutes later, he came inside carrying Brett, who was bleeding profusely from his face. He said Brett had run into a rusty rubbish barrel. We went immediately to Royal Jubilee Emergency Room. Brett needed quite a number of stitches in several layers along his eyebrow and down the side of his face. He couldn't go swimming for the rest of our summer. It left a large scar. I thought he could have plastic surgery when he finished growing.

A few days later, we drove further up Vancouver Island to Campbell River where we got a motel. Bernie and the children were in the pool. I'd had a recent surgical procedure and was not able to be in the water to watch our children. I noticed Bernie turning around and leaving the deep end of the pool where he had been playing with Melissa, who was six years old and a non-swimmer. A stranger jumped into the pool and grabbed her as she was struggling in the water. He brought her to the shallow end of the pool where I met them. What was wrong with Bernie anyway, I thought?

Brett got his permanent teeth early, at five years old. I was at my office, and Bernie was watching the children. We lived in a cul-de-sac, and Brett knew he was not to ride down the street and around the corner. This time, his dad was not watching. A car veered too close to him, and he was thrown off his bike. This was a hit and run, but I didn't think at the time to report it to the police. I was too traumatized by this accident. His face was bloodied, and two front teeth were missing. I left work early that day. I called our dentist, who met us at his office. The dentist was not able to reattach those two beautiful new teeth. In the meantime, Brett's head began to swell, so the dentist ordered us to get him to Evergreen Hospital Emergency Room. He recovered, but he now was missing his two front teeth.

I took Brett to a children's dental specialist, who made a plate with two teeth on it. Braces moved the other teeth closer and closer to the center. Then, he planned to cap each lateral tooth as a front tooth, and Brett's bone structure would not be jeopardized. Fortunately, this was at the age when all his friends were losing their baby teeth. It was unfortunate that Brett's dental treatment would never be completed.

Riding the bus back and forth to work in Seattle, I couldn't look at children who had their permanent front teeth. It saddened me for a long time. I had no idea what was in the future for my family, or I would not have focused so much on this one accident.

On a camping trip to Inn of the Seventh Mountain in Bend, Oregon, we drove up to Crater Lake and planned on driving around the rim. When it became obvious that Bernie's driving was jerking us from one side to the other on this narrow ledge of a road, I made the kids get out with the dog, and we waited for a park ranger to drive by and take us down to safety. Bernie followed the park ranger in our car. Thankfully, he was able to drive that narrow road to safety.

Huntington's disease was elusive for a long time. We all made excuses for Bernie's accidents. We didn't want him to have a life-threatening disease. His family physician suggested he might have Myasthenia Gravis; however, that diagnosis didn't get much attention as events started happening so fast.

Bernie worked as Traffic Manager for a Norwegian steamship company. While visiting a customer, he fell off his chair, and it was reported to his boss. He was fired for "having a two martini lunch." I fought it with the Human Rights Commission, but eventually lost. We had lost the breadwinner's income and benefits. There was no long-term disability with his employer. We applied for Social Security Disability. His claim was accepted rather quickly. This did not make up for his previous wages, but it certainly helped. I had to be thankful we only had a home mortgage and no other debt.

The next day I said I would "pound the pavement" for a job and not come home until I had one. I put on my new mauve pant suit I had gotten for Easter, mauve flowered chiffon scarf, cream patent leather shoes that pinched my toes, and off I went to Seattle. My first stop was at a medical employment agency. The owner told me flatly, "It doesn't matter how gutsy you are. If you don't have medical office experience, you won't get hired." Reluctantly, he did send me on an interview that day to a family practice medical clinic in downtown Seattle. I was hired as their office manager and worked there for over eight years.

Leaving Bernie alone during the day worried me, so I hired my neighbor, Inga, to come in through the garage and check on him. He quickly discharged her. He also refused to have a male personal attendant stay with him while I worked.

One night, Bernie was watching "Streets of San Francisco" while lying on the sofa and having a cigarette. His ashtray was on the floor beside him, but apparently he inadvertently shoved his ashtray under the hem of the sofa. Then he went to bed. We were all in our beds when smoke woke me up about 1 a.m. Our bedroom door was open. I went across the hall to each child and grabbed them and headed for the front door, but it was blocked by fire and smoke. I carried them back to our bedroom, opened the window, and pushed our heads out the window to breathe fresh air. I had to help Bernie keep his head out the window as well. In the ruckus, I neglected to lay wet towels down along the inside of our bedroom door to keep the smoke from coming in and choking us. By the time I heard that wonderful sound of the fire engines, my neighbor Jane was under the second-floor bedroom window, holding up a stick for us to climb down. It seemed to take forever for the firemen to find us in the bedroom at the end of the hall. Each fireman carried a child. The last fireman told me to crawl under the smoke as he was helping Bernie carry the dog. I was wearing only a thin nightgown. My closet door was open, so I snapped my bathrobe off the hanger as I was crawling along under the layer of smoke.

When we got to the front door, the fire was out, but there was plenty of smoke. A huge fan from the fire department was brought in and placed in the doorway. Our cul-de-sac was lit up by a searchlight. Most of my neighbors were outside, standing around and talking. I was glad I had grabbed a bathrobe to cover up.

Janice brought out cots into her living room so we could sleep there, and a neighbor brought over white twin-size sheets. At least we were all safe and could now take care of getting back to normal, quickly. That was a joke.

The next morning, I was able to go into the house and get enough things for us for a few days. We drove to Seattle and took the car ferry to Bainbridge Island and moved in with Bernie's parents. We were out of our home for almost one month. ServiceMaster was the company contracted by our insurance company to clean up the fire and smoke damage. Everything was meticulously cleaned with special chemicals to get rid of the smoke odor. One worker sat on the floor and delicately cleaned Brett's toy fire engine. Every item was tossed out, washed at a laundromat, or deodorized. I went back and forth to our home in Kirkland from Bainbridge Island to oversee the progress. I picked out new carpeting, paint, a chandelier for the foyer and a sofa to replace those things damaged in the fire.

When the last work was done, and the ServiceMaster crew left my house, I sat down in my wicker chair in the TV room and had my first panic attack. I began to sit in the back row at church and in movies. Grocery shopping became a frightening chore. More times than I care to remember, I'd panic and leave a full shopping cart in line at the register and run out of the store. My adrenalin worked overtime during the excitement of putting the house and our lives back together. Chaotic events occurred often enough that my panic attacks didn't get a chance to calm down. They lasted too long for my money, but eventually, in about a year, they went away completely.

This is not the way I had pictured my life. This was not the house with the white picket fence.

Fire number two changed all of our lives forever. After Christmas, the tree downstairs in the family room had all the decorations removed. I asked Bernie not to put the tree in the fireplace because it wouldn't fit and would be dangerous to burn. He promised me he would wait for my help after dinner. I had hauled a metal garbage can from the garage to put the tree in, then went upstairs to start dinner. The children were playing with the model railroad which sat on a ping pong table downstairs. There was a commotion, so I ran down the stairs. Bernie had put the tree into the fireplace lengthwise and lit it. He got too close and had burns on his face and hair. The flames spread to the new recliner his parents had bought him for Christmas. The fabric melted. Fire and smoke damaged the white stone fireplace and hearth. Again, the fire department was here. This time, Bernie was admitted to the ICU at Cabrini Hospital in Seattle, and a neurologist was called in for consultation. I mentioned to him that I saw Bernie's toes wiggling under the stark white sheet. The neurologist dismissed my observation; however, that was the first time I observed Bernie's small muscle movement disorder.

Huntington's disease could not be definitely given as Bernie's diagnosis as he had no family history. He was referred a genetics clinic to see a well-known neurologist treating Huntington's. I went through the same exam as Bernie and his parents to see if there was an environmental factor involved.

This is where we first met with a psychologist. She interviewed Bernie's father, then mother, then me, each privately. During my session, I threw out the suggestions that Bernie was adopted or somehow was not the biological son of Wilbur. Right then and there, the psychologist became openly hostile to me. She may have held the most important card, yet never divulged any information to me. A well-known neurologist at the genetics clinic at the University of Washington did diagnose Huntington's disease, as opposed to any other disease. This certainly was the closest he could come without a brain autopsy for comparison, as there was no DNA testing at that time.

The psychologist attended my local Huntington's support group monthly meetings. She scolded me because there was no HD in Bernie's family, so what business did I have being there? She told me I should wait until after Bernie's death, when an autopsy of his brain should be done. Of course, that would be another eight years.

Now I would have to wait to see if Melissa or Brett started showing any signs of the disease. When either of them dropped a glass or tripped over something, I thought to myself 'it' was starting. That was like living in limbo or waiting for the other shoe to drop. When they marry, should they start a family? If they have children, would they live to raise them? Would a spouse divorce them if they became difficult to live with? Should they bother to get a higher education? What if?

I could see my life disappearing into the unknown. At least I had my daughter, my son, and a job. I went to soccer games, school events, and therapy appointments for Melissa's and Brett's developing depression.

After our second house fire, Bernie's neurologist had said he was no longer safe at home alone while I was at work. His parents agreed to have him on Bainbridge Island from Monday morning to Friday afternoon. Now he could be home with me and his children over the weekend. The second Monday evening, a process server delivered divorce papers. I read and reread everything and couldn't see how this could happen to me. I didn't sleep a wink that night, yet had to be at work the next day.

In the paperwork, the Thompsons' high powered attorney stated that Bernie was capable of having total custody of the children. My in-laws wanted to live in our house with their son and grandchildren. For years they had visited, had their own bedroom and bath, and mingled with my neighbors. They were very comfortable there, and my mother-in-law would be closer to shopping in Seattle. Now I had to fight with all my might.

I hired a Christian lawyer, thinking he would do his very best for me. He was no match for the Thompsons' lawyer. They chewed him up and spit him out. They even attempted to change the venue of the divorce trial. I had to get busy and hire another attorney, this time a cut-throat. In the beginning, I was happy with her. Little by little, and at my expense, I felt she was losing ground against the Thompsons' attorney. That was when I told my lawyer to set the trial date. Bernie became so irrational during this period, he'd phone and yell at me, saying that I was going to jail. His parents had obviously worked on him to say that and also dialed the phone for him. How easy was it to brainwash someone with HD?

Bernie's parents signed him up for Parents without Partners, and he was assigned an "amigo." He did not attend any events that I was aware of, although I thought it was a sordid act on their behalf. They were determined to have their son act normal, but their attorney required him to have a Guardian Ad Litem.

When the divorce was final 18 months later, I had already cleaned out my savings account and could no longer afford to pay my attorney from my paycheck. Bernie's Guardian Ad Litem had been coming to my office in Seattle, taking me out to lunch and coaxing me to agree to the divorce. I held her off until I was worn to a frazzle. She also had to sign the decree, along with Bernie and myself. By this time, he didn't know what he was signing. He had been turned against me by his parents. I always thought they would have been much better off to support me emotionally in taking care of their son, rather than breaking up the family.

When we finally went to court, the judge thought I was the petitioner. There was a little snickering in the courtroom after it was clarified that it was Bernie's parents who had instigated this divorce, not me. Bernie's parents had promised him they would never place him in a nursing home, but told him that I was going to put him in a nursing home against his will right away. After he grabbed the steering wheel while his father was driving, they quickly found a place for him in the International District in Seattle. It was an awful place. I brought the kids there every Sunday. He was served a peanut butter sandwich. The kitchen staff plopped it down onto the bare table, no paper plate or napkin. He routinely spilled his coffee on the table. Now his sandwich was lying in a pool of coffee. At this time, he still smoked. The ashes fell into his food. He was oblivious to things around him, so this mess didn't bother him.

We sometimes picked Bernie up and drove him to Denny's on Mercer Island, his favorite place. He enjoyed his apple pie and coffee so much. I am sure he was not totally aware of where he was. We still had a great time as the kids loved being with their dad, and they treated him like a king.

I enrolled Melissa in a private Catholic girls' school that was paid for by my mother. Brett also attended a private school. I volunteered my time as their accountant in lieu of tuition. Brett was taught to crew a scull and thrived on the attention. My children's lives were kept as normal as possible. I took them up to Harrison Hot Springs near Vancouver, British Columbia for a long weekend. We played tennis, swam in the hot springs, ate in their beautiful dining room, and finally slept soundly. No television or phone in the room.

After a few years, a nurse at my office suggested I go with her to a singles' club that met once a month at a restaurant. On her first visit, she'd met a man whom she married six months later. She said she'd also met a nice man who seemed like "everybody's uncle." I was not really interested in dating, but I went reluctantly with her. Jos Zetz was the man she had mentioned. He not only was the treasurer, but was also the best ballroom dancer in the club, which made him popular with the single women. He was immediately interested in me, but I was not interested in him or anybody else. Over a period of six months, he called me a number of times, even on my birthday, and I politely refused to go out with him. Finally, at a home party at my neighbor's, who was also in the singles' club, I relented.

Although I was not attracted to him, I introduced him to my children, and they got along fine in the beginning. Jos came over to our home frequently and liked to cook. When his daughter, Caroline, came home from her Mormon mission, she asked if she could move into our extra bedroom, and I agreed. She and Melissa immediately took to each other. They took the bus together to Seattle every morning. Melissa went to school, and Caroline got a job. Jos kept his two-bedroom apartment in Kirkland for Caroline if she wanted to live there, but she never did. She had been engaged for the two years she was on her mission in Venezuela and married her fiancé three months later. She became pregnant, and my kids and I got caught up in being a family again. Jos proposed marriage to me, and I agreed. That was four years after my divorce from Bernie.

Melissa was suffering from depression and agreed to go to counseling at the University of Washington for that and for some bad behavior, such as hitchhiking with her girlfriend. She was mostly where we planned to meet after school so I could take her to the counselor. Brett, on the other hand, said he didn't need to go, the therapist was stupid, and therefore, he was not where he was supposed to be when I took time off my job to pick him up.

When he was 14, Brett's grades started to fall, he skipped school, and he was generally uncooperative with me. He refused to do even the most mundane of chores. I also found items missing from the house, including my stereo. He said he needed the money. He was not sorry for what he had done, but sorry he got caught.

I started looking for a Christian school where Brett could live and get therapy. I was praying that it would rehabilitate him. Remember, he didn't have the symptoms of HD that I recognized. I found two places, and we visited them both. I gave him the option of either one. He chose a Christian youth ranch in Naches, Washington. He had wonderful and caring counselors who also lived on the property, 600 acres of wilderness. The wives cooked in the big dormitory kitchen. His personal counselor was a retired football player with the Green Bay Packers. He did very well, and I visited him each time they had a parents' weekend, although I stayed in a motel in Yakima instead of at the ranch. We'd walk down the trail to the corral, and he'd show me his horse he was allowed to care for if he got enough good behavior points and did his homework.

Fourteen months later, the senior counselor said it was time for Brett to go home. It was one of the happiest days of my life. I sped over Snoqualmie Pass to Yakima, then Naches to bring Brett home. When I got there, he wanted time to spend with his horse down at the stable. He climbed the fence to hug and kiss his horse. I was so touched to see how tender he had become.

Before long, it became obvious Brett needed a refresher course back at the ranch, but he was difficult to convince. I had to bribe him to be in the house when he was picked up by a staff member. The ranch had a new counselor who came to our home to pick him up and drive back to Naches that evening. During the drive back to the ranch, it was the custom to remove the students' shoes and jeans, so they wouldn't jump out of the car at a traffic light. All went well for the drive. Back at the ranch, this new counselor forgot to take Brett's shoes out of the dormitory, and he ran away that first night. How he got back to Seattle, I never knew. They apologized profusely, but it was too late.

I searched for Brett on Broadway Avenue where teens hung out that wore the gothic black clothes, painted white faces, black eyeliner and a Mohawk. I drove along slowly in the evenings and called his name. I would not have recognized him, as they were all unrecognizable, and I never did locate him. I hoped he would see my car and come to me.

Brett was out alone in the world, and it made me physically sick.

The next contact I had was with a Catholic-based support program in Issaquah. They called me to say they would support Brett in a court trial for emancipation. Brett showed up to court wearing new clothes. His navy pullover and a short, traditional haircut gave him a new clean-cut appearance. I had not seen him look so good in a long time. I still hoped he would want to come home with me.

The judge denied Brett's request to be emancipated. His buddy's folks were there carrying Bibles to impress the judge. All along, they wanted to have Brett live in their house, along with his Social Security check from his dad's Huntington's disease. The judge agreed to this scenario. In six weeks, that honeymoon was over. They kicked Brett out of their home because he was a bad influence on their six-year-old son. Instead of calling me, they dropped him off in Seattle on Broadway, where the gothic crowd lined the street. Again, I would drive by myself along Broadway looking for him, yet probably not recognizing him if he were now dressed in that gothic garb. I never did find him. I had hoped he would meet a guy that had an apartment in Seattle. His other option was living on the streets.

Both kids were strong willed. Melissa was fortunate to want an education in order to support herself comfortably. Brett, on the other hand, did not like school, although he finally graduated from a Seattle school program. The building had been an elementary school and was surrounded with cement pavement. It was now a high school and littered with used drug needles and other paraphernalia.

Looking for a job, Brett lied about his age and was hired by Le Provencal French restaurant in Kirkland. He did dishes and also made the paté. At times, he came home with bags of shrimp and told me they were given to him. Other times, he brought home bags of coffee beans or Janet Lee ice cream. I thought it was very odd that a fancy French restaurant would serve a store-brand ice cream. I never knew when Brett was telling the truth.

Brett's jobs never lasted very long. It was never his fault, he would say. His longest lasting job was mowing lawns in Seattle with his friend, Art. Art was a role model for Brett, so I felt comfortable that an adult was looking after him and that he had a roof over his head and food. It rains a lot in Seattle, so Brett sometimes even had to mow grass in water up to his ankles, just to make enough money for food. When he and Art had differences of opinions, Brett had to move out and live in his car with his cat, Mia. Being so stubborn, he would never come home to live again because he didn't like living with rules. Renting a room worked at times for Brett, but he was not able to keep up his end of the rent over the long haul.

At age 18, Brett was living in a house in the University District in Seattle with a couple of guys. I finally was able to find out where he lived and drove to bring him groceries. When he opened the door, a dark haired girl wearing a black leather shirt and pants stood beside him. Her name was Danielle, and she was his wife. She was aloof and snarled at me. The only good thing was that he was truly in love with her. Looking back at his shortened life, I'm glad he had the love of his life. I was praying she didn't get pregnant, but I never heard of her or from her after that visit.

Melissa also had a marriage that I was not aware of. Also at age 18, she married a handsome boy from Hong Kong. They had gone to the same high school and dated, and he appeared to be a very polite young man. He lived with his aunt and uncle because his parents were unable to immigrate to America. One night, the doorbell rang, and a man from the Immigration Service stood there asking me if I knew my daughter was married. I said she definitely was not married. He showed me her signature. He came to see me because the following day they had a court date to verify that she didn't marry him so he could get a Green Card. With his

Green Card, he could bring his parents to the U.S., something he might wish to do since Hong Kong was scheduled to go back under Chinese rule in 1999. The next day, he was handcuffed, held overnight, and deported the following day to Hong Kong.

His buddy told Melissa he was now in Switzerland, going to school. I believe his parents were well off and owned a hotel in Hong Kong. Melissa called the number she was given, and a woman who spoke either German or French answered. Melissa did not understand either language and had to hang up without speaking to him. She never got to talk to him again, even though she loved him and wanted to, and later divorced him.

I believe my two children's marriages were due to HD's effect on the part of their brain that controlled their decision making. One of the first noticeable indications was their inability to make good choices. They each became irrational in their own way. Melissa purchased items such as a complete bedding set that cost $1,000. She also bought complete camping gear on her credit card. Brett bought junk cars that did not run. They were easily manipulated. How come they could be led by strangers and not by their mother?

After completing a program at North Seattle Community College, Melissa was hired as an Operating Room Technologist. When she got settled in her new job, she wanted to purchase a new car. She had her eye on a brand new, blue Mazda Miata convertible. She wanted Jos' approval, even though she was paying for it herself. He thought it was a good little car for her. She was so happy to be able to buy herself a unique car. She loved driving it with the top down and the heat on high in Seattle's damp weather. She told me she got no respect in the parking garage at Bellevue Square Shopping Center in her old but cute 1969 Super Beetle. With the new flashy convertible, she no longer got snubbed by people in the BMWs and Mercedes.

Melissa and I visited Bernie on Thanksgiving Day. When we walked in the front door back at home, the phone was ringing. Bernie had just passed.

Melissa got back into her Miata, drove to Seattle, and took the ferry back to Bainbridge Island to be with her grandmother. The cause of death was listed as pneumonia, not HD, on his death certificate. Huntington's should have been named first, as that would have been accurate. Edna, my former mother-in-law, told me not to attend the funeral. My girlfriends were also told not to bother attending. Their husbands were told she wanted them to be there with her, however.

No autopsy was ordered for Bernie, so his children still would not know if they were at risk for HD. A cruel trick, I thought at the time. Bernie's father had passed away a few years prior of natural causes, at age 77, and no autopsy had been done. That would have been the definitive answer. Several years after Bernie died, his mother died at age 85, and again, no autopsy was performed. Why would they refuse to cooperate with the neurologist who had recommended an autopsy? Why would they refuse information their grandchildren needed to know that could affect the rest of their lives?

Shortly after Bernie died, Melissa signed a lease at a new studio apartment in Seattle at Pike Place Market, a place she loved to shop and browse and have coffee at the very first Starbucks. This apartment building started on Western Avenue on the first floor and Post Alley on the seventh floor. Her studio apartment was on the seventh floor facing Post Alley. A French door was the entrance to her tiny balcony. She got a kitten and named him Mozart. One day, she forgot to close her balcony door, and the cat got out, climbed up on the railing, and lost its balance. Mozart fell four flights to Post Alley. An amputation of his right front leg saved his life. Once healed, he was back in action, this time climbing her bookshelves but never getting outside again.

One night Melissa worked overtime at the hospital, parked in her locked garage, and walked across the footbridge to her apartment building. Being exhausted after standing on her feet all day long and into the night, she went to bed immediately. In 1988, long before the genetic test for HD had been developed, Melissa had developed an unawareness of her surroundings and things going on around her. At about 1 a.m., she was awakened by a man leaning over her bed, holding a knife to her throat. He was there to rape her and, as it turned out, quite violently. She thought that this would be her last breath. He pulled her naked into different positions until his violent act was completed. He had put a pillow case over her head and tied it with the telephone cord he ripped out of her wall. Before or after the rape, she didn't know, he went through her jewelry and took several pieces. He told her not to call the police, or he would come back and kill her. She waited what seemed forever before she thought it was safe to untie the cord and remove the pillow case, lest he return. She crawled naked next door for help. Paramedics transported her to Harborview Emergency Room.

There is a protocol for rape victims. Melissa had a thorough physical examination, and DNA samples were taken. She was offered counseling, which she refused. She was released to me, and she never was able to go back to that apartment.

A Seattle detective was assigned to her. A portrait artist was called and was able to draw the rapist's face. Considering the rape occurred in the dark, it was difficult, but she did remember the outline of his head. She also reported that some of her jewelry was missing. Several times, we were called to come downtown to the Seattle Police Department to an area where these types of items are processed and stored. Melissa's jewelry was never recovered.

The detective investigated all aspects of the crime. He determined that the rapist had stalked her as she drove into her garage, probably because of her long blonde hair and her bright blue Miata convertible. The detective then told her how her apartment had been broken into. The rapist had grabbed a low balcony rail, then swung himself up to the next floor, then repeated it until he found Melissa's apartment. He had watched her light go out, and she had forgotten to lock her French door to the balcony, and that's how he gained entrance. Because of her unawareness, she had never noticed that he had been stalking her.

My husband, Jos, had already bought airline tickets for us to Amsterdam to spend three weeks with his two brothers and their families. We were able to get an extra ticket for Melissa, and this was the best therapy for her. She was adored in The Netherlands. With her blonde hair and blue eyes, she actually looked Dutch.

Two years passed before the rapist was caught red-handed. He had broken into another woman's apartment. Apparently, all his victims lived alone in apartments, not houses.

At Carlos Williams' trial, his DNA, found inside Melissa and six other women, was instrumental in his conviction on all counts. He is now serving life in the State of Washington's prison system in King County. He will be 94 years old before he has a chance of release on parole.

By now, there was a DNA test for Huntington's. Melissa was the first to be tested, in 1996, and the results were positive for HD. That evening at dinner when I got that phone call, my head dropped into my hot and sour soup at a Chinese restaurant, and I dissolved into tears. At that time, I lived in Newport Beach, California, and Melissa still lived in Seattle, 1200 miles away, and I couldn't comfort her.

Brett was tested the following year and also had positive results. Being a mother, I wanted to cure them and not have either of them suffer as their dad had done in a nursing home. Now they each knew what was in store for them, and I hated that.

After a few years, Melissa lost her job as an OR Tech because she kept dropping the sterilized instruments during surgeries. At first, she was given a part-time position answering phones and scheduling surgeries, but she couldn't perform that, either, so she ended up going on Social Security Disability at the age of 25.

I read in our local newspaper, coincidentally on her birthday, which we thought was significant, about a Fetal Cell Transplant for Huntington's and Parkinson's patients done in Los Angeles. In order to determine if Melissa was an appropriate candidate, she had to be seen by a neurologist in Phoenix, Arizona. So that is what we did. After making many phone calls for information on the surgery, I flew Melissa down to Newport Beach, and together, we flew to Phoenix for the day. She was deemed a perfect candidate for this procedure that was not yet accepted by insurance companies. Then she was examined and approved by the surgical team in Los Angeles at Good Samaritan Hospital. Everything was on schedule except that now the grant funds had run out after the third surgery, and Melissa was number four. I scrambled to come up with the $25,000 due on the day of surgery. My friends and relatives put money into a special account at the bank for her surgery. It was income tax deductible for them because if Melissa did not have the surgery, for any reason, the money was non-refundable. It would go to another stem cell surgery patient.

The abortion that yielded the stem cells was done on a Friday. After the procedure, the woman was asked if the fetal tissue could be used to save the lives of two people with terminal illnesses. The fetus could not be more than 42 days old. She agreed and signed the paperwork. On Saturday and Sunday, the tissue for Melissa was tested for diseases such as Hepatitis, then prepared for the two Monday surgeries, one Parkinson's and one Huntington's.

I was able to stay in a small hotel nearby so I could walk back and forth and be with her the entire time. Melissa was discharged on Friday, one day longer than planned, due to nausea. Melissa felt well enough to attend a family outdoor wedding on Sunday at her stepbrother's home. It was held in their garden. Because she was taking Cyclosporine, she had to wear a mask whenever she was near others. Even so, she looked lovely and bright that day. Melissa was a real trooper and never complained about her surgery or discomfort. She put up with a lot to have the chance for a cure or at least to lessen her symptoms.

Melissa improved dramatically after her transplant surgery. She began wearing her stylish clothes. She even wore a bikini at the Park Newport Apartment pool. We had our hopes high for a complete cure for HD, although no guarantee was given by the team of surgeons, because Melissa's whole persona changed. She was able to take the public bus and walk to class. The team said they would perform the surgery on Brett when new funding was available.

After the surgery, my husband and I took Melissa to Utah to visit his daughter and her family. We stayed a few miles away in a hotel next to a Wal-Mart store. We walked through the parking lot to get there. Melissa finished her shopping and left the store ahead of us to return to our hotel. A few minutes later, we started walking through the parking lot. In the distance, I could see a parked police car and a female officer questioning Melissa in the middle of the parking lot. There were no cars in that particular area, so I wondered what could possibly be the problem. It appeared the situation was escalating. Just in time, when handcuffs were in my sight, I walked faster to protect Melissa and find out what she had done to be grilled so harshly. It seemed that she had done nothing wrong except walk with a staggered gait as if drunk. I immediately turned to the officer and said, "I would like you to meet my beautiful daughter Melissa, who has Huntington's disease." At that, the officer backed down and said, "I was only checking to see if she was safe." I didn't think that was the truth at all.

This time period is when Melissa and I met Frances Saldaña and her daughter Marie. Marie was a strikingly pretty girl with naturally curly, dark brown hair and always a smile on her face. She was a happy girl. We met at Dietrich's Coffee House one evening and hit it off right away. They wanted to know more about Melissa's surgery. They both asked her questions. Melissa was proud she could help. The girls became great friends throughout their ordeal. Unfortunately, Marie was not a good candidate for the transplant surgery.

Sometime later, Melissa had an appointment with a female internist who was on a trial period in the office where I was the Practice Manager. A laboratory test revealed high cholesterol. Melissa was given a prescription for Lipitor. She took this for two weeks until her next follow-up appointment at Good Samaritan Hospital in Los Angeles. Her neurosurgeon was very disappointed that she had been given Lipitor. This drug had the potential to destroy her new brain cells. I was told it only takes one dose. Melissa had been on it for two weeks. Now it was a wait and see situation. She agreed to have Functional MRI's in Pasadena, at least a one-hour drive from Newport Beach. She had to be given a very light sedative in order to lie very still. We made the trip up to Pasadena for quite a while. On each trip, we went out to lunch and made a stop at Starbucks. In the line inside Starbucks in Pasadena, a few people could not help but stare at Melissa. I stepped up and said, "This is my daughter, Melissa, and she has Huntington's disease." I felt better letting others know that she actually had an illness, and wasn't on illegal drugs or alcohol. The Functional MRIs ultimately showed loss of the implanted fetal stem cells on one side of her brain, a side effect of the Lipitor, which was a huge blow to both of us.

Frances came up with the magnificent idea that she and I take the girls on a cruise out of Long Beach, California, to Mexico for a four-day trip. This was the first time Melissa needed to use a wheelchair. I rented it for a week, and she never complained about being wheeled around. I was always careful not to push her up to a blank wall, as in an elevator. Both Frances and I had special handicapped suites for our girls. They were glowing like sunshine during our entire trip. We took the shore excursions. We spent time by the pool. We dressed for dinner. Melissa had her hair done up in a French twist with a rhinestone hair clip. It was wonderful to see the girls having such a good time in spite of their disease.

On board ship, Melissa needed to use the public restroom by the pool. I parked her wheelchair, and she got up and gingerly walked toward the ladies' room. She had to step over a large door sill to enter, and she missed it and tripped. Help came running to assist her, along with Frances and myself. She did not want to see the ship's doctor, so I brought her back to our room to rest. That evening was the formal dinner on board, and she didn't want to miss it. Marie also had a mishap in their room. As I recall, she did get medical treatment in her room. Thankfully, she was not seriously injured, and we had a wonderful evening together. The girls were stunning.

In 1999, I looked for an apartment in Costa Mesa for my children. Brett had come down for New Year's and looked like he was doing really well. I had wanted him to help look after Melissa. She could walk across the street to the community college, as she no longer could drive, where she was in a class with other disabled students. Her teacher was a young man in a wheelchair. I went to check on her and Brett, and I brought groceries and anything else they needed. One morning, I opened the door to see strangers lying all over the living room floor and asked one, "Who are you?" She answered, "Who are you?" They all got up and scampered out the door. It appeared that this was a safe place to do drugs or anything else. One of the visitors was the apartment superintendent. On my next visit, my tires were slashed. I had no proof as to who had done it, but I did see that superintendent jumping the fence close to my car. I never saw him again hanging out around that apartment.

Another thing I discovered was that they were heating the apartment with the gas stove. Now it was getting really scary. That was the end of the apartment. Melissa moved into her stepbrother's first floor guest room in Santa Ana. Since Brett did not want live with me, he had no other options but a shelter. It was sad seeing him sitting on the pavement with others, waiting for the shelter to open each evening. I did develop sort of a friendship with the shelter manager, who ran the place, and asked him to keep an eye on Brett. This was so unfair for a young man in his late twenties with such a disability to live this kind of horrible existence. He was fed dinner.

Breakfast was only coffee and donuts. He was not allowed to stay there and rest during the day.

When Brett's thirty nights at the shelter were up, he had to leave. The night he was refused entrance, he carried his duffle bags with all his worldly belongings from Anaheim to Costa Mesa, about nine miles. As his bags got too heavy, he would place them behind bushes at the fast food restaurants along the way. In the morning, I drove him to pick up the bags. He found all of them. Now it was time to find another place for him, which he wouldn't like. I felt like I had no other options.

During this time, Melissa had been going to the county office for her free Prozac prescriptions and some counseling for her depression. She spoke with a terrific nurse who was always concerned for both of us. Brett also required medication, so I drove him to the same place. They determined that Brett needed the Dual Diagnosis Program at the department, for abusing drugs and alcohol and having severe depression. He was assigned a counselor. All went smoothly for a while, that is, until Brett had a problem. He had purchased a junk car, and it wouldn't run after he drove it to an Auto Zone store. He called me from there, and I rushed to him. He was curled up in the back seat, crying. He was more depressed than ever. I led him by the hand to my car and drove to his counselor's office. It was almost 5 p.m., and she let it be known that we were wasting her time. I begged her for help. She told us she could see that glassy look in his eyes, that he had drugs in him, and that she couldn't help him, and she told us to leave. We got back into my car, and I laid my head on the steering wheel and cried until I was exhausted. I didn't know what to do with Brett or who would help us. I was sure he felt bad at putting me through this, though he never said.

There was a psychiatric hospital in Costa Mesa that I had driven by many times. I didn't know anyone who had been treated there, but decided to give them a try. When the doctor saw how depressed Brett was, he was immediately admitted to the locked facility. That night, I breathed a sigh of relief and slept well. I knew he was safe and cared for. That night, he most likely slept well, also.

Such is the life of Huntington's disease patients. I never knew when the next accident would happen, yet it always did. My main job as a caregiver was to keep Melissa from getting injured. On our third floor apartment at Park Newport Apartments, Melissa had her own room. One day, she lost her balance and fell backward against the window. The vertical blinds she fell against saved her from going through the window. That was the moment that I realized she was no longer safe living at home.

Looking for the best assisted living places was not easy. The one that I decided upon was in Fullerton, about 25 miles from me. Melissa actually looked forward to the move and brought her cat, a Cornish Rex, with her. The facility did her laundry weekly and cleaned her room. She went to the dining room for all her meals. Since I visited her each day, I was allowed to eat with her.

After several weeks, the cat litter was not being contained in the box, but was strewn all over. Melissa certainly was not able to continue to sweep or vacuum her room. After complaints from housekeeping staff, I had to take the cat away and find it a home. I visited the veterinary office that cared for the Rex's check-ups and immunizations, and I asked if they would take this white, curly haired cat. They did not take in cats; however, the receptionist, who also had a Cornish Rex at home, said she would like to have it. Later, I visited the clinic to see how the cat had adjusted to his new home. I was delighted to know that he now had a new name and his own website with photos.

When Brett was murdered in Seattle, I still had Melissa in a nursing home in Fullerton, so I was kept busy every day with her. They were prepared to give her medicine if she freaked out over the news of Brett's murder. It wasn't needed. She handled the news very calmly. We took her to Brett's Celebration of Life at Bucca de Beppo restaurant. All my friends attended, but Melissa showed no emotion. That may have been due to the HD itself.

While in the assisted living facility, Melissa's neurologist at UC Irvine invited her to be a guest at a class he taught. I wheeled her out onto the stage, and students asked her questions about her illness. She was so willing to telling everyone about HD.

Since Huntington's disease care is so time consuming and the behavior is erratic, I was eventually told Melissa didn't fit the criteria of the assisted living facility any longer. Now she needed 24-hour care. Her first nursing home was in Newport Beach. I interviewed the place in detail and was satisfied she would get good care there. I soon noticed things going wrong, though. Her glasses were missing. Her speaking machine attached to her wheelchair was no longer wanted there as it had to be plugged in at night, and nobody would take the responsibility to maintain it. Soon after, Melissa complained about not getting her medicine, and she could not reach for her call bell. I found it tucked into her dresser drawer where it was not able to be reached. That was to keep her from calling the nurses' station. Then, I learned that every care home has a book of complaints from patients or their families that were reported to the Ombudsman and the changes they were ordered to make. I asked to see it. It was a loose-leaf notebook that was at least three inches thick. I called the number listed on the poster in the waiting room. An Ombudsman came to inspect the facility. Her report corroborated my complaints. Even though my reporting to the Ombudsman was not to be held against Melissa and me, I felt the distance from the staff. The way to get rid of a problem resident is to send them to the hospital and not accept them back.

The nursing home told me Melissa needed to be hospitalized, even though she was scheduled for her neurologist's appointment the next day. Medicare rules stated that she would need three days in the hospital to be admitted to a care home without a co-pay. After the hospitalization, the nursing home refused to readmit her. So now I had to find a place quickly. Several places told me they did not have to admit anyone under the age of 55, and said it was the California state law. Melissa was in her early thirties, and because of her movement and psychiatric disorder, she was admitted to several care homes and discharged to hospitals. Finally, I found a nursing home in Garden Grove, California. Melissa was interviewed upon her arrival. She was calmly asked if she wanted to have lifesaving treatments such as a gastric feeding tube and/or an IV if the nursing home physician ordered it. She sat on her new bed and talked about what she wanted. No hospitalizations, no feeding tube, and no IV lines. Only medicines for her comfort or urinary tract infections. I believe she came to her conclusion due to her years of working in hospitals.

I am not clear when the nursing home called Hospice to help in Melissa's care. At first, the nurse came weekly to go over her medications with the head nurse. Then gradually she came more often. At the end, she was there every day, almost all day. We never used the "H" word around Melissa. This nursing home was, finally, a wonderful place for Melissa. There was a garden path with babbling brook off the dining room. Lots of residents were out there chatting and smoking. I wheeled Melissa out into the patio area daily and read to her. Her favorite was the book *A Dog's Life*, by Peter Mayle. Some of the residents really took to her. John Hanson came every day to take his wife, Barbara, out on the patio and made a point to say hello to Melissa. I am still very touched at his kindness. After Barbara died, he came back to visit Melissa, and he stayed in touch with me after she passed, also.

Melissa's Hospice chaplain from Hope for Healing Hearts visited her weekly. I left the room when he came so they could have private prayer times. A personal companion was also assigned to her. She brought Melissa Starbucks coffee, always a venti frozen caramel frappuccino. She also brought small stuffed animals and sat by her for hours. I would leave to go home when her companion arrived. Melissa was not easy to care for. At times, she fought her CNA and nurses. Lying in her bed by the window, she tried to kick out the window. An attempt was made to give her an injection to calm her, but she kept fighting, kicking and screaming. One of the gardeners was asked to help hold her down long enough to give the injection. This was too hard on me to watch my daughter fighting with such vigor and strength. Fortunately, this didn't happen again.

Many times I went to the chaplain's office for a shoulder to cry on, yet I knew what the future held for us. Melissa was getting nearer to the end of her life, and I felt like it was the end of my life, also. It didn't matter how long I was prepared for the death of Melissa; I still grieved for a very long time and missed her in my daily life. I cried for two years and ate ice cream.

A few weeks after Melissa's passing, the Hospice chaplain invited me to speak to his students at his evening class at Vanguard University. The students asked me all sorts of questions. The class was four long hours. I felt drained going over Melissa's struggle with HD again and again. My main reason for this was to tell as many people as possible about HD and how to give them the respect they deserve.

I still have unanswered questions to this day such as why my in-laws filed for divorce on behalf of their only child and why they couldn't or wouldn't tell me the true story of his heritage. After all, they knew from the psychologist that each child had a fifty-fifty chance of developing the disease. Looking back, I've realized that my husband did not in any way resemble his father, Wilbur. He was six foot two inches, had blonde hair, was muscular and wore a size twelve shoe. Wilbur, on the other hand, was only five feet eight inches, completely bald, even in his class photos in his University of Washington yearbook, and wore a size eight shoe. Additionally, he appeared to be the puny, pasty, Caspar-milk-toast type man. Bernie's grandfather and great uncle also had the same appearance as Wilbur.

An interesting bit of information was given to me by Bernie's grandmother. In her eighties at that time, she told me a secret about her son,

Wilbur. He had been married twice before he met and married Edna. There were no children as a result of those marriages. After Bernie was born, there were no more babies, and Bernie was raised as an only child. Years ago, I calculated that Bernie was born 13 months after the marriage, yet Wilbur was home only two weeks after they married, then went back to sea as a purser for a well-known steamship company for almost a year. The numbers don't match. He could not have fathered Bernie, but then he may not have been able to father any children at all.

One year ago, I finally had both Melissa and Brett's ashes buried next to each other and their father. I had kept them with me, Brett for eleven years, and Melissa for seven years, both in beautiful, furniture-quality urns. I never felt that Newport Beach would be my home forever, and for that reason did not want to inter my children in a place I would not be able to visit. Now they are all together in the family plot at Seabold Cemetery on Bainbridge Island. I plan to visit them this summer.

—m—

Please consider making a donation to Frances Saldaña's foundation, HD CARE, a nonprofit organization.

Donations can be made via their secure web site, http://www.hdcare.org/, or by mailing a check to:

HD-CARE, UC Irvine, Portillo Children Memorial Fund
Account #3564 Appeal Code B5M10
P.O. Box 8036
Newport Beach, CA 92658

You can also contact HD CARE at 949-824-3061.

About Frances Saldaña

Frances Saldaña became an advocate for Huntington's disease (HD) in 1994, after one of her daughters was diagnosed with HD. Her children lost their father to the disease, and ultimately, all three of her children inherited the HD gene. Among her many accomplishments, Frances initiated the HD Orange County, California Affiliate, advocated for the HD Clinic at the University of California Irvine (UCI), and promoted the first Southern California Region HD Educational Conference in 2012. Wishing to further the state-of-the-art research being accomplished at UCI and to aid and assist the HD Clinic at UCI, Frances co-founded HD-CARE, a UCI 501(c)(3) Non-Profit organization, in November 2012, where she serves as president. Her advocacy work has been featured in several publications, and she has been a guest speaker on the radio and at HD educational events. Frances lost her two daughters to HD, her son is fully symptomatic, and her two grandchildren are at risk. Frances recently retired from the UCI Paul Merage School of Business and resides in Fountain Valley with her husband, David Saldaña. Her focus continues to be ending the suffering of HD patients and realizing a cure or treatment for this devastating disease in her lifetime.

CHAPTER 5

Marrying into a Family with Huntington's Disease: A Fight to End a Generational Disease

By Frances Saldaña

2015

Marrying into a family affected by Huntington's disease (HD) has taken me on the most amazing journey. Once your family is touched by this disease, you're on a winding road of obscurity and a never-ending fight to keep your family alive. Disbelief, despair, and devastation make life seem almost surreal. This only starts to describe the emotions that take place when a family member receives a positive diagnosis for Huntington's disease.

Huntington's disease is an orphan disease and what many call "a well-kept family secret." For a disease that screams out for help from specialized medical practitioners and every facet of social services, there is still an incredible lack of support for HD research and care for Huntington's disease families. They often find themselves bleeding in the trenches in an endless war, with no help in sight.

That's life with Huntington's disease. This journey has been a laborious one for me, and one for which there are so many tragic HD stories. Our families have become accustomed to hearing the inevitable, bowing our heads and crying every time we learn that one more HD family member has passed.

I have armed myself with perseverance, resilience, commitment, and love. My family and my memories form a collage of heartbreak and sorrow, love and warmth. The silver lining in the collage represents hope—our hope to make this the last generation of Huntington's disease.

Other Huntington's disease advocates and I have been working tirelessly and raising our voices about the urgency to have a treatment and put an end to this senseless suffering, and there is finally a glimmer of light on the horizon. It has been over 20 years since the gene for Huntington's was identified, and stem cell research finally holds a tremendous hope for a treatment. That is what took me to the World Stem Cell Summit in San Antonio, Texas, in December, 2014. It was just three weeks before Christmas. The scent of pine from the Christmas trees that adorned every area of the hotel permeated the air. Bright red and green lights and music created a joyful spirit, and everything was lovely and felt perfect. I was caught up in the moment of this wonderful holiday season when all too quickly sadness hit me like a gust of wind out of nowhere, and everything was suddenly in disarray. The joyful mood was interrupted and took me back to my memories of this holiday that was a favorite for my children. Why were my children not here to experience this beautiful life with me? Why? I asked myself that unanswered question. Joy and sadness run through my mind and now define the person that I am. Without thinking about it twice, I put on a smile to hide the tears and keep marching forward because there's so much work to be done.

Bernie Siegel, founder and Executive Director of the Genetics Policy Institute, had invited Judy Roberson, Katie Jackson, and me to speak at the World Stem Cell Summit about our advocacy work on behalf of the Huntington's disease community. I was preparing to go out and speak to a prominent audience from the scientific world. They had come from all over the world to share their knowledge. For me, this was a golden opportunity because I hoped that what I had to say would actually have some impact and speed up science and a treatment for HD. This is what I was wishing. I was so grateful to have this opportunity, but I only had a few minutes to speak so I had to choose my words carefully.

"Thank you so much, Bernie Siegel and The Genetics Policy Institute. It is a privilege for me to be a voice for the Huntington's disease community. I want to thank Dr. Leslie Thompson, Dr. Jan Nolta, and all who work tirelessly in search of a treatment to save our families. Thank you to my HD-CARE board of directors and to Linda Pimental, who is just as passionate as I am to have a cure for HD. You give us, as advocates, renewed strength to go through this amazing journey together, and thank you to my friends and generous donors who have partnered with us to make stem cell research possible.

"I met Bernie Siegel at the 2011 World Stem Cell Summit, and I showed him a photo of my three children. I told him I had just lost my youngest daughter, Marie, from HD. Fast forward three years later; I've lost my oldest daughter, Margie. My only remaining child, Michael, is in the late stages of HD. My children have been strong advocates for stem cell research, and all three donated skin cells, hoping their contribution would speed up science. I have heard several prominent scientists say, 'If there is one disease that we should be able to find a cure for, it is Huntington's, and if we can't find a cure for Huntington's, we can't find a cure for anything!' Why? Because the genetic mutation is known, and we can study the disease more effectively, and what is learned from HD can be applied to other neurological diseases, as there are so many things that they have in common with Huntington's disease.

"Before my daughter Margie died, she prayed for a treatment so her children, my grandchildren, would never have to fear inheriting

her devastating disease. My beautiful Margie passed away in her sleep eight months ago. As I said goodbye to my baby, I held her in my arms, and I vowed that I would never rest until we have a treatment for a disease that took the life of my husband, the life of my two beautiful daughters, and soon the life of my son.

"I have advocated for HD research for the last 20 years because our families re-live the Dickens Christmas Carol story each and every year of our life, with flashes of joy, love, and warmth. But generation after generation we live haunting moments of darkness, despair, sadness, fear, and ultimately death from Huntington's. As our family members fade away from HD, we find ourselves asking if they'll make one more day…one more week. Will Michael be with us next Christmas?

"So here's my Christmas wish: That stem cell research changes the future of HD families by conquering this fatal disease and the Ghost of Christmases Yet to Come, and that Huntington's disease will simply be a bad dream that happened sometime in the past. This is my wish. End Huntington's disease! Thank you, and in the words of Tiny Tim, 'God bless us, every one!'"

I didn't look back at the audience, but I hoped that my message would go back with them to the HD lab. I walked back to the left side of the stage where Bernie, Judy and Katie stood waiting. I could see in their eyes that they understood only too well. I hoped that the scientists sitting in the audience truly understood what our families have endured, generation after generation. Katie talked about her husband's diagnosis for Huntington's disease and her three children who are now at risk to inherit the disease, and I couldn't help thinking that her life was a mirror of mine 30 years before. Please, God, I often pray, please do not let my family's life be Katie's future. Judy talked about the progress in science and how we now have the tools to communicate and share information at a much faster pace and how different it is now from when her husband and my husband both received a positive diagnosis for HD. In a nutshell, we covered what was obvious to us: we have the science, we have the tools to speed things up, but the clock is ticking for our families, and now we need the cure.

Life was not always this way. There have been wonderful, warm, and endearing memories in my life, along with the many disquieting memories and a flurry of emotions that come from a disease that no one wants. The many warm, joyful, loving memories somehow pale behind the drama, passion, and suffering that is the hallmark of what HD families typically live through. My married life started out much like most marriages typically do with exciting and wonderful plans to raise a family. There was a brief time in the early years of my marriage to the father of my children when everything seemed perfect, and nothing seemed impossible. That time in my life often reminds me of the words from Camelot, *"Don't let it be forgot, that once there was a spot, for one brief shining moment, that was known as Camelot."* Of course, in the story of Camelot, the perfect world ended with a horrific war; such is my war against Huntington's disease.

It has been a long and arduous road. I don't know why life steered me in this direction. I don't know why the father of my children had to be a carrier of Huntington's disease. I don't know why all three of my children inherited Huntington's disease. I don't know why my two daughters had to die. "Why?" remains a haunting and unanswered question in my life.

<u>1963</u>

My introduction to a family affected by Huntington's disease started over 40 years ago. My sister, Isabel, had just turned 15 years old. Our parents agreed to let her have a birthday party at our home. She was a freshman in high school. I was only 13 years old and in the seventh grade. Isabel carefully selected the 45s that she would play for her party. She set them next to the hi-fi record player. She was glowing. The 30 or so school friends that she invited all crammed into the small living room of our home. There was standing room only, and that meant the party was a huge success. That's the way we had parties in those days—in the living rooms or garages, with parents keeping a watchful eye over everything and supervising the young people in their home.

There was one particular boy who stood out amongst the rest. He was standing by the door. I asked Isabel who he was, and she said his name was Hector, and he was a sophomore in her school. He was tall, had wavy brown hair and a big smile. I suddenly realized that his gaze was on me. I felt nervous and excited because a high school sophomore was walking toward me! He put out his hand and asked me to dance….it was a slow dance, and the rest is history.

The years flew by, but it was always understood between us that we would one day be married and start a family. He asked me to marry him when I was 14, and I said I would after he finished college. This was during the Vietnam years.

1969

Hector worked hard to finish college while also working fulltime. But in his fourth year in college, he was drafted into the Army. Normally, college students did not get drafted. His supervisor at Aerospace Corporation requested that he be excused as he was working on the development of a strong alloy component for a military aircraft, but Uncle Sam won over Aerospace's request, and Hector was sent off to boot camp at Fort Ord. Because he had four years in ROTC under his belt, he was later sent to North Carolina to serve in the Special Forces division at Fort Bragg doing administrative work. He was so proud to be serving in the Special Forces division, which was also the home of the Green Berets. Hector was always thin and not very strong, so he was not a Green Beret, but he simply enjoyed watching them train and often took photos during their drills. He would often remind me that they were America's best, the Green Berets!

It was a difficult time for all young people. We didn't know who would be sent overseas and face the horror of wartime in Vietnam, and who would actually return alive and in one piece. It wasn't long after his time in Ft. Bragg that Hector also received his order to go to Vietnam. He called to tell me he would be coming back home for three weeks before being deployed to Vietnam. We had originally planned on getting married after his discharge from the service, but this news alarmed us both, and knowing he might not come back, he wanted us to get married before he left for war. We planned our wedding in three weeks, and on April 12, 1969, I became Mrs. Hector Portillo.

1970

Expectations were different at that time—finish high school, go to college, get a job, get married, and start a family—so nine and a half months after my wedding day, I gave birth to my little Margie in Raymond W. Bliss Army Hospital in Ft. Huachuca, Arizona. I started having contractions at about 5:00 a.m. on January 22, 1970. This was the day I would finally get to meet my baby girl. She was born on a cold winter night. The nurses at the Army hospital whisked her away from me before I had a chance to hold her in my arms. I had a brief look at the little bundle as she screamed and cried. There was no doubt in my mind that she would one day be a singer. Army hospital rules were so strict in those days. I was alone during labor. To make things worse, they forgot to bring my daughter back to me after they cleaned her up. The following day at noon, the nurse came in the room and found me crying. It had been 18 hours since I had delivered my baby, and I still hadn't seen her. "Why are you crying, little girl?" the nurse asked me. I said I still hadn't seen my baby, and she laughed nervously and quickly went to get her for me. She was fragile and more beautiful than I could have ever imagined….a little baby doll, Margie.

Hector was loved by just about everyone who knew him. He was attractive, likeable, and possessed a sweet and kind manner that people liked.

There was also a sense of helplessness about him, as well as a desire to be accepted. As I recall, there was something very different about him. I couldn't put my finger on it then, but I knew he needed somebody to take care of him and help him achieve his goals. It all makes sense to me now, 25 years after he passed away.

Once he was discharged from the Army, Hector went back to school and graduated from Long Beach State University. He also got his old job back at Aerospace Corporation, and in less than one year, we bought our first home. Our little girl was growing up fast, and my hunch was right about her strong voice for singing.

Margie was quick at making a person feel loved. She would tell you, "I love you," over and over, with a sweet hug and a loving countenance. Margie loved to sing and dance and would later become very active in the Children's Community Theater. She was a very happy child, quick to laugh and ready to find fun in just about anything.

1972

Soon, we were expecting our second child. While watching the Olympics one summer evening in September, the baby started kicking harder, and I knew it was time. I became very uncomfortable. Hector grabbed my suitcase, and off we went. Michael came into the world on September 13, 1972, at Hoag Hospital, Newport Beach, weighing 9 lbs. 11 oz. and 22 and ½ inches long—a big baby! He looked like a three-month-old baby at birth, beautiful and strong. I remember vividly the day he was born. One of the happiest moments for me was sitting in the hospital bed with my baby boy in my arms and looking out the window at the glorious sunset over the shimmering water of the Pacific Ocean. The nurses laughed because the newborn diapers were too small for him. I spoiled him rotten, and he was very attached to me. I called him my Koala bear.

1977

My third pregnancy was a happy surprise for us. This time, the baby was coming much faster than my first two. We drove to the hospital, but after seeing that Hector was driving down the same street two or three times, I realized that he was actually lost. I couldn't do much more than to try to breathe and stay calm and hope that I wouldn't deliver the baby in our van. We had rehearsed the drive several times before. I felt very insecure at that moment, but I just blew it off, thinking he was probably just very nervous. I was in no condition to give it much thought, but these were the first clues that HD was giving me about what was to come. Fortunately, we made it to the hospital, and Marie was born on February 24, 1977. Michael was not happy about having a new baby around the house and asked me to take her back to the hospital, but I kept reminding him that he was my baby, too, and he got used to her after a couple of months.

By now, Margie was seven years old. Looking back, I now realize we were living an enchanted life. Our children brought us more joy and happiness than we could have imagined possible. Hector adored his children and wanted only the best for them, maybe more than most fathers do, and I was ridiculously in love with my babies.

Hector left his job at Aerospace Corporation to work closer to home and started working as a land surveyor in Huntington Beach. Those were great years of camaraderie with his co-workers, raising a family, and a flurry of activity. My children were active in Little League, soccer, ballet, the Fountain Valley Community Theater, district choir, Mini Scouts, Boy Scouts, and 4H. For the children of these two adoring parents, anything was possible! We jumped in with reckless abandon. Hector was a Boy Scouts Master, and I was on the Board of Directors for the Fountain Valley Community Theater. Those magical years went by fast.

Sometime after Marie was born, Hector started showing some very peculiar symptoms. He crossed his arms and shrugged one shoulder continuously. No one thought anything of it; however, his movements accelerated. There was continuous and annoying sniffing that we couldn't figure out. He didn't have a cold or a runny nose. It was an involuntary symptom that he couldn't stop. There were also significant changes in his personality. He wanted only the best—a custom-built home, a Porsche for me on our tenth wedding anniversary, and whatever our children wanted. Nothing seemed impossible to him. I did my best to support him, but after two or three years, his erratic behavior escalated.

The beginning of the end of Hector's career happened while he was working at a site in El Segundo, California, when two airplanes collided in mid-air and landed on the job site that he was surveying. Amid all the shock and confusion, the workers pointed to a carpenter who was trapped in the wreckage. The building was on fire, and as there was no time to waste, Hector's military training came in handy, and he quickly climbed up the scaffold of the building and grabbed the man and brought him down before he burned to death. Both he and the carpenter were taken to the hospital. Hector's hair and skin were singed from the fire. After going through that trauma, he broke down and was unable to stop crying. The doctors diagnosed him with post-traumatic stress syndrome. He was written up as a hero by *The L.A. Times* and received a letter of commendation from his employer. Soon after this event, however, he was fired for making too many mistakes on the job.

Hector went from one job to another and soon was labeled as unemployable. No one would hire him. His movement disorder escalated after the job site accident, and it seems that the stress triggered the onset of what we now know were clearly symptoms of Huntington's disease. He had grandiose ideas of what he thought he could achieve. When I tried to reason with him about the numerous bad decisions that would affect our entire family and jeopardize our stability, he blew up with emotional outbursts and physical attacks on me and on my children.

His family practitioner referred us to a neurologist. After many tests, they still could not figure out if Hector was suffering from post-traumatic stress disorder or something else. I started digging for family history and going to the library for information on HD. I tried being sensitive in probing Hector for information about his mother's symptoms before she passed away. As foggy as his responses were, I was able to get more information than I was ever given before. He was adamant in telling me again that his mother's neurologist had told him his chances of getting HD were one in a million. By now, I simply couldn't believe that, as his symptoms resembled what I had been reading about HD.

At his follow-up appointment with the neurologist, I asked if Hector could possibly have Huntington's disease. The expression on the doctor's face was like a lightning bolt had just struck him. Nothing had been mentioned to him about a family history with this disease. At that time, there was still no blood test for this disorder. All we had to go on at that time was a family history and physical symptoms. The doctor's face turned somber, and he replied that in his opinion, considering Hector's symptoms and the family history, Hector had Huntington's disease. We were told there was no treatment for the disease and that it was fatal. Just like that, with one simple question, the mystery was over. We walked outside into a new world, different from the one we left behind before receiving the fatal diagnosis. It felt as if we were walking in slow motion, holding on to each other for support, but the weight of the world was on our shoulders. It took monumental strength just to put one foot in front of the other. This was one of the darkest moments of our lives. What would happen to my Hector? He was going to die! How was he going to die? How would this disease make him suffer? Would it be painful? Why him? Why was he randomly chosen to suffer like this? He was so good and loved life and his family with all his heart! Why, why, why! There was that question again. Yes, I would take care of him, I immediately decided. I would learn everything I could about Huntington's, and I would take care of him and never let him suffer!

This diagnosis now explained so much of his behavior. There were some tough times early in my children's lives. They were only eleven, eight and four years old when their father became very sick, but I could now explain to the children about their father's illness; however, then came the question from my oldest daughter, Margie. I did not have the heart to answer truthfully. "Mom, will we get Dad's disease?"

I sugar coated the truth with a lie. "No, Honey. You won't have your dad's disease because you look like me, so you have more of my genes than his."

That comforted Margie, but what I was really trying to do was to buy time, hoping we'd have a treatment before I had to tell her the truth. She learned that she was slowly losing her father to a disease for which there was no cure. Margie loved her father, and the care and affection with which she treated him amazed everyone.

My direction in life took a quick turn. I needed to learn all I could about this horrible disease. In 1980, there was very vague information about Huntington's disease. Even doctors had no real knowledge of what Huntington's disease was. Hector would become weaker and weaker, both physically and mentally, and ultimately die. The possibility that my children would also inherit this demon disease was something that I couldn't even give myself the time to think about. I had to stay strong and make a decision about how our lives would continue moving forward.

No one really gave me facts about the illness that had taken his mother's life before I had married Hector. Whatever I was told was presented pretty much like gossip. Hector took me to his grandmother's house to see his mother only once. She was lying down in bed, and Hector led me to her bedside.

"Mama, this is my honey," he said to her. She turned to me and smiled. She was a beautiful lady.

"She's smiling at you, honey!" he said, looking very proud and very pleased.

That's about all I knew about his mother. She was very sick, and she passed away a year later at the age of 46. I was later to learn that this illness was the unwanted inheritance that no one wanted to talk about. Forty years later, his family still behaves in the same secretive manner. How does his family handle the situation? When they see one more family member demonstrating what are without a doubt HD symptoms, they tell each other to, *"Shhhh! Don't say anything!"* This is sad but true and common among many HD families.

When Hector was diagnosed, my primary concern at that point was simply to survive. The shock of what our family was to endure and the knowledge that our lives would be nothing like what we had planned set in like a ticking time bomb. This realization left me mentally and physically frail with just enough strength to focus on caring for him and my three young children. Beyond that was too much for me to deal with. Keeping busy was my therapy, but behind my busy life was the subconscious knowledge that my three young children were now "at risk" for inheriting this fatal disease, "the unwanted inheritance."

I made numerous long distance calls to New York and all over the country, but very little information or hope was to be found. The internet had not been invented yet, so the library was my destination for medical information on Huntington's. I read through stacks of medical books from the library, but not much information was to be found, even in medical books. I contacted a holistic doctor and told him about my husband's decline, and he said to give him two pieces of toast with honey every morning, some orange juice, and some multivitamins. I was hopeful and willing to try anything, but of course, that did not halt the progression of the disease. Hector and I gathered with fellow church parishioners and prayed for a healing, but his decline continued. At one particular prayer circle, I had such a sharp pain on my back, left side that the pain brought me to my knees. That was the end of the occasional kidney infection that I had experienced for seven years. Maybe it was just a coincidence—I don't know. One thing for certain was that Hector did not receive a healing, and he continued to decline.

Not many people had ever even heard of HD. In spite of being at a loss for knowledge about the disease, this was not the time to crumble and let a fatal diagnosis bring my family down, especially when they now needed me more than ever. I was determined to do all I could to care for them and shield them against the challenges that awaited us.

Hector's family had always behaved secretively and treated me with distance. Although they rarely carried a conversation with me or looked me in the eye, they were keenly aware of my presence. These visits were never pleasant for me, but I accompanied my husband. Whenever there was a death on his side of the family, there was mention of various causes of death, but never Huntington's. Several of his family members always appeared to be intoxicated—the grandfather, the uncles. The family would laugh and brush it off as amusing. I never visited long enough to suspect otherwise. As time would tell, I don't believe it was intoxication at all, but Huntington's disease.

I just recently learned that Hector knew well before we were married that he, too, was at risk for inheriting Huntington's disease—not one in a million as he had told me, but one in two chances. A sense of betrayal washed over me at learning this. I felt betrayed by him and by his family... a family that had countless "accidents" and unknown causes of death. My future children would be at risk of being born with a fifty-fifty chance of inheriting HD, but no one said a thing. All I remember is the mysterious side stares that I would get, and I mistakenly took their behavior simply as being socially inept.

Personal goals and what seemed so important before now seemed so insignificant and were seldom thought about anymore. Life with someone with HD would teach me about the profound effects on a family at war with a fatal disease. I became mindful of seizing opportunities to laugh and to create happy moments in whatever touched my family.

Hector's symptoms worsened as the disease progressed. The disease was a daily threat to his life. It was destroying his body and his mind. I was distraught to see what it was doing to him. The disease rendered him helpless, and loss of autonomy threatened his dignity. He became weaker every day and was forced to rely on help from people for some of the simplest tasks that one takes for granted. The feelings of worthlessness were changing him. He was now truly disabled, and friends who surrounded him in the past no longer came around. Anger over the way life had turned out put him in a horrible mood that caused depression and insomnia. Like an emotional avalanche, all this turmoil made his symptoms accelerate.

In spite of the hardships that we had endured, my children were growing up in a playful family setting where there was much laughter, music, singing, playing, and a burst of activity. All three of my children were my treasures, generous with their love and their innate desire to make people happy, but Marie, my youngest, was so sweet that I truly felt she was an angel sent from heaven. She was sweetness and radiance that could soften any heart with her funny little expressions, her laughter, and her smile.

<u>1983</u>

Things got more difficult for everyone as Hector's symptoms changed him into a different person, one that we loved but of whom we became fearful. What used to be a routine part of raising a family now became a hardship for him, and he began over-reacting to even the slightest annoyance, lashing out violently and becoming combative. He was unrecognizable, no longer able to reason and to handle simple things calmly. The daily outbursts of violence soon became life-threatening to my children. Loud noises and screaming further triggered his symptoms and made him very nervous. We were afraid of him and never knew when he was going to blow up. On several occasions, he beat either Margie or Michael, and even little Marie, so severely that I feared for their lives. With no one to care for my children while I was at work, he was now a danger to my children and to himself.

It became necessary for me to protect my family, so I filed for a legal separation. This was another blow in my life—to separate from the person I had been with since I was 13 years old.

As it turned out, the separation actually gave him peace of mind, as he didn't have to deal with the everyday pressures and responsibilities of a young family. We were then able to have the children visit with him at his beach home as often as he wanted, and when he got tired, I would pick them up to let him rest. My dad continued to take him to the doctor and drove him to run his errands, and my sister would clean his house and cook for him. He had been a part of our family for so long that it was heartbreaking for my entire family to see him getting so sick. Margie went to see her father almost daily and treated him with the love and attention with which he'd treated her before he became sick.

While we were dealing with the challenges that Huntington's brings, Margie was feeling her own freedom as a teenager with a driver's license and her own car. She was a vivacious teenager who saw no obstacles in whatever she wanted to do. She got her driver's license the day she turned 16, and soon after that, she bought a car. Of late, I learned from one of her closest high school friends that while driving to a concert in L.A. with several of her friends, she was speeding, and along the way side-swiped several cars on the freeway. Her friends were stunned and kept yelling out to pull over, but Margie never stopped. She was focused on getting to the concert on time, and nothing else mattered. No one stopped her—neither police nor any of the drivers in the cars she had side-swiped. There were no cell phones then, so she was never given a ticket either. This was one more clue that Huntington's disease was on its way. I never knew about that incident until a few weeks after Margie had passed. I just wonder what else I'll never know. While I was chasing after Margie and trying to keep her on the straight and narrow, Marie started having trouble with schoolwork at about the age of 8, but there was still no test available for HD. I knew something was wrong, but I brushed negative and frightful thoughts away.

Margie attended Fountain Valley High School. After high school she moved to Los Angeles and attended L.A. City College, where she studied cinematography. She learned to write screen plays and produced several student films. She was vivacious and driven and so persuasive that several of her family members reluctantly agreed to participate in her films. Now, we look back at these films and are so grateful that we had her in our family to push us to do things that we never would have done on our own.

She attended The John Robert Powers School of Modeling and got a few jobs in fashion shows and promotional modeling. Some of her fondest memories included performing in the annual summer workshops at El Modena High School, where professional actors and students came together to study theater arts. She loved being on stage. Perhaps that was where she was able to escape the reality of her own life. She would shine in whatever she did. It wasn't just her quick smile; it was her warmth, her openness, and her spirit! She was fearless and completely confident that she could do anything she set out to do.

1989

Hector was a free spirit and loved his independence and autonomy. But on Good Friday, 1989, he was taking his daily walk to the beach to watch the sunset, but he never made it. He was struck by a motorist and passed away while being transported by helicopter to UC Irvine Medical Center. It has been 25 years since his death. The police report indicated that he was jay walking. That's what they said, but I'll never know. All I know is that he fought to retain his autonomy. He was such a free spirit that it just seemed inconceivable to me to have him confined to a nursing home. I am pretty sure that most individuals will fight for their autonomy, but with HD individuals, there are so many tragedies that occur because they truly are not able to care for themselves and be out on their own. The disease affects all areas of the brain, behavior, cognition and movement. I loved Hector, but I hated his disease, and I hate what it has done to our family.

A few more years were all I had to breathe. They say things happen for a reason, although I don't know why. HD is definitely a parent's worst nightmare. The script is entirely rewritten, and the family can expect nothing less than suffering, sacrifice, unexplained chaos, often financial devastation, and ultimately death. I soon embarked on a passionate appeal to researchers and elected officials to bring awareness about HD and to solicit support for HD research.

It wasn't long after Hector passed that Marie started exhibiting symptoms of the dreaded disease. She was 12 years old. I strongly suspected that the traumatic events around her father's death triggered the onset of the symptoms. I was horrified, broken-hearted, and almost at the point of hysteria in my urgency to do something! The fear and "fight or flight" phenomenon set in as the impending disease threatened my daughter's life. I brought the most wonderful children into the world only to have fate knock them down with the cruelest disease imaginable.

Marie took life in stride. She was such a trouper and tried her best in everything she did. She tried being athletic. Her activities included soccer, gymnastics, and Girl Scouts. Some of the happiest teenage years for Marie were spent boogie boarding in Huntington Beach, attending summer camp, and participating in the high school youth in government program.

1993

A blood test for the disease had finally been developed in 1993, so when Margie became engaged, she elected to have the DNA test. To everyone's shock, the results were positive. This diagnosis further motivated me to work faster to save my children who were all "at risk."

1994

Margie's fiancé loved her, and I made sure to tell him exactly what that diagnosis meant. Nevertheless, they decided to marry a couple of years later.

I don't believe I remember Margie ever looking happier than on their wedding day. There was so much love in the way they looked at each other that I couldn't help sobbing. They started a family immediately, and her focus quickly shifted to her husband and their two beautiful children. Margie started becoming symptomatic when her daughter was about two years old. Fortunately, we have a big family, so our entire family helped her with the babies while Craig was at work.

At Margie's insistence, Marie also participated in the Miss Teen Orange County Beauty Pageant. With my heart in my throat, I supported her participation in the pageant, knowing well what her limitations were and that they would be totally exposed before the other contestants and her audience. True to my feelings, she stood out when the contestants performed a group dance. Her movements were not in time, and she followed the other contestants' lead, and it was clear that she had not memorized the choreography. During the Q & A segment, she stuttered and didn't respond the way she had hoped. I knew what that meant, but Marie had still not been diagnosed with Huntington's disease. In spite of everything, I was so proud of her and can say without flinching that she looked like a Disney princess during the evening gown segment of the pageant. She had the courage to get up there and do what most girls who are perfectly healthy would never have the nerve to do. I know she agreed to be in this Teen Pageant to please her sister.

Soon, Marie started stumbling, and her speech became sluggish. She had a way of camouflaging her disabilities with her happy and sweet personality. While still in high school, she was fortunate to have a wonderful English teacher who recognized that she required special education. She helped Marie make it through high school.

1996

Marie was now 18 years old. I wanted it to be her choice whether to be tested for Huntington's. I asked the question in the gentlest way that I could, and she agreed to be tested. Always a trouper, once given the positive diagnosis of Huntington's disease in 1996, she quickly became an advocate and spiritual warrior in the fight against HD. Her strong will enabled her to continue doing many things in spite of her illness. She attended Orange Coast Junior College and hoped to someday be a kindergarten teacher. While representing the HD community at many levels, she was poised, hopeful in spirit, and a joy to behold.

While attending junior college, she often stumbled and fell, and she would get so frustrated when campus security repeatedly pulled her into the trailer to check her for drugs. She hated having to explain over and over again that she had HD, which didn't make any difference to the security staff because they had never heard of it anyway. It was humiliating and demeaning for her, and after two years, she decided she didn't want to continue with her education.

I had heard about work being done on HD patients at the neurosciences institute. They were doing embryonic stem cell implants and reported some positive results. I called them for a consultation. I then asked to meet an individual who had undergone the procedure. That's when I was introduced to Jeannie Zetz and her daughter, Melissa. I met them at a coffee shop in Newport Beach. Melissa was a beautiful, blue-eyed, blonde young lady, and she and Marie quickly became friends. She showed Marie the scar on her head from the stem cell implant and told her the procedure was not painful at all. Marie quickly decided to have the procedure done as well. We went through all the pre-surgery tests required, and it was found that Marie would not be a good candidate for this surgery, as they found that she also had Von Willendbrand's disease (a bleeding disorder that prevents the blood from clotting normally), and they could not risk losing her on the operating table due to hemorrhaging. I agreed and said I could not risk that either. What good came from this was that Marie and I became lifelong friends with Jeannie and Melissa.

While I was maneuvering through the stages of HD with Marie, Michael was on his own. He lived in Seattle, Washington, and would wait for the fishing companies to call him for the various deep-sea fishing expeditions where he went out to sea for several months at a time. He was determined to save enough money to start his own restaurant in Manhattan.

Margie had already been advocating for HD research long before her own symptoms escalated to the mid stages of the disease. One of the kindest gifts she had given Marie was a trip to the East Coast. They toured all the way down the coast, visited the Hershey Museum in Pennsylvania, and made a stop in New York for a Broadway show. She wanted to do all she could for her sister for as long as she could. Margie encouraged her brother, Michael, to live out his dream of one day owning his own restaurant in Manhattan, but it wasn't much later that he, too, became symptomatic with Huntington's disease. This doubled her dedication. Margie was a patient and a patient advocate. She attended many events in support of HD research, including Team Hope Walks, organized "Margie's Bake Sale," attended the Strike Out HD Bowl-a-thons, and attended the national Huntington's conventions.

1997

I met my current husband, David, at work, and we were married in 1997. It seems that he came into my life at a time when I needed so much moral support. Michael was in Seattle at the time, and I asked him to come home for the wedding. I wanted all my family there, and I wanted Michael to walk me down the aisle. He was so proud to have this honor. As we walked down the aisle, he suddenly tripped. This happy occasion was marred for only a split second, as I knew very well what the beginning symptoms of HD looked like.

2000

Michael fought being diagnosed with Huntington's disease. He continued to be in denial, although it was very obvious even to him that he was not well. He fought to keep his driver's license, but allowing him to continue driving would have ended in a very bad way not only for him, but for anyone else on the road.

Four years after Marie tested positive, Michael also tested positive for HD. It was the worst domino effect imaginable. I felt like I was doing a juggling act, with all three of my kids now very symptomatic. But rather than feeling helpless, I felt an intense urgency to do something to change the course of this disease. Internet access was a tremendous help in allowing me to tap into knowledge that would have taken a lifetime to obtain in the past.

It was necessary for me to get conservatorship over Michael as he wanted so badly to maintain his autonomy, and he did so for much longer than what he really should have. During the years when he was still going out on different jobs, he rode his bike and was struck by a car two different times and miraculously survived. He thought I was being too dramatic in worrying about him and would tell me, "Don't worry, Mom. I know how to roll. We learned how to do that when I played football."

I had learned from my friend, Jeannie, about her challenges in wanting to protect her son who also had HD. She had appealed for conservatorship over him, but her son was able to convince the judge that he could take care of himself, and the judge ruled in his favor. Jeannie cried, but there was nothing she could do. Her son went on his way to Seattle where she learned six months or so later that he had been murdered. From this lesson in life, I knew the time had come when Michael needed to be conserved, and I knew I had to hire an attorney if the judge was going to rule in my favor. I hired an attorney, and I was granted conservatorship over Michael.

2001

All three of my kids wanted to continue doing some of the same things they had done before but were now unable to do. Marie had attended the annual summer youth camp since she was 14, first as a camper and later as a counselor in training. She was getting older, and the symptoms were limiting her activities. I received a call from the summer camp director telling me they could not allow Marie to attend any longer as a very scary incident had taken place. A bear had come charging, and all the little girls had run, but Marie had a horrible time, stumbling while running to get the girls in the cabin. One of the counselors had had to run back to get Marie, putting his own life in danger. It terrified everyone, and that was the end of the summers that Marie loved so much. She was heartbroken and cried for days. I had to try really hard to console her by begging her to let me take her on a cruise. The neurologist that she was seeing at that time also begged her in his British accent to, "Go on the cruise, Marie! You will love it. You'll like it much better than camp!"

Marie laughed to see her doctor begging, as she had never seen that look on the face of a grown man. Margie and Marie both went to the same neurologist, and they really loved him. He always told them they looked lovely. What a great doctor! He couldn't take away the disease, but he knew how to make them feel happy. He was finally successful in convincing Marie to let me take her on the cruise. I called my friend Jeannie Zetz and asked her if she and Melissa would join us, and they loved the idea. The girls had a wonderful time, although they each fell during the cruise. Marie fell in the bathroom and cut her lip, and Melissa fell while walking out on the deck and scraped her elbows and knees. In spite of these incidents, the cruise was worth it. Marie was able to get over not going to summer camp, and for Melissa, this cruise was the last outing where she was able to walk independently. Four years later, our girls would be in the same care home where they would sit and watch TV while holding hands.

Marie's disabilities continued to progress, and it was time to get her a hospital bed. On the day it was due to arrive, I had been crying for hours before she knew what would take place, but I put on a cheery attitude and told her how great the hospital bed would be and how cool it was with all the buttons to raise or lower the bed in different positions. But when she saw the movers taking her bed away and bringing in an ugly looking hospital bed, she cried. She knew that it was a moment of transition in her life. Her friends slowly disappeared so that in time all she had was me and her brother and sister, who by now had also been diagnosed with HD.

I explored traditional and non-traditional approaches and treatments, integrating attention to personal care and curative treatment. My efforts did not halt the progression of the disease, but I do know that the overall quality of her life would have been worse without the supplements that I provided for her. My drive and passion led me to the startup of an HD chapter in Orange County. Along with fellow HD advocates and HD researchers, we were successful in advocating for an HD clinic in Irvine. That was a blessing to many families who had previously driven long hours to receive care from a medical staff with expertise in Huntington's. Our hope was that through this clinic, HD patients would be treated with dignity and provided with the comfort and care that they deserved.

I worked on providing Marie with outings that didn't require a lot of walking or transferring from the wheelchair. Some of our favorite girl-time was the drive through the countryside to Julian. We drove along the winding Highway 76 and enjoyed the vibrant beauty of the countryside—horses, old country stores, and lots of fruit stands and fresh air that simply mesmerized her. I'd roll down the windows, drive slowly, and let her take in the scent from the hundreds of orange groves. We'd stop and have lunch, walk to the old fashioned candy store, pick up some apple cider and a pie to bring back home, and that was about all we could fit into one day.

I participated as a member of a peer group that authored "Lifting the Veil of Huntington's Disease," a publication supported by the Robert Wood Johnson Foundation. At the conclusion of this project, I felt comfort in knowing that if no cure was to be found in my children's lifetime, I would provide them with comfort, care, and meaningful interaction to which everyone is entitled.

2004

Californians voted for Proposition 71, The California Stem Cell Research and Cures Initiative, which was authored by Bob Klein. The initiative created the California Institute for Regenerative Medicine (CIRM) to fund stem cell research in the state. I voted for Proposition 71, but I truly didn't realize how quickly things were going to move in the direction of stem cell research.

2005

Dr. Peter Donovan, the Director of the Stem Cell Research Center at UC Irvine, and Dr. Hans Keirstad invited me to be a part of the UC Irvine Patient Advocacy Committee, made up of the leadership from various disease organizations, some of which included Parkinson's, Multiple Sclerosis, Alzheimer's, Retinitis Pigmentosa, the hearing impaired, and cancer. I took every opportunity to be a voice for the HD community at the various CIRM board meetings. When I was not able to attend, I asked other HD advocates to represent our cause. Our voices were heard from northern to southern California. CIRM created collaboration among researchers, doctors, clinicians, pharmaceutical companies, HD families, and state and federal governments in support of stem cell research and clinical trials and has been a model template for the world. Through this movement, I found another boost of courage and renewed stamina to continue in my mission to be a voice for the HD community.

It was necessary for me to work, so a care home became the only option I had for Marie, as I was waking up every couple of hours or so when I heard her call for me because she was hungry, or after hearing her fall down. Marie was admitted to a convalescent home at the age of 26 and felt perfectly comfortable with senior citizens. They loved her and named her "Snow White." She expressed pleasure in sharing quality time with them, much as she did with people her age, as well as with children. She was pure of heart, and in spite of the extraordinary challenges in her life, she quickly became very good at adapting to whatever came her way.

Although residents loved Marie, there were many incidents where she was mistreated by the staff. I now wish I had never placed her in a care home. She was sexually abused at the very first care home she went to, and the next four years were a roller-coaster of one care home to another, all pretty much the same. Sadness transformed her happy spirit, and she was never the same after that. Her life ended just when she should have started living.

2006

It had now been more than a decade of tireless advocacy, fundraising, and hoping for a cure for my children, but the disease was taking them down. As I saw all three of my children looking very weak and only a semblance of who they used to be, I came to terms with the fact that my children were not going to make it. Margie was requiring help with all her activities of daily living. Marie had been in a care home for over a year and was no longer ambulatory or able to feed herself. Michael was losing his balance and falling while walking, and he was often choking on his food. The cure was not here in time for my children. What could I do, I asked myself. I got on my knees and prayed. I asked God to help me take care of my children in the best way that I could as I went through this illness with them till the end of their time with us. I had resigned myself to face the inevitable, but my resolve to keep fighting for a cure continued even stronger. At that point, my focus for a treatment for my children switched over to my grand-children and future generations at risk, who I hope will never have to face the fatal diagnosis that Huntington's disease brings.

All three of my children had already experienced so much suffering. There are still so many areas that fall below the level of awareness and care that families are crying for. Law enforcement, healthcare providers, social services and general public education about Huntington's disease have truly missed the mark.

2009

I went to stay with Marie several hours every day. In her last days, Marie was talking—mumbling, but we could understand what she was saying. She was smiling and humming while I sang to her. Margie went to see her several times, but seeing her little sister in the hospital at end of life was too painful for her to endure.

Yes, she was leaving me, but I think she was smiling and humming just to make me happy. Everyone was surprised at how alert she was, but that may have been because we had taken her off all the medications and just made her comfortable. She was responding better, but she was truly not getting better. HD was finally destroying her. She smiled and nodded, "Yes," when I ask her if she loved me. When I asked her who the love of my life was, she answered, "I am."

Her eyelids and the skin under her eyes were purple, and her skin tone became grayish. She was so thin that it was unbelievable that anyone could be that thin and still be alive. We had taken her off of food and she mumbled, "I'm hungry."

That just killed me. She could no longer have anything by mouth, and prolonging her suffering would have been cruel. Her seizures were horrific and left me feeling limp and lifeless. Life has truly tested me to the limit, and this was the most excruciatingly painful experience I had ever had. I loved my little girl so much, and I just wanted to take her in my arms and rock her to sleep, but I couldn't even do that, as she was hooked up to a pick line, a catheter, oxygen, and she was so fragile that I was afraid I'd break her little bones. All I could do was massage her neck, stroke her face, sing to her, and tell her I loved her. She knew that all too well. She never stopped thinking about summer camp. She smiled when I recounted the happy memories that she had shared with me, and I sang camp-fire songs for her until the day she passed away.

One year before Marie passed away, I was still very hopeful for a treatment, although I secretly knew it would probably be too late for Marie. All of my children were skin cell donors for stem cell research. UCI was setting the infrastructure for induced pluripotent stem cells (IPS). They were collaborating with UCLA and UCSD stem cell centers to obtain fresh skin samples to generate both the cells for nuclear transfer and also for generation of induced pluripotent stem cells from the patients. But for my Marie and so many other HD family members, the clock never stopped ticking, and their time ran out. Marie always believed she was going to be cured, and she fought to stay alive till her last dying breath. I want to keep that hope alive.

I cherish this letter from my friend, Tammy Schuff, because it gave me so much comfort when she stood by my little girl in her last days:

"November 1, 2009—Please let me know if you need me for anything. Marie will definitely be free, happy, healthy, and dancing once again when God brings her home. That's what I pray for. I had a dream the other night that she was sitting up in bed, laughing and talking, and she looked healthy and free of HD. I want to remember her and think of her that way always. Give her a kiss from me. Stay strong. Call if you need a friend. Tammy"

One day later, she wrote:

"November 2, 2009—Frances, I am not sure you'll be checking emails; however, in case you do, Vera called to tell me that Marie is with God and is in peace. I see her now dancing in heaven, full of love and free of HD. My thoughts go out to you and your family as I know how sad you feel. I will call you Tuesday as I would like to stop by your

house tomorrow night for just a few minutes if you are up to having company. God bless, and I'll talk to you tomorrow. Tammy"

Michael is still fighting the good fight. My little guy . . . the fighter . . . the strong one. I always thought he would be the one to escape this disease, as he was strong from the day he was born. He, too, went to a care home. The challenges for him were unimaginable. He was not the sweet person that Marie was in accepting having to be confined to a care home. He fought to get out, and the neglect and abuse that he received in the first six years were inhumane and cruel, especially for someone who is disabled through no fault of their own.

Privatized care homes are definitely not in the best interest of the patient, as I and so many other HD family caregivers have learned. We have learned that care homes routinely send a patient out to the hospital in order to push the patient out of the facility and then refuse to take them back. I suspect it has something to do with benefits and profit.

In the first year that Michael was admitted to a care home, he was moved around to five different facilities with a handful of hospital stays in between. There is something terribly wrong with the way patients are treated in the majority of care homes. I was finally able to have him admitted to a care home in Los Angeles, where he lived for five years. I still cannot accept the fact that the care homes in the county where he was born refused to accept him as a patient. They all stated the same reasons: they didn't have a bed available—when there were visibly numerous beds available; we don't accept young patients; we don't have programs for young people; we don't have sufficient staff to care for a patient with Huntington's disease; some actually had the nerve to say, "We don't accept HD patients."

Michael was almost killed at his first care home. I was told that he had tried to run away three times in that first week. Because of the symptoms of HD and the medical staff's unfamiliarity with the disease, I felt a sense of urgency and knew that it was critical that I have a social worker do an in-service for the staff so that they'd know how to care for a Huntington's disease patient. Not being successful in getting a social worker to the care home soon enough, I arranged for my brother-in-law, Dr. Malcolm Casale, to join me in presenting the in-service for the staff ourselves. He presented the medical aspect of the disease, and I presented the palliative care of HD and the patient dynamics. After our presentation, the nurse didn't even bother to say thank you. Malcolm and I didn't know if we were done or if we had to stay to present an in-service to the next shift. After 15 minutes or so, I went over to the station where the nurse was standing and asked her if we were done, and she said we were. We were both stunned and puzzled, and as Malcolm started to leave, he looked at me with a concerned look on his face and told me that I'd better check on Michael because he looked really dirty, and he smelled awful.

Just one week after I had Michael admitted to a care home, I went to see him, and all his clothes had been stolen. When he heard my voice, the first thing he said was, "Hi, Mom. Give me a kiss."

I kissed him and immediately saw that his eyes were swollen almost shut and bloodshot. The nurse played dumb and asked me if his eyes had always been red like that, and I said, "No! His eyes have never been red at all!"

I don't know what could have happened to him to make his eyes so swollen and so incredibly red. They had him dressed in old, dirty clothes that didn't belong to him. I freaked out at seeing my son in this condition. I found him in rags—rags that were not his own clothes! He was unshaven and dirty and wore cut-up green pants that looked like leggings and no underwear. He wore an old shirt. I was appalled and asked why he was wearing those clothes. He smelled terribly. No one had an answer for me. Everyone was running around back and forth, ignoring my desperate call for someone to tell me what was going on.

Michael was sitting in an old wheelchair, so I decided to come back the next day to deliver the new chair that had just been given to him from his medical insurance. I finally got someone's attention and asked them to show me his room and his closet. When I opened his closet, I found that everything was gone—his entire new wardrobe that I had purchased when he was admitted to the facility. Even his socks and underwear were gone! The director of nursing and the social worker assured me that they would find his clothes. I asked what they would dress him in tomorrow if they didn't find his clothes. They assured me that they would clean him up and dress him in clean clothes. I returned the next day, and he was wearing the same clothes as the day before—cut-up green leggings and no underwear, and an old shirt. They had still not located his clothes. I was horrified.

I left the care home, and on arriving at my home, there was already a voicemail message for me from the nurse at the care home. They called to tell me that Michael had fallen down and lacerated the back of his head. I called the care home, and they said they had sent him to the ER, where he received seven staples on the back of his head. I made a mad dash to the ER, and after they treated him, they sent him back to the care home.

I went to see him again the next day. Michael heard my voice and woke up. He started rolling over to the side of the bed, and the nurse and another person, a male, just stood there and looked at him. I was standing by the bed parallel to Michael, so I couldn't run around fast enough to hold him by the arm to help him sit up. I told them to hold him because he was going to fall. The nurse said, "No, Michael gets up by himself all the time."

I said, "He needs help."

She asked why, and I said, "Because he'll lose his balance."

She asked, "How do you know that?"

I said, "Because he has HD, and he needs help transferring from a sitting position to the wheelchair."

She said, "We don't do that here. We want them to do as much as they can for themselves."

Because they were blocking me from running around to help him before he fell, with my foot I pushed two beds together, Michael's bed and the bed next to him, to protect him in case he rolled over to the side. They looked astonished at my quick reaction and the fact that they were not able to stop me from protecting my son. It would have been awful if he had fallen again after just receiving seven staples in his head. I repeated that he needed help in getting up from the bed, especially after just waking up, and the nurse said, "We are a convalescent home, not a skilled nursing home. We don't do that here."

I looked her right in the eye and said, "Well, we'll need to talk about that."

She seemed pleased to hear my response and said, "That's fine."

It was so clear to me that that was their whole intention—to get the ball rolling to get him discharged from their facility.

Just three weeks later, I received a call from the nurse. She said Michael had fallen and that he had been sleeping quite a bit. They were going to monitor him. The next day I received another call from the nurse informing me that they were going to send Michael out to the hospital for an evaluation because he was sleeping quite a bit and had not woken up since the day before. She added that there was swelling on the right side of his head and that they were going to send him out for evaluation and a change of ALF, which I learned stood for Assisted Living Facility.

I knew immediately that there was a problem when they said he had been sleeping since the day before. I called my friend, Paula, and asked her to grab her camera. I knew something was terribly wrong. We drove out to the ER, and my heart sank. When we arrived, my son looked so bad that I knew immediately that he had been brutally beaten. He had a cut on his eyelid, and his nose was broken. He had a shoe mark on his back where he had been kicked. There were bruises the length of his forearm, and he could barely open his eyes. Once he was stabilized, I started asking him questions:

"Do you remember what happened to you at the care home?"

"Seven guys beat me up."

"Why?"

"Because they don't like me."

"Was Jared one of them?"

"Yes."

"Did Jared hit you?"

"Yes."

"Where did he hit you?"

"On the face… twice. Four guys hit me on the face twice."

"Who punched you on the nose?"

"Tim."

"Who is Tim?"

"The little one."

"Who hit you on the eye?"

"The lady's son. He lost his ring when he hit me."

"Does he work there?"

"Yes."

"Where was Jared when all this happened?"

"Jared was there."

"How did all this start?"

"Another guy gave me attitude. He told me to shut up."

"What was his name?"

"William. The guy who works there started it. They pushed me off the wheelchair and threw me on the floor."

"Why?"

"That's the way they operate, Mom. They're gang members."

I was infuriated and heartbroken. They had almost killed my son. I went into battle mode and made sure the staff that attacked Michael were all fired. The sad part about a privatized care home system is that those individuals who were fired will simply go to another care home and get hired there with no thorough background check.

It took months to find another care home for my son, and all the while, the hospital kept threatening me to take me to court if I didn't find another care home for him. He was still semi-ambulatory, he was strong, and he wanted his autonomy. He was finally accepted at a care home somewhere in Sun Valley. It wasn't long before they were calling me to complain about Michael. Once more, I was appalled by what I found. His sheets were soiled with blood from scabies. I called the director of nursing and asked him to look at Michael. He said he would have him evaluated. A few days later, I received a phone call informing me they were sending him out to the hospital for evaluation. When I arrived at the hospital, he was all hooked up with monitors and needles. He was in sepsis, dehydrated, and had pneumonia and scabies. Once again, it was a wonder that the care home staff didn't kill Michael. I went into battle mode again and reported the care home to the Department of Health. A slap on the hand and a relatively small fine is probably all they got.

What is so ironic and hard for me to understand is how he was accepted and loved when he was growing up in Orange County, but when he became ill, no care home where he grew up would take him. It appeared that the directors of admissions had an unspoken covenant not to accept HD patients. This is how Michael wound up in Los Angeles County for six years, away from the places and people that he knew, and why he would cry and beg, "Take me home," every time I went to see him.

The director of a care home in Los Angeles was kind enough to accept him. I made the drive up there twice a week, but it was not often enough to really watch over him. There, too, he was attacked by other residents all too often.

2010

I found myself making a dash to check on Margie during the week and making trips to L.A. to see Michael. Margie was now nearing the late stages of HD, but that didn't affect her courage. She was brave, putting aside her pride, and with the typical symptoms, slow gait, sudden and smooth movements of her hands, she spoke before numerous international scientific coalitions in support of HD research. She wanted to make a contribution by sharing what scientists don't know about HD patients and will never learn about in the lab. She left a lasting and powerful impact and inspired some of the most brilliant researchers in the world. She continued making presentations until she became so weak that it was too difficult for her make the trip and sit for long periods of time.

As the disease progressed, she had moments of depression, anger, and the other roller-coaster emotions that come from the disease itself. But in spite of these challenges, it was common for her to confront her day with boldness, with wanting to get the most out of life, with wanting to be a good mother and wife, and with a boundless love for her children. She was relentless in her hope for a cure in time for the next generation. As she was less able to do things like cooking breakfast for her children, she worried that the day would come when she would be unable to care for them. She prayed, she screamed, she cried, but nothing could ever bring her peace of mind until she knew that there would be a treatment to end this generational suffering, to allow her to care for her children, and to spare them from inheriting her disease.

2013

After five years in the Los Angeles facility, Michael was once again sent to the hospital with pneumonia, sepsis, and dehydration. He was now non-ambulatory and so weak that upon his discharge, I insisted that he be transferred to a care home in Orange County. They no longer had a valid reason to turn him down in Orange County. He was no longer able to walk or even stand, much less to run.

Margie was now pretty much confined to her home. She missed her brother terribly. She would mumble, "Michael, Michael," so I made special arrangements for her to see her brother. On the fourth of July, 2013, I hired a transportation company to drive Michael from the care home to Margie's house. Margie was so excited and kept turning her head to the side to look at her brother. She had not seen him in five years, and I still wonder what she thought when she saw what the disease had done to him. Would looking at him make her realize what it had done to her? We tried making it a happy celebration for them, and the effort was emotionally exhausting, as they were both so sick. The effort was well worth it, though. Margie got her wish. She spent an afternoon with her brother. This would be the last time that they would be together as she passed away seven months later.

As the disease progressed in her life, Margie became more passive and caused less drama if her husband didn't run off to get her the list of things she wanted from Target, or if he didn't get annual passes for them to go to Disneyland. Her children have gone through their young lives wondering, just as Margie, Marie, and Michael had wondered, if they would inherit this disease. They have witnessed unpredictable and unreasonable behavior, never knowing what to expect, and wondering if in their mother they may be looking at their own future.

Margie's time was running out, and I was caught completely off guard. It was astounding to see that her features became softer as she came closer to the end of life. Her face was taking on a radiant and angelic look, much like she looked before she became sick. God was preparing her for life as an angel in heaven.

Margie had done everything she could to fight this dreaded disease. It took her away from us at the prime of her life. On Friday, February 7, 2014, she was called home to eternal life. I'm still numb from having lost my beautiful daughter. She left us in her sleep on a cold winter night. It was unexpected and shocking beyond words. I didn't have a chance to hold her in my arms when she was born, and once again she was whisked away from me without a chance for me to kiss her and tell her one more time how much I loved her. Just four years after Marie's funeral, I was once again going through the motions of funeral arrangements. Margie was all about family and love. It was so fitting that her funeral and celebration of life should fall on Valentine's Day, February 14, 2014.

2015

I am now able to see Michael on a daily basis, although the staff always give me a sideways glance when they see me coming. There's no doubt that they believe I'm too particular and too protective of my son. They are right, and my son deserves to be treated with the utmost care and dignity. Because I'm relentless in accepting nothing but the best care for my son, he is now well taken care of and looks happy and content most of the days. It is amazing what providing comfort, proper medical care, and meaningful interaction for a patient will do. For now, if that is all we can do as caregivers, that needs to be high on our priority list, and it is definitely worth the challenges that we face with care home facilities.

All of this is still incomprehensible to me. Nothing has been as painful and hard to endure as seeing my little family slowly withering away and ultimately dying . . . first, the father of my children, then my sweet and delicate angel, Marie, and four years later, my darling Margie. How could so many young, loving, and vivacious souls come to this world only to be so senselessly silenced and so permanently gone from everything and everyone they touched and everything they created in their brief lifetime? The words keep repeating in my mind. Marie is gone. Margie is gone! My beloved daughters are gone forever. It seems surreal that they were here for such a brief time. My Michael will be gone soon . . . I can write these words, but I just can't process and accept the reality of this truth. Every time I walk into his room at the care home, I feel as if I'm getting a gift to be able to physically see him there. I treasure each day that he is still with us as I understand only too well that children are only a borrowed gift from God. Michael's dreams of running his own restaurant in Manhattan, getting married, and having lots of children are something he is no longer able to talk about, but I hope he can still fantasize about his goals in life and feel contentment from his thoughts and dreams.

This is the legacy of Huntington's disease. This hereditary disease causes so much suffering and pain from one generation to the next. Families are often dealing with numerous family members who are affected by Huntington's disease at the same time. They are juggling caregiving for several individuals with HD, advocating, and often feeling like they're fighting the world for their loved ones. They are often holding a job and working tirelessly to provide for their family, educating as many people as they can so their loved ones won't be misunderstood and mistreated. They're most likely financially strapped, yet they are fundraising to support HD research and patient care, and often donating a lot of their own money; and yet, most of the people in the world do not know about or have never heard of Huntington's disease.

I try to dismiss the feelings of betrayal and seek to forgive Hector by remembering my beloved children who were a product of our marriage. If only pre-genetic diagnosis and in-vitro fertilization had been available at that time, life would have been so different for my family and for the thousands of families who have been touched by the tragedy and suffering that Huntington's disease brings. I can imagine how lovely and joyful it would have been, but only for a split second because the painful truth of Huntington's disease is so powerful that the heaviness blurs my imagination and steers it back to the reality of the disease.

As my children are leaving me, I want to know that there will be something for those at risk of inheriting Huntington's and that my children will not have suffered and died in vain. I continue to fight for my grandchildren and other generations of HD families who await a treatment that will change the course of their lives. Like Dorothy in "The Wizard of Oz," I, along with my fellow HD advocates, continue looking to scientists as the wizards who will one day have the answers and the cure.

To put some balance in my life, my husband, David, and I will sometimes take a drive to the beach. When I watch the ocean waves, they resemble the rhythm of life in a family with Huntington's disease. The peaceful ocean waves are exhilarating, like the birth of a newborn child. There is peace, joy, love, and beauty, followed by deadly waves and an ocean of sorrow and tears, and then a brief calm, and a new cycle of waves starts again…another wave of beautiful newborn babies with Huntington's disease, so much like the cadence of the ocean tide and the rhythm of life with Huntington's. The only solace I create within myself is to envision that those who have passed from Huntington's, along with Hector, Marie, and Margie, are now reunited in heaven with only love and happiness and no more pain and sorrow.

Yes, I cry every day, and I suspect I will do so for the rest of my life. But I've learned that it is okay to cry. It is an emotional cleansing of the soul and a show of the love that I have for my babies who will always be a part of my mind, my heart, and my soul. Perhaps by default, I've also learned to make the most of what good there is in our world. I make a point of creating good times, cultivating the blessing of good friends and all who have become a part of my extended family in my journey with Huntington's disease.

This is how Huntington's disease became part of my reason for living. As long as I have the strength to get up each morning, I'll continue to advocate and be a voice for HD families. I have surrounded myself with fellow HD warriors who have also persevered with resilience, hope, and strength and survived the painful challenges that HD brings. The fight goes on!

Please consider making a donation to Frances Saldaña's foundation, HD CARE, a nonprofit organization.

Donations can be made via their secure web site, http://www. hdcare.org/, or by mailing a check to:

HD-CARE, UC Irvine, Portillo Children Memorial Fund
Account #3564 Appeal Code B5M10
P.O. Box 8036
Newport Beach, CA 92658

You can also contact HD CARE at 949-824-3061.

About Vicki Owen

Vicki Owen was born in Wheeling, West Virginia, in October 1945. She grew up in a little village called Beech Bottom and graduated from Wellsburg High School in 1963. She worked at Wheeling Hospital in the Purchasing Department for a year before moving to Washington, DC, to work for the Department of Health and Welfare, Foreign Studies Division, as a secretary. She met her first husband, Deral, at Andrews Air Force Base and then moved to Hamilton, Ohio, where he was from. She has one daughter, Dawn, and one grandson, Cody. Her first husband passed away at the age of 28. She then met her present husband, Tom, and got married to him in Las Vegas in 1989. He has two children. His son gave them four grandchildren, Bradley, Heather, Hannah, and Haily, and five great-grandchildren, Cason, Easton, Lucas, and twin boys Brettly and Benjamin. Vicki moved with Tom to Florida in 1992. She worked for AllMed Infusion, Watson Publications, and Academy at the Lakes before retiring to take care of Tom. They now live in Sun City Center, Florida and do volunteer work to help bring awareness to Huntington's disease.

CHAPTER 6

I'm Not Sick ... I Just Have HD
By Vicki Owen

"*I*'m not sick....I just have HD." These are my husband, Tom's, words when asked how he feels.

Our journey with Huntington's disease began in late 2009, when my husband decided he needed to see a psychiatrist. After reading a book about ADHD (Attention Deficit Hyperactivity Disorder) that my daughter had sent us to help us understand the symptoms our grandson was dealing with, my husband thought it sounded a lot like what he was experiencing. His focus on work, inattention to detail, and angry outbursts for no good reason sounded like an adult version of ADHD, and he asked me who we could see to help him. We found a psychiatrist and made an appointment. While he was seeing the doctor, my husband received a call from his nephew, checking to see how his uncle was doing. It was this phone call that triggered our journey into HD.

Tom's nephew asked if we'd had him tested for Huntington's chorea because he thought his mother, my husband's sister, had told him that his grandpa (Tom's father) had had Huntington's chorea. On a recent visit, Tom's nephew had noticed that Tom had some movement issues, especially in his fingers, feet, and shoulders, and this prompted him to ask about the chorea. When we mentioned it to the psychiatrist, he suggested we see a neurologist right away. I don't know if Tom's parents knew his dad had HD, but we had never heard the term before and asked Tom's nephew why he thought that. He said his mother (Tom's older sister) had said his grandpa had Huntington's chorea. By this time, Tom's father, aunts, uncles, and sister had all passed away. We asked Tom's brother if he knew anything about it, and he did not.

Our neighbor was a nurse, and she suggested we go to see the neurologist at the University of South Florida (USF) and talk to him. We made an appointment, and the doctor determined after the initial examination that Tom should have a DNA test to confirm what the doctor suspected. Tom's test came back positive with a CAG of 39. Since the number was low, and being diagnosed late in life (my husband was 64 at the time), the neurologist told us that Tom's symptoms wouldn't develop at a fast rate. My reaction was more one of disbelief, like what the heck is it? We didn't think anything horrible about it because we knew he'd gotten it from his father, and we hadn't really seen anything horrible with him. This was in January of 2010. We were invited to attend a support group meeting, and since we knew virtually nothing about HD, we decided to go. When we walked into the meeting, it was a rude awakening for both of us. There were people there in wheelchairs, using walkers, or using canes. Most were younger than my husband and were much more advanced. One had JHD and was already in a wheelchair. They all had a lot of movement.

After seeing what this disease could do to you, my husband refused to go back to support group meetings for three months. He thought that he was going to advance more quickly, and it scared him. That, I think, was the point that we first realized just what Huntington's is. After that experience, I called the clinical coordinator and started to learn more about the disease. I shared with Tom what I had learned. I learned that the disease doesn't affect everyone the same way, that it doesn't progress in everyone at the same rate, and that everyone reacts differently to finding out they have it. Because his family has a history of late onset and mild symptoms, we thought it wouldn't be so bad and decided to try and stay positive. Once we understood what to expect, we started going back to support group meetings. Understanding that everyone progresses at a different rate made my husband realize that he may never have the symptoms that affected everyone else in the group. He decided he would try to be very positive and to keep a good attitude toward this disease.

I started researching Tom's family history and talking to other members of the family about what they knew. It was then that we got our first shock. His father was one of nine children (two died in infancy), and five of those had HD, including Tom's father. He has six first cousins and at least four second cousins with HD and at least eleven cousins at risk. The more I investigate, the more we are finding out. We now know that all of his aunts and uncles were misdiagnosed, but we don't know for sure about the symptoms they had. Apparently, it has been known for a few years by some members of Tom's family that HD was in the family; however, Tom and I didn't know about it until he was diagnosed in 2010. We're not even sure how the family found out about HD.

In researching Tom's family, I noticed there seems to be a pattern of onset in ages. The first generation, Tom's dad and his siblings, all had very late onset with symptoms seeming to be no more than chorea and anger issues. Parkinson's disease seemed to be the prevailing guess of what they had. All of them passed away from more or less other causes, i.e., heart attacks, cancer, dementia, etc., late into their 70s or early 80s. The next generation, Tom and his cousins, also were diagnosed later in life, if at all, passed away into their 70s and were not clinically diagnosed. The third generation seems to be getting symptoms earlier in life, 30s and 40s, with some passing away in their 30s.

The best I can understand about why the family didn't share this information before now is because most of them lived in separate parts of the country and didn't see each other or talk to each other much. It's only been in recent years that it's started to be talked about with the family members and the younger ones wanting to be tested for their children's sakes.

When I found out about the history of HD in the family, I was surprised, but it didn't really make any difference to me. We were already dealing with it, so knowing about the family history didn't change anything. I did want to know more, though, about this disease that was affecting my husband.

When I asked Tom why he didn't know about HD being in the family and how he thought all of his aunts and uncles had passed away, he gave me surprising answers. One aunt had passed away in a mental hospital when she was very young. It wasn't known at the time that she had HD; she was put in the hospital because of her chorea and angry outbursts. She wasn't diagnosed with anything; they just thought she was "crazy." The other two aunts were thought to have Parkinson's and died of heart attacks. His uncle was an alcoholic, so Tom thought that was the cause of his death. His own father died of prostate cancer at the age of 78, without our knowing he had HD. Looking back, we can see that some of his actions could have been HD-related. He had an uneven gait, anger issues when Tom was growing up, and constant movement in his hands and shoulders. His driving was very erratic, and when we came to Florida to visit, I always made my husband drive because his father's driving made me nervous. Because other members of his family actually knew that HD was in the family for a few years, they just assumed everyone in the family knew about it. His cousin said he thought he'd noticed it in Tom when he'd seen him at his brother-in-law's funeral but didn't mention it. He assumed we would know about it since he knew that Tom's dad had it. I didn't go to the funeral, or I might have learned about it at the time, but it was only a couple of years later anyway that Tom was diagnosed.

I asked my husband if he had ever heard anyone mention the words Huntington's chorea to him. He said he didn't recall ever hearing about it in regards to his family or anyone else. Tom moved away from his family in his twenties, and didn't really keep in touch with anyone other than exchanging Christmas cards. He never lived close to any family members until we moved from Ohio to Florida to be near his parents, and they passed away from other health issues within a year of our moving here.

Knowing all of this sooner, though, would not have changed anything for either of us. We might have been able to plan our retirement a little better financially, but nothing else would be different. I guess knowing how many family members are affected by this horrible disease makes it easier to accept, and Tom chooses to have a positive attitude.

We went to see the movie "Alive and Well" in Tampa, and Tom had a few qualms after seeing it, but the NBC reporter from the United Kingdom, Charles Sabine, said in the movie that he was convinced that having a good attitude is what keeps his symptoms under control. He was a great inspiration for my husband. I encourage Tom every day to take walks and to talk about what is going on in the news to keep his mind and body as strong as he can. We both believe that's why his progression has been slow. He has had several sessions with a speech therapist, occupational therapist, and a physical therapist, and when he feels like he is slowing down, he requests that they return. The speech therapist works on exercises for his tongue and throat muscles. She gives him VitalStim treatments to strengthen his throat to help with swallowing. His physical therapist works on strengthening his legs and lower body as well as exercises to help with balance. His occupational therapist works on his upper body to strengthen his arms and back. She also works his core muscles to help with his balance. They are very positive and encouraging, and that helps him to stay positive.

Looking back over the years since meeting my husband, I can see when his symptoms started to show. I met him in 1983, at volleyball for Parents without Partners. I don't know what it was, but I was attracted to him instantly. Him….it took a little work! One of the things that attracted me was that he was such a sweet, old-fashioned gentleman. I even had to learn to sit in the car until he came around to my side and opened the door for me! He was raising his two kids alone and didn't go out much without them. It took six long years of dating to get him to pop the question! I didn't notice any significant symptoms in the beginning of our relationship. The more we were together, though, I started to see that he had a lot of finger and foot twitching, which I attributed to his nervous personality. He had some very angry outbursts, most of which came out of nowhere, and those frightened me when they were happening. I tended to step back whenever this happened, but his anger was never directed at me, so I just attributed it to something like a bad day at work. Now we've been together for a total of 32 years, and I wouldn't have it any other way. I love his sense of humor and positive attitude toward life, despite the fact that he has a fatal illness.

Tom was a national account sales manager for a company that printed the PGA (Professional Golf Association) tour programs. His inability to learn new things on his job, mainly when they brought computers into it, and he more or less refused to learn how to operate them, led to the loss of the job he'd had for nine years. He blew up at work after a run-in with another salesman over one of Tom's accounts, and that ended up being another reason he quit the job. After leaving that job in 2003, he changed jobs frequently because it was too hard to learn new things. We didn't worry too much because we were always confident he'd find another job. His last job at a major grocery chain lasted about four years because it was repetitive work, no computers were involved, and he didn't have to think about what he was doing. The customers loved him, and he had no problem with that aspect of his job, but when asked to do something in addition to what he normally did routinely, it would throw him off, and so he started to get bad job evaluations. He quit his job in 2010, after he got lost coming home from work one night and started losing focus at work. He could have stayed on because his boss and the people there really like him, but we were worried about his driving at night. Once Tom was diagnosed, the bad job evaluations, getting lost, and losing focus started to make sense. Since he had been diagnosed with HD just a couple of months before getting lost, we thought it best that he not work any longer to keep him and everyone on the road safe. Because he was old enough to collect Social Security, he was able to retire and not worry about the money, but he missed being able to be around people. He hated losing his independence and was a little depressed about it at first, but he rallied around pretty quickly and decided being retired wasn't all that bad. It wasn't too bad at first, but just a few months later, I lost my job as a teaching assistant at a private school, and things started going downhill financially. I was not prepared for this, as I'd never had to be in charge of finances before. Tom had always been in charge of major decisions and finances, and finances had gotten pretty shaky as they often do with Huntington's disease.

I guess the hardest part in adjusting to the disease, besides the knowledge that someday it will take my husband from me, is the financial burden it has caused us. We ended up filing bankruptcy, losing our home, and moving to a community we thought would be better suited to us. After three years, that didn't work out, and we moved to a rental, so at least I didn't have to worry about the upkeep of the house. It is still very hard to make ends meet, and we have gone through our savings very quickly. Being considered my husband's caregiver doesn't allow me to have much time to earn money to make ends meet. I get a very small stipend as his caregiver from the county we live in, but if I leave him alone, I lose it. We get this from Hillsborough County Aging Services Department, and I know that neighboring counties in Florida have this same program. I have had to learn to balance the checkbook (which I hate, by the way), pay the bills, take care of the house inside and out, do the laundry, etc. etc. etc. Some days the stress of all the everyday tasks gets to me much more than anything that has to do with my husband's HD. I take a sedative sometimes to help me sleep when things just get too overwhelming. When that happens, I feel like I have an elephant sitting on my chest and can't breathe. Tom is the easiest part of my day.

I guess another thing that was hard to take was the loss of a lot of our friends. Not knowing anything about the disease and apparently not wanting to know much has pushed them farther away from us. Yes, Tom eats a lot more slowly than everyone else, his speech slurs, he walks slowly, and his gait is uneven, but he is still the same man inside. Patience is a virtue, and I guess our friends were not blessed with it. It's their loss because he's still the wonderful man I married twenty-six years ago. Our friends in the HD community, though, have been wonderful. They came into our lives at our lowest point. They are now and will always be very special to us. I know I can call anyone in our support group or at the Center of Excellence and get support if I need it. My daughter is also a great source of support for us. Without her, I would be very depressed; I count on her positive attitude to pull me out of my moods. I can vent to her about things I can't tell anyone else or if I'm just having a bad day. She offers a lot of moral support for me.

What do I miss most about the man I first met? His genuine love for life. He made everything we did FUN. We laughed a lot, even about silly things. He would call me and see if I would like to go do something, skeet shooting, archery range, water skiing. We went on picnics, went to fireworks, went dancing. Oh, how he could dance! We went on sleepovers with the kids at Parents without Partners events and played racquetball half the night. All were things I had never done before. He would call me late at night, and we'd talk for hours on the phone about anything and everything.

The night he proposed was cold and rainy, and we were supposed to go out to dinner. His parents were due in town for his son's wedding, and I was baking cookies for Christmas and trying to get ready for them, so when he called to say he was running late, I just decided to make something warm and quick so we didn't have to go out in the rain. After we ate, I continued baking and cleaning up, and finally Tom called me into the living room. He'd been waiting all evening for me to get done. I sat next to him on the couch, and he reached behind it and pulled out a pink velvet box. My heart started beating so fast I thought it would jump right out of my chest. He opened the box, and a beautiful solitaire diamond winked up at me, and he asked me to marry him. I immediately started crying and said, "Yes, yes, yes!" He then explained to me about the beautiful candlelight dinner he had planned at The Hamiltonian Hotel where he was going to ask me….I didn't care….he had FINALLY asked me, and that was all I cared about!

I then jumped up and called all the kids. He then told me his plans for getting married, and I was flabbergasted because he wanted to get married right away! Just a month later, we flew to Las Vegas, found a darling little chapel on the strip called the Silver Bell Wedding Chapel, and it was done! We didn't tell anyone we were going, just our bosses, and sent "by the time you read this" announcements, "we'll be Mr. and Mrs. Owen." Needless to say, the kids weren't too happy with us, especially my daughter, since she and I had lived alone for 11 years, and she thought she should have been there. Of course, everyone was happy for us, both of our families and all of our friends who had suffered that six-year journey with me. I miss those days of late night phone calls, spur-of-the-moment outings, etc., but I still have the man, and that's all that counts.

Tom and I are now both very involved in helping to raise money for our local Center of Excellence, where Tom's neurologist is working on a procedure to slow down the progression of the disease. Tom loves to help and goes with me to get donations for raffles for our events, obtain venues to hold our events, and then help out at the events. I am the "Cocktails for a Cure" chair and hold quarterly cocktail events to raise money and awareness for HD research at USF. I have also hosted "Drag Queen Bingo" and hope to have a walk and other events soon. We also help with and attend events that our local HD group holds.

Recently, we attended the annual conference for the International Association of Chiefs of Police in Orlando, FL, with the Help4HD-International foundation and talked to law enforcement officers about their knowledge of neurological diseases, specifically HD, and their treatment of people with HD in situations leading to arrests. Tom is always game to attend events where HD needs advocacy. He was happy to hand out pamphlets at the conference and talk to officers about how he feels. He has no problem talking about his disease to anyone who wants to know about it. He was always very sociable and still has a wonderful sense of humor. He hasn't lost the ability to make people laugh, but he doesn't talk much when we are in a group of people who have no association with HD. Everyone in the support group loves him because he makes them laugh, and he doesn't dwell on the disease itself.

More recently, we attended a class for speech language pathologists as guest speakers with the social worker for the Center of Excellence. After her presentation to the class, we had a question-and-answer session where they asked Tom and me what we have learned by having a speech therapist treat him. We gave them examples of one speech therapist who was very ineffective with Tom and why, then compared him to Tom's present speech therapist who is excellent, and why. They asked Tom how he benefits from speech therapy, and he willingly answered all the questions put to him. He did a fantastic job, even though some of his words were slurred, of getting his point across. The speech language pathologists were all very pleased with the session and thanked us both for our input into real life situations. My main thought to leave with them was to "know what disease you are treating." Everyone should be treated according to his/her personal situation, e.g., Huntington's disease, stroke, Alzheimer's, etc. The same goes for physical and occupational therapists. If they don't understand the disease, then they won't know what exercises and treatments to administer. That's the big lesson we learned from having an ineffective and then a very effective speech therapist.

Tom has one son who has tested negative for HD. His son has four children with three grandsons and twin grandsons on the way, all of whom don't have to worry about inheriting this disease. Tom also has one daughter who has chosen not to be tested. She doesn't want to know and is not married and doesn't have children, so there is no pressing need for her to know whether she has the expanded CAG. I'm sure one day she will decide to test if she starts to show any symptoms, but for now, she is living her life as normally as possible. I'm not sure that Tom is even aware that she's at risk.

Tom and I participate in Enroll HD at the Center of Excellence at USF. We have been involved for three years and hope to help researchers learn more about the progression of this disease. We both do the same tests, like identifying colors and the Stroop Test and naming animals whose names begin with a certain letter, and the researchers compare our results from year to year. We like to get involved with anything that will help to find a cure for this horrible disease. This is also why we volunteer so much of our time to raise awareness and money for our local research department. We are firm believers that there is a cure around the corner, and we pray for all those afflicted with this disease.

How is Tom doing today? He can still shower, dress, and feed himself. He does have choking issues, and he gets tired very easily. When he chokes, I try to keep calm and to keep him calm. He usually chokes on liquids and still hasn't learned that he cannot put more into his mouth than he can swallow easily. He uses a straw now, and that has helped tremendously. He slurs his speech when he is very tired and walks like he's drunk if I don't hold his hand. We can live with that. If he thinks he needs it, we take a walker with us to go out. We recently got a wheelchair for those times we want to go to a park or festival, where he would get tired really quickly. This way, we can both enjoy a longer time out, he won't get cranky and want to go home, and I can take my time. Other days, he says he's fine and doesn't need the walker or the wheelchair. He gets his words mixed up and forgets how to change the channel on the TV. He's obsessive/compulsive when it comes to drinking fluids. He HAS to have a glass of juice at his fingertips at all times. Yes, his medication has caused his sodium levels to drop, and so we add sodium tablets to his daily regimen of medications, and that makes him even thirstier, but since his only vice is juice, it's okay. Tom tried Xenaxine, but it magnified all his symptoms—his anger issues came to the forefront, and it made him highly agitated—so his neurologist weaned him off that. Risperdal also didn't do a thing for him, so the doctor took him off that one. Tom currently takes Zoloft for anxiety and depression, thioridazine for chorea, and olanzapine for chorea and mood (anger) at night. Trazodone is a different type of antidepressant he takes at night to help with his sleep, and he also takes Seroquel (quetiapine) for restlessness and mood (anger). I often tell people at our support group meetings that not everything works for everybody.

Would his symptoms be worse without the medications he takes? Yes, I'm sure they would. He knows that and makes sure he doesn't forget to take them with every meal and at bedtime. Sometimes I forget, and he reminds me. I'm not getting any younger, so one of us has to remember! How I wish he didn't have this dreadful disease because it has taken the man I married away from me. I love him regardless and will always be there for him. You never know; he may outlive me, if it's God's will. In going forward, all we can hope for is that God blesses him with a long life and that the disease is very slow in progressing. I won't put him in a nursing home. I'm just going to keep on trucking, and I will keep him at home, even if I have to get someone to come in and help. We don't really talk about or make any plans about the future, other than what's on the calendar for the month.

After all, he's not sick; he just has HD.

—⁂—

Please consider making a donation to the University of South Florida's Huntington's Disease Research Fund, a nonprofit organization.

Donations can be made via their secure web site, http://www. usf.edu/ua/FUND?fund=250068, or by making out a check to

Huntington's Disease Research Fund at USF, Acct. # 25-0068, and mailing it to:

Dr. Juan Sanchez-Ramos
Huntington's Disease Research Fund
Morsani Center for Advanced Healthcare
13330 USF Laurel Drive
Tampa, FL 33612-4799

You may also wish to consider making a donation to Help 4 HD's Law Enforcement Education Program.

Donations can be made via their secure web site, http://help4hdin-ternational.org/LEprogram.html, or by mailing a check:

Help 4 HD International, Inc.
436 Playa Blanca St.
Santa Maria, CA 93455

In the "memo" section of the check, please specify "LEEP."

About Roberta Brink

Roberta Brink was born in the Midwest. Her love of writing began at an early age. She writes poetry, fiction, non-fiction, short stories, and children's books. She has lived in Virginia, Tennessee, and California, but always returns to her home state of Iowa. She found out Huntington's disease was in her family at the impressionable age of fourteen. As a shy teenager she kept her feelings buried deep inside instead of sharing them. She states her life would have been quite different if she had known then what she knows now and had shared her feelings more. Having said that, she has no regrets about the way her life turned out. She is the mother of four sons and is a grandmother. She states she has the best daughters-in-law she could have ever imagined. She belongs to several non-profit organizations and donates her time to many causes, but mainly HD and shelter animals. She has five dogs of her own.

CHAPTER 7

❧

Accidental Discovery
By Roberta Brink

I grew up in a small Iowa town, the youngest of three daughters. My dad owned his own business, and my mom was a school teacher. One of my favorite memories was having Dad come home for lunch when my sisters were in school. Mom, Dad, and I would eat lunch, and then Dad would lie down with me to take a nap. There were a few days that he would be out of town at lunch time, so he wasn't there to nap with me. I had a hard time falling asleep without him. The radio played the same songs every day, and every time I hear one of those songs today, I smile as I remember my special nap time. Dad was always gone when I woke up, but I don't ever remember being awake when he left. My mom stayed home with my two sisters and me until I turned four. I had a babysitter that year, but she was one of Mom's friends, so she wasn't really a stranger. It was wonderful having a school teacher mother because I got to spend the summers with her. She was such a loving, caring mother. Her children always came first. She and Dad rarely went anywhere without us. She felt that if her kids were not welcome, she wasn't welcome. We were all very well behaved (really) except for an occasional hiccup. Girls cannot be good all the time!

Life was pretty normal most of the time. My dad was Justice of the Peace when we were young. He held court in the old tin-sided town hall building in Orient, Iowa. Later, he became mayor of our town. I was very proud of him, but it did kind of mess with his daughters' social lives. Kids didn't tell us anything because they knew we would tell Dad, and their "fun" would get interrupted. We were never invited to parties. It kept us out of trouble, which is every parent's dream anyway. Although I didn't have much of a social life as a teen, I wouldn't change a thing. I had a very happy childhood.

Halloween was always a pretty scary time in our small town. The teenage boys would walk through town, vandalizing anything and everything they could. Dad sold and serviced citizen's band radios and police receivers, so we always had a scanner going during my entire childhood. I always enjoyed hearing what the cops were doing and learned the "lingo" at a very early age. The teens usually did harmless things like upsetting outhouses, filling the trees with toilet paper streamers, putting old tires in the middle of the road, and soaping business owners' windows. For a couple of years, Mom and Dad let the three of us "go out" on Halloween. We would follow the guys doing the dirty deeds and clean it up as fast as they messed it up for the things that were easily fixed. We had a blast and never got caught. We giggled and laughed all night long at our own "clean, dirty tricks"! It was hilarious to hide in the dark and hear the guys doing the dirty tricks come back through our handiwork and make comments like, "What in the *&#@ happened here? We had this messed up, and now everything is put back. What's up with that?"

Mom was the matriarch of our extended family because her mom had died while she was in college. She rarely talked about her feelings of losing her mother when she was so young. She made sure that our extended family got together every Thanksgiving and Christmas and usually on Easter as well.

Some things in my life started getting strange when I was in junior high school. I remember going to my aunt and uncle's home one time. We rarely saw them, but always enjoyed visiting. They had five kids, three older than me and two younger. We always had a good time, and my aunt and mom were both excellent cooks. I noticed "something" was wrong with my uncle. He had strange facial expressions, and his language was "different." I had not seen him like that before, so I had no idea what to think. I thought he must be sick and would soon be better. He had a very strange gait that looked like he was drunk, but I could not smell alcohol on his breath. When we left, Mom and Dad mentioned that something seemed to be wrong with him. Mom said that she would call my aunt and talk to her about it.

A few weeks later, Mom said that she had heard back from my aunt. My uncle had undergone some tests, and the doctors thought he had multiple sclerosis or Wilson's disease, or something else. They were still doing tests. I asked if he was going to be okay. Mom said she hoped so, but they didn't know what they were dealing with yet.

Time passed, and I didn't hear any more. As I mentioned earlier, Mom was a school teacher. She taught in a neighboring town about thirty minutes away. Part of her duties included selling tickets to the high school sporting events on a rotating basis. On one particular evening, it was her night to stay late and sell tickets. That meant she would not be coming home until around ten o'clock or after. It was a cold, wicked, nasty Iowa winter night. It had started snowing earlier in the day. After supper, Diana and Dad had gotten out a bunch of papers and had them spread out over the dining room table. They were discussing them in low voices. Diana had told me Dad was helping her with her homework for an essay. About forty-five minutes later, Mom walked in the door. Dad said, "What are you doing home?" She said one of her school teacher friends had decided it would be best if they switched nights, so Mom could go home early. Her friend lived a few blocks from the school. I was thrilled to actually have her home early. However, Diana and Dad apparently had that "deer in the headlights" look on their faces. She saw the guilty looks on their faces and asked what was going on. They told her that Dad was helping Diana with a school essay project. That seemed quite unusual, so she asked why Diana had not asked her for help. They stammered around and didn't have an answer. I could tell the situation was becoming a confrontation, so I disappeared into my room with my other sister.

A few minutes later, Diana came into our room and started whispering. She told my other sister and me what had happened. Diana said that a few weeks before, Dad had gone to my grandpa's house to fix his television. He was behind the television getting ready to work on it when Grandpa started sobbing. Dad asked him what was wrong. Grandpa said that he was afraid his son had the curse. Dad had no idea what he was talking about. Grandpa proceeded to tell him that they had a "curse" in the family. The curse took Mom's mother. That was why she had died so young. He had seen my uncle and noticed the same symptoms in him that he had seen in Grandma and the other relatives who had the curse.

Dad asked what the curse was called. Grandpa said it was Huntington's chorea. Dad had never heard of it. Grandpa filled him in on what was in my uncle's future, and it wasn't going to be pretty. Dad was curious as to why Mom had never mentioned it. He guessed she didn't want to talk about it. Therefore, he consulted his mom for answers and advice. He asked her if she would do some research for him and find out what this Huntington's chorea was because Mom had never mentioned it. Grandma did some research and told him she couldn't find anything more than a small paragraph in the encyclopedia. Dad wanted more information, so he had talked to Diana and asked her if she could do some research with him. She had been gathering genealogy information about our family and writing notes on her findings. I think she'd even sent away for some information. That is the paperwork they were going through when Mom walked in the door.

Mom had absolutely no idea what Huntington's chorea was, let alone that it was in the family. Dad and Diana explained everything to her. She was in shock. Diana also told me that Mom had a 50/50 chance of inheriting the disease and that each of us had a 50/50 chance of getting it if she had it. My life changed forever that night. The black cloud started hanging over my head. I was fourteen years old.

Mom called my aunt the next day and told her to tell the neurologist that it was in the family. Shortly after that, it was confirmed that my uncle had Huntington's chorea. We found out that the disease had been renamed Huntington's disease because not all HD patients had chorea. Mom immediately became my uncle's advocate. She said that she'd known something had been wrong with her mom, but she'd never known what it was. She thought she had a mental disorder. When her mom died, she'd asked the doctor what was wrong with her. The doctor's response was, "Nothing that you ever have to worry about." Back in that time, it was thought that sons inherited the disease from their mothers, but daughters could not get it. Therefore, he didn't think she needed to know.

Mom started connecting with other relatives and people she found through her own research who had HD in their families. She was like a sponge, hungry for any kind of information available.

Meanwhile, I started living as if I had the "curse." My dating years were pretty much non-existent. For one thing, I was very shy. I didn't want to date anyone because I would eventually have to talk about the disease. I thought it would only be fair to let my future spouse know what might be in store for him. I met my first husband when I was a senior in high school and eventually married him. He was the only guy I dated prior to my marriage. I remember the night I told him about HD. I told him I wanted to tell him early in the relationship because it was going to get ugly if I had the disease. He said that he had heart disease in his family, so it was no big deal to him. Hardly the same, but I felt I had done my due diligence by at least telling him about it.

I made up excuses for not wanting to go to college. I got married instead. I desperately wanted to have a baby. My motherly instincts were deeply rooted. I lived in a dream world and felt that there were enough researchers working on a cure for HD that there would be one long before my children would ever have to worry about it. I had two sons five years apart.

I lived my life in five-year increments, never looking beyond five years. I gave myself that time frame for "being okay" from the time the symptoms start until I would start to become a prisoner in my own body. Every twitch made me believe that I had HD. Every stumble made me believe I had HD. I would stand in front of the mirror and watch my face to see if it made the faces I saw in other HD patients.

A few years went by, and Mom seemed obsessed with learning all she could about the disease. All she really knew was that there was no cure. She had to save her brother. She joined a support group in Iowa for families and friends affected by Huntington's disease. The support group had been started by Marjorie Guthrie, wife of Woody Guthrie. Woody was a famous folk musician who had started showing symptoms of the disease during their marriage. When Woody started having symptoms, they'd had absolutely no idea what was wrong with him. Marjorie had done mountains of research before they got a diagnosis, then more research after they knew what was wrong. Marjorie named the support group the Committee to Combat Huntington's Disease. Marjorie, like mom, wanted to know everything she could about the disease and set out to connect families affected by the disease and to educate the world about it. Marjorie made the trek to Iowa to help get the Iowa support group up and running. I had the pleasure of meeting her at that time. What a wonderful, down-to-earth woman. She had a heart of gold. She treated all of us like friends she had known forever.

Through that group, Mom found out there was going to be a Huntington's disease convention in Boston, Massachusetts. By this time, both of my sisters were married. Mom told Dad it was very important to her that she attend the convention, so she went. This was her first time flying, and she did great, but was pretty scared. When she came back, she was so excited. She said, "Guess what I did at the convention?" Of course, we had no idea.

She said, "I donated our family to science!"

I said, "You mean the five of us?"

"No," she said, "my whole family; all of them, as in aunts, uncles, cousins, spouses, everyone!"

I said, "Now, how in the world are you going to get all of them to participate?"

She put her hands on her hips, stomped her foot, and said, "Because I said so!"

Since she was always the matriarch of our whole family, I had no doubt she would be successful. She said that she'd heard a speech at the convention given by a doctor named Dr. P. Michael Conneally. He said that Dr. Nancy Wexler was doing extraordinary research on Huntington's disease in Venezuela, where there was a large family that had the disease on both sides of their family. He said that, although that research is critical, it would be very helpful to do research in the United States as well. However, he could not find a family large enough and willing to participate. After his speech, Mom approached him. She asked if he was serious about needing a large family for research. He said indeed he was. She asked how many family members he needed. He said fifteen would be great. She told him she could get him at least fifty and possibly more. You can imagine his immediate excitement.

Thus began a lifelong friendship between our family and Dr. Conneally. He made arrangements to come to Iowa with staff members to get samples for his research. He conducted a huge workshop at a local college gymnasium. The college was state of the art at the time and had co-ed bathrooms. We have joked throughout the years that this was the strangest family reunion that we had ever attended. Dr. Conneally and his staff collected scrapings of skin, took blood and urine samples, had a taste test, and did a few other things that I cannot recall. He collected samples from blood relatives and also from their spouses. He went to a couple of other locations to get samples from relatives who could not come to our "reunion" due to health reasons. I helped him with one of the other locations and was blown away by the mental games that HD plays on affected patients. One of my cousins had advanced chorea and had difficulty eating and talking. However, when I went over the intake questionnaire with her, she stated she was so glad that Dr. Conneally was doing this so he could help her relatives. She was so thankful to God that she did not have the disease, but she hoped he could help her relatives. That experience had a profound effect on me. Dr. Conneally said that was typical. He gathered information from well over 100 family members.

When I found out HD was in my family, I was embarrassed. I did not want anyone to know about it and didn't want to talk about it much. However, Mom took me aside one day and asked why I didn't want to talk about it. I told her it was embarrassing. Her words have stuck with me ever since. She said this was a disease, for Pete's sake, and we didn't ask for it. It is hereditary. She said that it was her job, our job, to educate the world and let anyone and everyone know about this ugly disease, or there would never be more than a paragraph in the encyclopedia. She said she would scream it from the mountain tops if she had to because educating people about it would bring about change and a possible treatment or cure. She also said that the support group needed a treasurer, and she would really appreciate it if I would volunteer to help. I was 23 years old. With a little reluctance, I joined her journey for a treatment/cure, and I've never looked back.

At one point, there were two national Huntington's disease support group organizations. It was decided by both groups that they needed to meet and join as one. Mom was a part of that meeting. She didn't know how it would come out, but she said she was going to stand her ground on what the organization would look like. She came home and said the two groups agreed to join together and picked out a new name. She said this was a national organization, and we would be a part of it. I thought the name was strange, but if she was okay with it, I was okay with it.

In 1978, my husband and I were on our way home from a visit with our families. Our parents lived in neighboring towns. We lived an hour away from them at the time, so we tried to visit both sets of parents in the same day. My husband asked me if I had noticed my mother's movements. I told him I had not. He told me he had been watching her and he thought she was starting to show signs of HD. I told him that was ridiculous. He told me to start watching her the next time we were there and see what I think, but he was paying close attention and was sure he saw her reach for a cup the way my uncle does, and we discussed a few other movements he had noticed. I was devastated! She was 48, and normally, HD patients start showing signs in their mid-30s. I was sure she had dodged the bullet and did not inherit the disease. He also mentioned that she wasn't caring for herself quite as well as she used to do. I told him she was very busy and didn't have time. He asked me to just observe. That is the one thing that HD families have a tendency to do. We watch each other closely and analyze one another. But what do we do with the information? Nothing. It becomes the big white elephant in the middle of the room. We may notice symptoms in one of our relatives, but we don't mention it because then it makes it real. We know it is happening, and everyone notices, but we don't mention it.

I started paying closer attention to my mom and her movements. I did notice that she seemed to have a few symptoms, but nothing was happening on a regular basis, just subtle things here and there. I went to our Huntington's disease support group meetings and, as treasurer of the board, I went to all of our board meetings. At the meetings, she would be at the front of the room, usually sitting at a table, and the rest of us would be in the audience. She was president of our group for many years because no one else would run for (or want) the office. I noticed that her legs would start to make a random choreic movement, and she would purposely move her leg. She did the same thing with her arms. I also noticed that she was not caring for herself as meticulously as she normally did. I knew how busy she was and offered to style her hair here and there, but she said, no, it was fine. My husband and I never mentioned it to anyone other than one another.

Mom was getting moody. She always loved to have her grandchildren spend the night with her on weekends. However, she was starting to lose her temper with them, and it seemed like my oldest son was in trouble more than he wasn't when he stayed there. We loved her, but he didn't want to stay with her anymore. I noticed one of my nieces was getting disciplined a lot more than what I felt was necessary, too. That just wasn't like Mom. She usually loved having the kids around and spoiled them rotten. Now, it seemed they couldn't do anything right. She would pick sides when there were fights instead of getting to the bottom of the situation. The older kids used that to their advantage and blamed the younger kids when it was clear the story just wasn't adding up.

In 1983, it was announced that scientists had discovered a gene marker linked to HD on the short arm of chromosome 4. Dr. Conneally told Mom that the data he'd gathered from our family confirmed the findings they had from Venezuela, which helped find the gene marker. He said that searching for the gene was like searching for a needle on a 100-acre farm. Finding the marker narrowed it down to finding a needle in a haystack instead of on the whole farm.

Predictive testing was started once the marker was found. It was very expensive and not 100% accurate, but it was a way to find out your destiny. I wanted so much to find out. It would break up the dark cloud hanging over my head. Ever since the day I found out HD was in my family, I have not had a single day go by that it does not enter my mind at some time or another. Finding out would give me a future. However, I did not have the money for the test, so I waited…and waited.

As time went on, I watched several more of my relatives start showing signs of Huntington's disease. I watched several more of my relatives die. It was heartbreaking. Going to the funerals of HD patients is much different than any other funeral I have attended. An HD patient's funeral is more of a celebration of their life, the good years. We know they are no longer suffering the effects of HD and are finally free of this ugly disease.

Mom became caretaker for her brother while another brother and several of her nephews and cousins started showing signs of the disease. Later, she became caretaker for some of her nephews. I know how much it hurt her to watch them get progressively worse, and there was nothing she could do except to keep working with the researchers and fighting the battle to end this disease.

In 1988, Mom told me that one of my dad's cousins was having marital issues, and it was looking like he may get a divorce. He said his wife was acting strangely, and he had no idea where some of her ideas were coming from. Mom told me he and she had mutually decided to get counseling and have her go through some medical tests. He said that if she was truly sick, he would care for her, but life was getting pretty tough. Mom called me one day and told me I would not believe what she was about to say. She was pretty upset. My cousin's wife was diagnosed with Huntington's disease. The doctor (a local general practitioner) told them that he had an idea he knew what was wrong with her. He said he would have some blood drawn and would send the sample away for testing. When he got the results, he called them back into his office. In a matter of fact way, he told them she had tested positive for Huntington's disease. He told them there was no treatment or cure, and she would eventually be bedridden. He told my cousin to take her home and love her because there was nothing more he could do for her. THIS is exactly why there is a protocol for testing. My cousin was unemployed and had no health insurance at the time! If the doctor had used the protocol that was used by researchers, they would have had a chance to prepare prior to getting a devastating diagnosis. Once it was in her records that she had HD, she was no longer able to get life insurance or long term care insurance. With him being unemployed, with no insurance, his new insurance at his new job could use "pre-existing condition" against them. I am a strong advocate for the protocol. This situation is why.

In early 1989, my husband decided to plan a trip for us and several of our friends. He planned the whole trip, start to finish. It included a bus ride from Des Moines, Iowa, to Dubuque, Iowa, to the greyhound races. We would leave on Saturday, May 20th, and return on Sunday, May 21st. We had seats at the races, a night of dining, a stay in a local motel, then a ride back on the bus. He meticulously planned the whole trip. His parents, as well as many of our friends, were going. My parents hardly ever went anywhere, so my husband and I offered to pay for their trip if they wanted to go. They thought that would be fun, so we made arrangements for them to go, and we footed the bill for them.

In February of 1989, my paternal grandfather was attacked in his home when someone tried to steal his car. He took a pretty good blow to the head. From that time on, my dad became his caretaker. The blow to the head gave him something we referred to as instant Alzheimer's disease. He had dementia that left him unable to fend for himself. He would forget to take his medication. He would wander. Dad and Mom started taking turns spending the night with him, and I don't believe they ever spent the night in the same home after that. The neurologist said Grandpa had suffered severe brain trauma from the blow to the head. His perpetrator was never brought to justice, but in our minds, God took care of the situation in his own way. That's all that needs to be said.

In mid-April, my mom started getting sick. She went to the doctor many times, but was never accurately diagnosed in time to help her. A couple of weeks before the bus trip, she called me and told me she didn't think they would be able to go. She was still feeling sick and just didn't think she would be well enough. She told us to see if we could get our money back. I thought that was strange for her to say. She had seemed so excited about the trip, and it was still two weeks away. My husband was able to get back a 50 percent refund. The trip was sold out, as I recall.

Mother's Day was coming up. I worked at a college, and some of the students were holding a fundraiser. They were selling a dozen roses for a very reasonable price. I bought a dozen for my mom and a dozen for my husband's mom. We received the roses on the Friday night before

Mother's Day, so I begged my husband to take a drive to our parents' homes to deliver the roses. When we got to my parents' home, my husband suggested we go to my grandpa's house first. My dad was staying there, and my sisters were both there that evening. My oldest sister, Diana, told me she really wanted me to observe Mom when I went to the house to give her the roses. She said her complexion looked ashen, and she was really worried about her. She said at the time that she felt Mom may have an intestinal blockage, but the doctors were not in agreement with that.

I took the roses over to her by myself. My husband had bought me a brand new car for my birthday in April, and Mom had not seen it yet, so I was excited to show it to her and excited to give her the roses. When I got there, she was in bed and seemed very weak. Her face was drawn and ashen, just as my sister had said. I got a vase for the roses and put them in her bedroom for her. We visited for a few minutes. I told her about the car. I told her if she wasn't up to it, she didn't have to look at it, but she insisted on going outside to see it, even though she was in her robe and slippers. It took her a long time to climb down the stairs, and she moved very slowly to the car. After just a few seconds of looking at the car, she said she felt like she'd better go lie down again. Once back inside, I sat on a chair in her room and visited with her. Every few minutes, I would hear a loud noise. I asked her what that was. She said it was her stomach growling. I asked her if she was hungry and offered to make her something to eat. She said she didn't want to eat because everything she ate came back up. I told her it was very important that she keep her strength up and tried to get her to eat something. She asked me to get her some ice chips, so I did. She had been to the doctor that day, and he said he thought she had diabetes or the flu. Really? Hmmm…I wasn't happy with that diagnosis. I asked her to please come home with me, and I would take her to the hospital so she could see my doctor. She absolutely refused to go with me. She made up every excuse she could think of and would not go. I went back over to my grandpa's house, and we all discussed her dire situation. We all agreed she needed to go back to the doctor on Monday.

We went back home, and I called her every day to see how she was doing. I hated calling her because the only phone my parents had was in the dining room. They had a portable phone, but it wasn't always reliable. That meant she had to get out of bed to answer the phone, but I was really worried about her. I noticed her voice was getting weaker and weaker. When I talked to her Sunday, she said she was sitting in a lawn chair, watching Dad plant the garden. She said she wasn't up to helping, but it felt good to be outside in the sunshine. She had the portable phone, so she had it in her lap already. I insisted that she go back to the doctor on Monday. My sister took her to the doctor. My other sister, Diana, seems to know an awful lot of medical stuff. She is a school teacher, but I have always told her she should be a nurse. Diana still said she felt like Mom had an obstruction in her colon. Nothing was passing through, so it just made sense. My sister mentioned that to the doctor. His response was that Mom was not in nearly enough pain for something like that. He thought she just had the flu, but he would order a lower GI. He couldn't get her in until Friday. I about went through the roof when she told me it would be Friday. I begged her again to let me come get her and take her to a hospital in Des Moines. She said no, she'd rather wait until Friday. Friday never came.

The following morning, my sister woke me up early in the morning. She said that Mom was undergoing emergency surgery. In the middle of the night, she had called my middle sister and asked her for help. They live a few blocks from one another. My sister said she didn't recognize her voice, but she knew it had to be Mom. My brother-in-law had rushed over to find her collapsed on the bathroom floor. An ambulance was called, and she was taken to the hospital. Lo and behold, an obstruction was found, but her colon had burst and was leaking into her system. It was a very serious operation. When my husband and I got there, my mom was just coming out of surgery. It was a long, grueling surgery. The surgeon said that she had a tumor in her colon that had caused a major blockage. We later found out the tumor was cancerous. With the blockage going untreated, the colon burst. Mom went into septic shock and was in very serious condition, but we could each see her for a few minutes.

Diana and Dad went in to see her first. After a few minutes, Diana came out, and I went in to see Mom. Tubes were connected to her everywhere. Machines were making noises, and lights were flashing here and there. She had a drip of something connected to her arm. She felt so cold to the touch. She was moaning and groaning. She was in obvious pain. She kept drawing her legs up, then putting them down, then drawing them up again. Dad announced to her that I was there. I grabbed her hand, and she squeezed to let me know she knew I was there. I was holding her hand with her arm bent when the nurse came over and told me to leave her arm straight so there were no bends. She said we needed to make sure there was a good even flow of fluids going into her arm. The nurse kept apologizing for the pain Mom was in. She said she was trying to get in touch with the doctor to let him know how much pain she was in so she could possibly give her something to ease some of the pain.

Seeing how much pain she was in made tears roll down my face. I stayed at the top of her bed so if she opened her eyes, she wouldn't see me crying. She was my mom, my hero. I couldn't stand seeing her like this. I would have gladly changed places with her. It wasn't fair. Mom was such a good person. Why did this go unnoticed? Why did she have to suffer so much? After a few minutes, the nurse was on the phone with the doctor. She got off the phone, disappeared for a couple of minutes, and then came over with an injection of some kind. She injected a substance into Mom's intravenous tube port. Mom immediately relaxed. Her legs stretched out. The groaning stopped. I breathed a sigh of relief. She was finally not in pain.

It was only a couple of minutes afterwards that the nurse came over and said Mom's blood pressure was dropping and dropping fast. She started trying to wake Mom up. She told us to try to wake her up, too. We were both saying her name and trying to get her to wake up. I was worried something horrible was going on, so I thought I'd better give my middle sister a chance to see her. I left the room and told her Dad needed help trying to wake Mom up. They were in there together for about five minutes. We heard someone call Code Blue over the loud speaker. All of a sudden, people came from everywhere and went into Mom's room. My sister and Dad came out of the room. They said Mom's heart had stopped, and they were asked to leave so the medical crew could work on her. I started sobbing and sobbing. No, no, no! Not now! Not Mom! I need her! I need her! Please, God, NO! This cannot be happening. I could not hear anyone else. I kept my eyes shut tight. At one point, I felt someone holding me. I needed my husband, but it was my aunt. She had been in the waiting room the whole time. She knew I needed someone, anyone. Where was my husband? Why wasn't he holding me? My whole world fell apart. Mom was my mom, my best friend, my confidante, my everything.

I don't remember who came out and told us she was gone, and I don't even remember everything that was said. I just remember that it was confirmed that she was gone. I finally stopped sobbing. We all just sat there dumbfounded. When someone finally spoke, it was my dad. He said, "Well, at least she never had HD."

I looked at him and said, "What are you talking about? Yes, she did have HD."

He said no, she didn't. I insisted she did. He said that if there was a possibility that maybe she did, we'd better follow her wishes and make sure we had her brain donated to the brain bank. We knew we only had a few minutes to give the doctors instructions so they could harvest her brain and get it to the brain bank. I called Mom's cousin's husband and told him what had happened. I asked him if he had one of our newsletters. The instructions were in each newsletter. His wife, my mom's cousin, had advanced HD at the time. She went to pieces, sobbing uncontrollably. He was trying to comfort her and find the newsletter. He finally found it and gave us the information. Mom's brain was donated that day.

My whole life fell apart May 17, 1989. I never in a million years would have guessed my mom would die so young. She was so strong and strong-willed. She was invincible in my eyes. The next couple of years were extremely painful. A few days after I went back to work, I was sitting at my desk and looked at a document that I needed to fill out. I worked at a community college. My mind went blank, and I had absolutely no idea what to do with that form. I sat there for several minutes and could not believe that I didn't know what to do. Over the next couple of weeks, it happened several times. Also, I would have moments when I would have to run to the restroom and sob for a few minutes. I had five bosses at the time. One of my bosses came to my desk one day and told me that she had a major problem. She had students show up for a class, but there was no classroom reserved and no instructor hired. Part of my job was setting up the classes and contracting with the instructor to teach the class. My boss said she had taken care of the situation, but she wanted to see me in her office right away. I knew I was in big trouble.

I went into her office, and she told me that she thought I needed some help. I told her I did not know what was going on, but I felt like I was losing my mind. I couldn't remember how to do my job, and I was crying out of the blue for no apparent reason. She told me that was a common depression symptom. She thought it would be a good idea for me to go to the doctor to get an anti-depressant so I could get through the grief from losing my mother. She also gave me the name of a counselor so I could talk through my feelings. She literally saved my life that day. I had been having the crying spells at home, and they continued off and on for several months. The medication helped immensely. I don't think I would have gone to the doctor without her prompting, and the way I was feeling was very scary. My husband kept telling me to "get over it." He offered no comforting of any kind. Losing my best friend and my mom in the same motion was devastating. I needed his close bond to help me get through it, but he had no compassion. Every time he told me to get over it, another brick went up in the wall between us.

Within a year and a half, I had become very cold toward him and just wanted out of the marriage. We had other issues, too, so I wanted out for a culmination of reasons. I knew he and my mother never really saw eye to eye, so I felt he was halfway glad she was gone so that he didn't have to share me anymore. I don't know that he consciously felt that way, but that was the impression I got, and perception is reality.

Finally, in November 1990, I left him. I had planned it in the back of my mind for months, but the night I left was just an out-of-the-blue thought. I knew I would be taking my younger son with me, but my older son was fifteen and a handful. I wasn't sure I could handle him, and I wasn't sure he would go with me because he and his dad did a lot of things together. He spent a lot more time hanging around his dad than he did hanging around me. Therefore, the night I left, I asked him if he wanted to go with me or stay with his dad. He said he wanted to stay. I packed a very few things for my younger son and me and left the house. Now, where was I going to go? I had no idea. I went to my oldest sister's home. I showed up unannounced. She was having a party. I wasn't in a partying mood, but tried to be happy. Mostly I just cuddled my nine-year-old son. About an hour after I was there, the phone rang. My sister answered it, of course. After she got off the phone, she told her friends that she was really tired and probably better have everyone leave. In truth, my husband had called her. He asked if I was there, and she said yes. He said that was fine. He just wanted to make sure I was safe and said good-bye. At that point, she knew I was there for more than a visit. We talked until the wee hours of the morning. I moved in with my best friend the next day. I stayed with her for a couple of weeks, then got my own apartment.

My husband begged me to come back home. He kept me on the phone for hours, trying to work things out. I tried going back around Christmas time, but I felt like a caged animal in that house. I could not wait to get to my quiet, peaceful apartment with my youngest son.

Four months after I moved out, my current husband, Bruce, moved in next door to me in my apartment building. When he was carrying in his first box, I was standing in the hallway, talking to our landlord's maintenance man who lived across the hall from me. I didn't see him come in and backed right into him. I was so embarrassed, and he looked more than a little annoyed. I apologized, and he said that was fine. I didn't really pay much attention to him that day. I was so embarrassed I went back in my apartment and stayed there. However, I did notice he was quite good-looking.

Over the next few months, we got to know one another through our kids. My son told me one day that the guy living next door had a couple of kids. He wondered if he could go knock on his door to see if his kids could play. I told him I thought that was okay, so I met his son weeks before I met Bruce. Every other weekend, the boys would play, and they seemed to really get along well. Bruce and I became good friends long before we fell in love. We met one another at the race track for our first "date." After the evening was over, we headed to our cars. My car was parked much closer than his, so I told him to hop in, and I would drive him to his car. We sat in my car and talked until 3:30 in the morning! Neither one of us ever wanted to get married again. We still joke about it sometimes as to how our marriage ever happened when neither one of us wanted to get married. We thoroughly enjoy one another's company, though, so it is great.

I remember thinking that I needed to introduce Bruce to HD before things got too serious. My best friend had never really been around HD, either. I decided to have a potluck dinner at my house and invite my HD support group friends. What a night! We had such a wonderful time, but one of my friends had HD and had a lot of chorea and choked very easily. She choked several times that night. Bruce left before my best friend. After everyone was gone, my best friend grabbed me and hugged me. She said that she had no idea that was what I meant when I talked about HD. She said she didn't ever want me to have to go through that. I told her I didn't want to either, but I really didn't have much choice.

The next day, I called Bruce. I slowly asked him what he thought of the dinner. I told him why I'd invited him and told him I wanted him to be aware of what he was getting into if we decided to move our relationship to the next level. I told him I felt like I had HD, but it had never been confirmed. He was pretty quiet during our whole conversation. I ended the conversation by telling him that I'd thrown a lot at him over the last twenty-four hours. If he wasn't able to handle it, I understood, and we could just part as friends. However, I really wanted him in my life, and if he was willing, we could try to get through it together. It took him two long days before he called me back. After the first day, I was sure I had lost him. When he called, he told me he was ready to jump in with both feet, and whatever happened was fine with him. I know I cried myself to sleep that night.

My oldest sister and I went to the national convention in 1989 and again in 1990. The 1989 convention was in San Francisco. We had a great time and learned a lot. It was at that convention that Dr. Conneally confirmed to us that he knew our mom had had HD. He said he'd made monthly calls to her to ask her about relatives he had tested, but he was also trying to get a feel for her HD status. He noticed small things over the years in her voice and composure, but he, too, was so glad that she didn't have to deal with the true ugliness of the disease.

The following year the convention was in Atlanta, Georgia. At the convention, we listened to a speech by someone representing the brain bank. He stated that they had received a brain from a woman in her late 50s the year before. She was HD-positive, but not symptomatic. He said the studies they'd done on her brain confirmed several things for them. He said they were so grateful the family chose to donate her brain. Diana and I looked at one another and grinned. She had made a difference even after she died. It was never confirmed that the man was talking about her, but in our minds, we knew.

In 1992, I received a call from the national office of the Huntington's organization. The executive director was on the phone and told me he wanted me to give a speech in front of a joint Congressional committee. I asked, "Why me?"

He said that it was mostly because I am my mother's daughter. She'd had such a huge impact on the organization, and they needed an HD family member to deliver a message to Congress so we could get national funding for research. I was humbled and honored to be asked to do this. An Iowa senator was head of the committee, so the executive director felt it was vitally important that we have an Iowan give the speech. I made the trip to Washington, DC, all by myself. I met the executive director outside the chamber office where we would be meeting with the committee. Mary Tyler Moore was there to give a speech in support of Juvenile Diabetes. Ben Vereen was there to give a speech on behalf of the hearing impaired. There was a total of about a dozen groups giving speeches on behalf of their organizations. During my speech, I got emotional and had to pause for a few seconds to regain my composure. The executive director was by my side. After my speech, the Iowa senator complimented me on my presentation in front of the joint committee. He also said it was fine that I'd lost my composure for a bit because that showed what an emotional disease this was, and he would rather hear from someone who lives it rather than from a lobbyist or employee. I got a call a few weeks later from the national office to let me know we'd gotten the funding!

In 1993, I was still working for the same non-profit organization that I was working for when I'd met with the joint Congressional committee. The non-profit organization lobbied for the local twelve community colleges. I got a phone call from the national office. I knew the employee who called me. She said she needed my fax number. She said she was going to fax over something that she wanted me to read. We had a board meeting going on downstairs, and there were probably thirty people at the meeting. I got the fax and read it. I read it again and again. Tears started rolling down my face, and I wanted to scream with delight. The fax said that the Huntington's disease gene had been found! Wow, the needle in the haystack was found!

I had to tell someone. My oldest sister was a school teacher. I looked up the phone number for her school and called her. The secretary said that she was working at a different school that day. I told her I really, really needed to get in touch with her. She gave me a phone number where I could reach her. I called that secretary and told her I needed to talk to Mrs. Fisher. She said she was in class. I told her this was very important, and I needed to talk to her right away. The secretary pulled her out of class. I told her the HD gene had been found. She and I cried and cried on the phone. If there was ever a hug through the phone, we did it! We were both ecstatic. She got off the phone and had to explain why she was crying. She said she was crying happy tears, not sad tears. Next, I had to call my dad. He and I cried together. Then I had to call my cousin's wife, Vicki. She and I cried together. I was so glad that all thirty people had stayed downstairs in the meeting throughout my joyous rant with my relatives. They would not have understood. They probably would have thought I was crazy. Maybe I was, but at that moment I was so, so happy! I also called the national office to make sure I'd read what I thought I'd read. They assured me I had read it correctly!

A whirlwind of activity followed the finding of the gene. The Huntington's disease community has the best researchers in the world, in my possibly biased opinion. Every one of them is "approachable." Most of them have given their whole heart and soul to Huntington's disease research. I have come to know many of them very well. Dr. Conneally was the first researcher who entered my life, and I will be forever grateful to him. In 1993, our family won an award at the national convention. We would never have won the award were it not for him and my mother's chance meeting years earlier. Mom had already passed by that time, but it felt wonderful to have her noble work recognized.

Dr. Nancy Wexler is another researcher who has done monumental work for HD her entire life. Her mother died with HD. She and her father took it upon themselves to try to find a treatment or cure. I had the distinct pleasure of meeting her many times over the years. I have the utmost respect for her and the awesome work she has done and is continuing to do.

In early 1995, my sister Diana called me and was very excited. She said there was a doctor in California that was originally from Iowa who had contacted her. The doctor was finishing her internship and was looking for a permanent location. She specialized in Huntington's disease and wondered if there was a large enough base in Iowa to make it worth her while to move here. Diana told her there was, but she wanted to talk to me, too. The doctor's name was Dr. Jane Paulsen. I called Dr. Paulsen and told her that we have a huge family, and we are not the only large family in Iowa with HD. She said she would be moving back to Iowa then. I am one of Jane's number one fans. She has been there for our entire HD community world wide! She has done mountains of research on the subject and has written mountains of papers about it. She has travelled world-wide, giving presentations and workshops to other researchers, and never fails to come through for our entire HD community. I have the utmost respect for her, and I am thrilled to say I know her. She has headed up countless research projects and continues the fight.

There are so many other researchers I could mention, but they would not want me to focus on them. The researchers do what they do because they have seen the disease first hand and know that any research done will help not only HD patients, but it will also help Alzheimer's patients, Parkinson's patients, and muscular dystrophy patients, as well as patients with countless other diseases.

In 1995, I was reading a newsletter that is still published today by the University of Iowa. I knew there was a genetic test for HD, but I thought

I would have to travel to Indiana University to get tested. The researchers had set up a "protocol" for testing that involved several meetings with a counselor prior to getting the results of the test to attempt to avoid the possibility of someone with a positive result committing suicide once they knew their fate. Suicide is the major cause of death for Huntington's disease patients. Finding out if you carry the defective gene prior to actually showing symptoms of the disease was something I had waited for since 1970. I desperately wanted to take the test, but knew I could not afford to make multiple trips to Indiana University over several months to go through the protocol. As I read the newsletter from the University of Iowa, I was drawn to a story about the genetic test. The article said that the University now offered it! I was ecstatic. I made a phone call to set up an appointment the very next day! I told no one except my husband (because you have to have a support person for the final results) and my boss. Some may find it strange that I told my boss. However, I knew without a doubt he would not use it against me in any way. He is actually the best boss I have ever had throughout my working career, bar none. I knew he would support me, no matter what the outcome.

I talked to a nice woman on the other end of the phone when I made the call. She was very kind and empathetic. Then, she told me the best news yet. Not only were they offering the test at the University, but they had travel dollars available so that they could bring the testing to me! Wow! I was amazed and oh, so excited! The appointment was set up for two weeks later at Lutheran hospital in Des Moines, Iowa. Time seemed to stand still. I met with the counselor by myself for my initial time. It was November 1995. Our first appointment was more or less filling out paperwork and getting background information on me and my family. During my interview, the counselor told me she thought there was an HD support group in the Des Moines area. She said she didn't know how to get in touch with the group, but wanted to make me aware of it. I started laughing and told her I was treasurer for the group! We both had a good laugh, and I gave her our group's contact information that day. She said she was so glad she had the opportunity to meet me so she could share our organization's contact information with all of her patients. I had follow up meetings with her in December and January.

At my January appointment, my counselor said she had two very important questions for me. Number one: If you find out you are gene positive, what will you do? My answer: If I find out I am gene positive, I will just continue on as I am doing, but will be a stronger advocate. In my mind, I had Huntington's disease, so it would just be confirmation of what I always thought was true. I will do my best to try to get myself out in the forefront so people all across Iowa can see me slowly get worse and worse so they really understand the disease. I told her that I felt that is the only way to really get the word out. Most HD patients do not want to draw attention to themselves, but I wanted to so I could carry on my mom's mission. Number two: If you are gene negative, what will you do? My answer: If I am gene negative, I will celebrate. I will scream and laugh and be so grateful. I will, however, still continue with my advocacy to educate Iowa, if not the world. She smiled and said I passed. It was now time for the blood draw. She said they always make HD patients wait a month after the blood draw to get their results so they can ponder whether or not they want the answer. She said I could back out at any time prior to getting the results, and it was no problem. I said, "Are you kidding me? I have waited twenty-five years for this! I will not back out."

She told me not to call the clinic prior to my appointment. She said they have had a lot of people call to see if they can detect something in the counselors' voices as to their gene status prior to the appointment. I promised her I would not do that.

The month between my test and the results was the absolute worst month of my life. I got very "bitchy" and dwelled on getting the results almost constantly. Tiny little things irritated the dickens out of me, and I found myself crying for no reason again. I thought, oh, no, here we go again. What is WRONG with me? In reality, I thought, okay, this is HD starting. Here we go!

The day I got my results was February 15, 1996. Iowa had a fresh, white blanket of snow, and it kept snowing and snowing and snowing. The site of my counselor's clinic had been moved to a different location. It was getting close to the time to head to the appointment. I called my husband and told him I would like to head there early because of the weather. He said that was fine, so he stopped by and picked me up. After we started down the road, I panicked. The roads were so deep with snow, it was a challenge to get through. We were leaving downtown Des Moines and heading just a few blocks to the west. What should have been an easy ten- to fifteen-minute drive turned into a very treacherous, nerve-wracking drive. Bruce was a mechanic at the time and used to driving all kinds of vehicles, so I knew I was in good hands. However, we were going much slower than we expected. I didn't have a phone number for my counselor, so I called the hospital and spoke to a very kind volunteer at the receptionist desk. He found her for me and transferred the call. I told her I was on my way, but we had run into road blocks of snow. She told me that they were snowed in, so if it was too treacherous, we could meet the next day. I shouted much too loudly into the phone, "NO! I have waited much too long for this!" If she was willing to wait for me, I would be there.

After her eardrums recuperated, she laughed and said she would be waiting. We got there about twenty-five minutes after we left my office. She showed us into a very neat, clean, quiet office. She let me sit on a stool and gave my husband one right beside me. She had not met Bruce yet, so I introduced them. She said that normally she makes the support person come to all appointments, but since Bruce had a difficult time getting that much time off work, and I have a long history of HD advocacy, she let us wait until the final appointment to meet Bruce. She said it sounded like we had a solid enough marriage that she wasn't concerned. She then handed me a piece of paper with a lot of printing all over it.

My eyes searched frantically for something that said negative or positive. After a few seconds, I looked up at her and told her I didn't know what I was looking for. She pointed to the box in the middle that showed my CAG repeats. The numbers there said 17 and 19. I looked at it and studied it, trying to absorb what I was reading. I slowly looked up and said, "Does...this mean...I am negative?"

Only then did she smile and tell me, yes, that is exactly what it meant. I distinctly remember I was leaning forward and had my legs crossed with my toe pointing to Bruce. About the time she said that was what it meant, my foot flinched. I looked at my foot, then looked at her, then looked at Bruce. I said, "You mean that twitch happens to everybody?"

She laughed and said, "Yes, that happens to everybody!"

I was dumbfounded. I was speechless. I thought I would jump up and down and squeal with delight, but all I did was sit there, shocked. I said very little. The three of us small talked for a few minutes, and then we were headed out the door. As we were walking to the car, my phone rang. It was my boss. I answered the phone and he said, "Well?" I told him I had tested negative.

He said, "See, I told you so. You didn't have to go through all that. I knew you would test negative. I don't know that you are 'normal,' but I felt it in my gut that you would be okay."

I said, "Okay, then why did you call?" We had a good laugh, and I told him I would see him later.

I told Bruce that I just had to go see my dad and share the news with him. We lived in Orient, an hour away from Des Moines and the same town as my dad, so he said that was fine. I immediately called Dad on my cell phone and asked if he was up for a visitor that night. He said he was, so I told him I would see him later. My boss had offered to let us spend the night with him and his wife instead of making the drive back home to Orient, but we told him we would be fine. Besides, I was just way too anxious to tell Dad the good news.

After supper, I walked through Dad's front door. I told Dad I had something I needed to tell him. After Mom died, he had told all three of us that he hoped we never took the genetic test because he did not want to know if any of us was going to get HD. I knew he would be so happy for me now, and it would stop one third of his worry. I knelt down beside his easy chair and handed him the piece of paper. He said, "What is this?"

I told him that I'd gone against his wishes and taken the genetic test, and I was negative. He stared at the paper, and I swear, he read every word on the page, something I hadn't done yet!

His next words were, "Bert, I told you not to do that, but...I'm glad you did!"

We then cried and hugged and hugged and cried. I told him all about my experience and what it was like. He said he was not aware the test was available in Iowa yet. He asked me if I was going to tell my sisters.

I told him, "Of course!"

However, the longer I sat there and thought about it, the more I dreaded telling them. After all, they were both still at risk. I didn't want to sound like I was bragging. Suddenly, my happiness turned to despair. Wow, I hadn't thought about what it would be like to tell my sisters. It was too late to call either one of them that night, so I thought I would go home and tell my kids, then deal with my sisters...later.

Telling my kids was easy. I told all four of them, my two sons and Bruce's two sons. They really didn't know what to think. It was many years later that I realized I'd skipped the part about them being gene negative because I was gene negative. I thought they knew. I had talked about it my sons' whole lives. I felt so bad when I found out they still thought they were both at risk!

My middle sister lived in Orient as well. I thought, well, she's just down the street, so I'll tell her sometime this week.

The next night, I decided to call my oldest sister, Diana. I told her, and the first words out of her mouth were, "Wow! That's awesome! Why didn't you tell me? I would have gone through the testing with you! How can I get tested? Do you have the phone number?" We talked for a long time, and she took down the number and called the very next day.

It took me six days to finally call my middle sister. I just found one excuse after another to not call her or go see her. When I finally did call her, she said, "I know. Your kids already told me!"

I will never forget the next words out of her mouth. "How do you know the test is right? Did they run it twice to be sure?"

What? What? I could not believe she said that. This test was a major, major test that impacts lives in a huge, huge way. I had and still have no reason to believe that they would make a mistake. I was slightly offended, but never told her.

Over the next few months, I went through something quite unexpected. I finally figured out that it was survivor's guilt. I found myself not being overjoyed about being negative because I still had numerous family members and friends who were either at risk or positive for the disease. I went to a national convention and told the people who were caretakers or gene negative that I was negative, but I could not find the words to tell my gene positive or at-risk friends. One of my at-risk friends was starting to show quiet signs of the disease. I could not bring myself to tell her, but I told her sister. My friend confronted me at a bar the first night of the convention. I love her so much and always will. It broke my heart to have her know, but she told me she was really thrilled that I was okay.

At a support group meeting in Des Moines, I finally found my relief. I was sharing how guilty I felt and that it really bothered me. I said that I couldn't be happy for myself when so many others were still suffering. My cousin's wife was there. My cousin was in a nursing home at the time. She started crying and told me I should be so happy for myself. She said that she and her husband were so very happy that I was not going to get HD. I should be happy as well. She was the turning point in my life that made me realize my good fortune and made me aware that it was ludicrous to continue on this guilty path. I had no control over my gene status, so I had nothing to be guilty about.

Diana's experience was unique. She was a part-time newspaper reporter and photographer for a local small town paper. She had contacted the *Des Moines Register* and asked what reporter to call to do a human interest story on Huntington's disease. As it turns out, the reporter was a man I had babysat for seventeen years before when his son was just a little guy. I adored his son and his wife. I barely knew him, though, even though I saw his name in the paper daily.

Diana lobbied and lobbied to try to get him to write a story. She got down to the month after her blood was drawn and had the same experience as me during the waiting period. She said she was growly and grumpy. She called the reporter one more time. He had recently done a story about another disease that his mother had, so Diana got pretty brutal. She told him she thought it was shameful that he would do a human interest story on his mother and her disease, but he wouldn't do one for her on Huntington's disease. He told her he would make her a deal. He wondered if she would let him and his photographer come to her appointment with her when she got the results. She said, "Sure! Be there!"

She gave him the date, time, and place of her appointment, then immediately called me and told me she may have done a bad thing. I told her I thought it was a great idea, but I would like to be there with her in case I needed to fend off inappropriate questions. She said that she really appreciated that.

The day of her appointment was a much nicer day than the day I found out. All of us met in the hospital waiting room. The reporter stood off to the side with his photographer. The counselor invited us into the quiet, dark, tiny room. There were only enough chairs for the counselor, my sister, and her husband, so I stood up against the wall at the side of the room. The photographer and the reporter stood quietly at the rear of the room. Diana had a different counselor than me. I was so sure Diana had HD because she tended to be pretty klutzy at times. I thought I saw other movements in her as well. The counselor handed her the paper, but told her at the same time that she was negative. As I recall, Diana said, "Are you sure?"

The counselor smiled and said, yes, she was sure. Then all three of us burst into a flood of tears. I glued myself to the wall to keep myself from jumping in the air and high-fiving the ceiling! I let Diana and her husband hug and kiss, and then I pulled myself from the wall and hugged and kissed them, too. The three of us clung to one another for quite some time. The photographer snapped a few pictures, but otherwise, the two men stayed silent. When we walked out of the room, the reporter approached us. He told Diana that he'd had no idea this was such an emotional test. He apologized for being there and said he felt like he intruded. She told him it was fine and asked if he was going to run the story. He said of course he would run the story. He interviewed her and also a friend of ours who had advanced stages of Huntington's disease. His story was brilliant. He did a very good job.

As I write this, I have to say that I realize I let HD run my life. I hope that my story will help educate others so they don't make the same mistakes I made. I would have had a much different life had it not been for the ugly, dark cloud that hung over my head about this disease. And in the end, it was all for naught. It was many years down the road of my HD journey that the mother of a friend of mine taught me something that I wish I had known in the beginning. She said, "Plan your life like you have HD. Live your life like you do not."

What a profound statement! I have repeated that statement over and over in the hope that people new to this disease will learn from it. Having said that, I would not change one thing in my life. I feel very blessed and happy about the way this journey is going. I have noticed that I became much more positive after finding out I was negative. I go to bed every night praying for a cure or treatment for HD. I wake up each day just happy to be. I also wake up each day hoping this will be the day that the announcement of a treatment or cure will be made.

I have met so many amazing people through my HD journey. If this were not in my family, our paths may never have crossed. And that would be sad. Thank you to all of the wonderful friends I have made. I love all of you.

—∞—

Please consider making a donation to the University of Iowa's Huntington's Disease Fund, a nonprofit organization.

Donations can be made to Dr. Jane Paulsen's clinic at the University of Iowa via Help 4 HD International's secure web site, http://research4hd.org/Researchers.html, or by making out a check to:

University of Iowa Huntington Disease Clinic
Craig Stout
500 Newton Road
1-317 MEB
Iowa City, IA 52242

In the "memo" section of the check, please specify "HD Research."

About Pat Wolf

Pat Wolf was born in 1951, in a very small town of Sussex, New Jersey, the first of three children, to a dairy farmer and his wife. She says living on a farm was the BEST! They had cats, dogs, cows, and a pond to catch frogs and snakes. She would go fishing with her grandmother in the pond and row around it with her dog, Blackie. She even had a horse for a couple years. She says the best thing was freedom: "Back then, it was nothing to hop on your bike and ride a couple miles to visit a friend, and there appeared to be no worries." The worst thing that touched her life was when her dog Blackie was shot and killed by a neighborhood delinquent, which for a young 8-year-old was the end of the world. She says she struggled somewhat through school and did one year of college. She married Ken, whom she met in college, in 1972, and that lasted just four years. In 1979, she married Jay. She says she's been a Jack of all trades and hopefully a Master of Some. She did data entry, babysat, worked as a teacher's aide for autistic children, drove a school bus, and was a home health care worker. Pat is now happily retired.

CHAPTER 8

⚜

Woody, My Wife-in-Law, and Me
By Pat Wolf

I have a very vague memory of hearing a news report sometime in the 1950s about an announcement that Woody Guthrie was going to stop performing because he didn't want his fans to see him suffering from his disease. I didn't hear the name of the disease, but I remember being very sad that anyone would feel this way. Little did I know that many years later I would not only learn the name of that disease, but I would also learn how it would affect so many people that I knew and loved.

Jay and I first met at a party and started dating. I'm guessing I was about 27 years old. I loved how kindhearted he was, especially with animals, and we both liked scary movies. On our first date, we went to see "The Omen"! I married Jay in 1979, and of course, we were madly in love. What could go wrong, right? Three years later, we had our first son, and life was good. There were times Jay acted a little odd, almost childlike, immature, but I just thought he was in a good mood. He sometimes would talk in a baby voice, which creeped me out a LOT.

There were also a few times that he made some pretty poor decisions. When my car needed to go in for repairs, and we had to come back in HIS car (a two-seater), he wanted to either leave our baby in his crib while we left OR just stick him in the hatchback section of the car. I just tried to explain to him why that would be a bad idea, and I thought it was because he was a . . . (sorry, guys) a *man* and didn't have that protective mothering instinct. I started to not feel comfortable leaving him alone with the baby as he also thought it was fine to put our baby in the crib and go outside to mow the lawn while I went grocery shopping. Jay really was not happy when I put my foot down over that, as I knew our baby could be in distress and Jay would never hear him.

We had another son a couple of years later as Jay mostly was a very good dad and a good provider. He enjoyed playing with the kids and taking them to the park. When times were tough financially, he took a part time job, sometimes two. I really started to worry, though, when we got a kerosene heater, and I put a dog play yard (like a bottomless playpen) around it so the boys would not accidently run into it. My husband did NOT like that as he felt the play yard was in the way. He also felt that leaving it unprotected would be a good way for them to learn. If they did get too close and fall on it, well, then they would learn not to get too close, wouldn't they?? This was the same time that one of the Philadelphia Eagles player's young child did exactly that and had very serious injuries. I was really frightened at this point, and I made sure the pen was up at all times whenever the heater was on.

We moved into our third home in another town when the boys were in sixth and third grades. It was a great school district; I got a job with the school and loved it. Jay had been having trouble keeping jobs, which was a great worry. He worked for Michael's, and one time someone dropped a vase, and it made a very loud noise. He shouted, "WHAT THE F***!!!" Another time, he was substitute teaching and had lunch duty. One boy didn't like his lunch and turned around and spit it out on the floor. Jay yelled, "What are you, a F'ing ANIMAL??" Now that was humiliating to me as I worked in the same school. He lost manager jobs at Channel and at many other stores. I don't believe he ever truly told me why he lost the jobs, but I believe he just wasn't doing his job. It was absolutely nerve-wracking, and I had NO idea what our future would be. I don't have a college education, so my job as a classroom aide and later as a bus driver was basically for extra income. Just as we were about to be approved for the mortgage for this house, he lost another job. This one was for outside sales with Sears, selling roofs and air conditioning. Actually, this was NOT his fault; Sears had decided to cut that part out of their business. I didn't know whether to worry that the mortgage company would find out, and we'd not be approved, or worry that they wouldn't find out, and we *would* be approved. Well, we were approved.

Thankfully, right after we moved in, he got another job as a co-manager in a home improvement store. Of course, he lost that one also when the mother company closed that store down. The company said the store wasn't doing enough business. And so he moved on to another job. He also worked for Woolworths and had problems there as well. One day, he split his pants, REALLY split his pants. Now here he was, working in Woolworths where they sell pants, but what did he do? He Scotch-taped them together. Can you imagine how that went over? He was depressed over losing so many jobs, but didn't talk about it. I was beyond scared and so extremely worried. I believe he really tried his best at all his jobs. I'm thinking he may have said or done something inappropriate to keep losing them (like tape up his split pants or yell F***), but I know he wanted to excel and move on to be a district manager. That was not to be, though.

It was around this time that I knew something was truly wrong. Jay's dad was in the hospital, having a hip replacement, when the nurses noticed he could not swallow his pills very well. They requested that a movement specialist examine him, and BINGO. That's when I heard about the name of that disease that Woody Guthrie had had: Huntington's disease. Everyone referred to it as disease, although onset was judged by chorea. We all had to gather at the genetic counselor's office to get the news. Dad had HD, and his two boys were each 50 percent at risk. Dad was one of eight children, and we had never heard of anyone else having it, which I find hard to believe. We did figure out that Dad's father was told he had lead poisoning as he was a house painter. Now we are sure that it was not lead poisoning, but HD. Well, Jay had already said to me, "Whatever Dad has, I know I also have." He had noticed he was "antsy," and with all his job troubles, he knew there was something wrong. I don't think he and his dad were very much alike in their disease, though. I knew that he had it also. Jay had movements and obsessions. He couldn't let one piece of laundry just sit there; he'd have to start a load of laundry, although he was fine with wearing stained shirts himself. He had to keep checking things over and over and over, like checking to see if his camera was in the camera case on a trip, even though he had just checked it five minutes ago.

I didn't even have a computer back then, so I called a friend from the last town we had lived in and asked her to look up Huntington's disease. Bad news. She did, and she didn't want to tell me about it. I told her, "YOU MUST." She hated telling me about the psych symptoms, and that there was no treatment and no cure, but she did. That was the beginning of my crying jags and memory loss that lasted for months. I know this sounds really awful, but I could barely stand looking at Jay with his shrugging shoulders and tapping feet. All that meant to me was that my boys could have the same thing, and this gave me more heartache than I ever knew was possible. I am sure I went into a state of shock. I truly was of no use to my boys at that point. All I could do was cry. I would get into the shower and blast the radio to mask my sobs. At work, I would go into the room with the gigantic Xerox machine and do my sobbing there. Any chance I had, I would go on drives to nowhere, mostly to nearby forests. We gave no details to the boys, just told them that Grandpa had a brain disease, but we loved him all the more. I wanted to get a grip on myself before we told the boys anything about it. I knew I had to accept it before we talked to them about it. We just didn't discuss it at all with the kids.

I was on a mission, though, to learn all I knew about HD and any medication that would help. Jay decided to get tested, but I knew what it would show, and of course, I was right. He got tested in a different state, three hours away from where we lived in New Jersey. We went together, and we went to Maryland as we didn't know where else to go. We decided we'd make a day of it and go to the aquarium and just played tourist. He really wanted to test so our boys would have the information. He tested free under a program for at-risk, no symptoms and at-risk with symptoms. He was switched back and forth twice, and ended up in at-risk with symptoms. We were supposed to go for three years in order for this program to pay for his test. They told him they were not prepared to give him his results unless he had a psychiatrist near where we lived as they thought he could be suicidal. I was very glad they insisted on that.

Before Jay even got his results back, his doctor, who happened to be one of a national HD organization's fair-haired boys, gave him a prescription for Haldol. Back then, I still thought doctors were Gods and trusted him blindly. My online HD family tried to tell me that Haldol not only was contraindicated for HD, but Jay also was having no meltdowns, was not violent and barely had movements, and those are the things that Haldol is sometimes prescribed to control. At that time, I also allowed Jay to take care of his own meds and to pay the bills, also. After a few months on the Haldol, I noticed his mouth was in a grimace, and I thought he was mad at me. I kept asking him what was wrong, and then I had my light bulb moment and realized it was the Haldol, just as my friends had warned me.

About a day or so later, I got a call at work from him, telling me he had run out of his Haldol and was suicidal. He went to his general practitioner and got an antidepressant from him, then went to his shrink and got another antidepressant from HIM. I left work and called the pharmacist. Together, we figured out what Jay could take and couldn't take, and I was told Jay should have been weaned off the Haldol. I called this famous doctor in another state, as he had told me that whenever I needed any help at all, to call him, and it didn't matter if it was night or day; he'd call me back. So I did that. About five times, including faxes and emails. His secretary sounded embarrassed when I talked to her, and she assured me she had personally put the notes on his desk, and she didn't know why he hadn't called. I guess you can say that was the beginning of the failure of the HD "system" for us. This was also the beginning of my knowing my online HD family were the ones I should actually rely on. Jay had another appointment set up with that doctor, and not only did we not go, but I also didn't cancel; I guess I showed them, huh?

I then found a neurologist in our state who specialized in HD, and I kept a huge notebook with all the latest and greatest new developments and took notes when we went to his neuro visits. THEN I was pulled aside by the social worker there, and she told me that the neurologist felt uncomfortable and intimidated by me and my notebook. HELLLLLO?? I told her, "I guess he has a problem he needs to work on then, as my notebook will be staying with me."

Around this time Jay's boss noticed he wasn't doing his job properly and talked to him about it. I believe he just couldn't get his thoughts together to do his job as was expected of him. Jay and I had a conversation about it, and we decided he should probably tell his manager about his illness. The manager was wonderful and gave Jay fewer responsibilities but never reduced his pay, and Jay then applied for Social Security Disability. He was approved the first time, maybe because his neurologist wrote, "Jay has Huntington's disease. There is no treatment, no cure, and then he will die." No argument there.

We decided, since Jay was going to be home all of the time, and not working, that this was the time to tell the boys. We started by telling them the disease their grandpa had was Huntington's disease, and that we had since discovered that Dad also had it, and he would be going on disability. My oldest said right away, "HD???? THIS means that I can get it, too, right?"

Well, folks, it seems that in most schools around the country, they teach a class, sometimes in science, about genetics and DNA. I had no idea that my boys already knew about this disease. As a matter of fact, I ended up calling my youngest son's English teacher as they did a class about debating, and had split the class in half with this topic: "A man has a high-profile, high-paying job and was diagnosed with Huntington's disease. I want this side to debate why he doesn't have to tell his job about it, and THIS side (my kid's side) to debate why he should tell." I was HORRIFIED. I told his teacher immediately that my husband had HD and also let her know that I knew of one other child there whose father had HD. Now it was her turn to be horrified. She thought it was sooo extremely rare that she'd never have to be concerned. I have no idea if that lesson plan got tossed or not, but parents, PLEASE be aware that our kids ARE taught about this disease in around sixth grade, and it's NOT always accurate information. My stepdaughter was told by her teacher that only men can pass on the gene, and it's impossible for women to get it. Never mind that it was her grandmother who had died of it, and her mother had it as well.

We tried as a family to hold things together, but we were a group that kept things to ourselves and didn't talk about our feelings. We should have. Jay would do strange things, like want to bake oatmeal cookies, even though when I checked the oatmeal, I found it full of bugs, so I threw the oatmeal away. He decided, after I left for work, to make them anyway. I came home to the aroma of baked cookies, and found them. I asked Jay how he had made them since I had thrown out the oatmeal. He told me he'd removed it from the trash, and then he had a meltdown about it, telling me the bugs were killed during baking, so it was not a problem.

Our marriage was all but over, due to me losing a partner and the inappropriate things he expected from me when we were alone. Even though our kids were pretty much grown, I hated leaving him alone with them, I just didn't trust him. He'd hit them, and when I told him he couldn't do that anymore, he started pulling their hair. That was stopped by me, also, of course. I had considered a divorce much earlier, but decided to wait till my kids could be on their own. I could not face him having them alone for visitation. Around extended family members, Jay could hold things together pretty well, but when he and I were alone, he was highly inappropriate with me, and nothing I could say, nothing I could do, no deals that I made helped. We were just waiting to make the end of our marriage official.

In 2003, our youngest boy was ending high school, and our oldest was in college, so we got our divorce and sold the house, splitting the money four ways. Jay moved into an apartment near his mother in Pennsylvania, my oldest had already moved out, and I helped my youngest find an apartment. I packed up and drove to Michigan to live near Steve, a buddy from my online support group, not *with* Steve, as many thought. I got a job as a school bus driver, and later I became a home health care worker. It was a scary time for everyone. I think Jay had been in his apartment for a year or more, and one day the kids visited him with Jay's mother and found Jay all disoriented and all his pills gone. He couldn't remember what day it was, and so he'd taken too many pills. They called an ambulance, and the hospital kept him for over a month until there was an opening in a nursing home.

We all see Jay, who is now in a nursing home in Pennsylvania, and he will always be loved by me as a close family member. I wish I could say that Jay's family circled the wagons and got closer to my boys, but no. There's just one brother, two nephews, aunts, and uncles who sometime send him cards. They are only about 30 minutes away, but his brother never visits Jay and has never invited my children over for a holiday, barbecue, ANYTHING. His brother never visited his dad either, and I think the last time I saw him was at Dad's funeral. Jay's brother never tested, but we can assume that he does not have the gene, as he is now over 70 years of age and not showing any symptoms. Call it what you want, but I will never forgive them for their cowardly behavior.

The only thing that kept me going those years in New Jersey and finding out about HD was the online HD chat room I found. I just kept searching till I found it. The first person I talked to became my best friend. I met people from all around the world, HD positive, HD at risk, HD caregivers. They were family to me. I met my best friend there, who lived about an hour away, and we managed to get together at times. We would try to have gatherings. I had one at my house in New Jersey, and my buddy Steve had one in Michigan. We met our buddies from London, Missouri, Kentucky, Long Island, well, you get the picture. We made lasting, forever friendships, and I gained a future husband.

Steve and I fell in love, and after my house in New Jersey was sold, I moved up by him, rented an apartment in his building, and we married about two years later. Steve's former wife, Kay, had HD, too, and they also have two kids at risk. His former wife had become very symptomatic, and eventually, their beautiful home looked like it belonged in an episode of "Hoarders." She was very argumentative, and she fought with her children over petty things. They tell us she even had tantrums and lay on the floor screaming, crying, and kicking her feet, just like a child. She told her son that she hoped he would get HD. She kept insisting that her son come stay with her, and Friend of the Court also said he needed to stay with her. But it was filthy in her house and the last time he had been there, the animals had used his bed as a toilet. He chose to live with his dad. We encouraged him to visit her, but he would not. Nothing was going to make him go there.

Kay kept borrowing money, supposedly to pay her mortgage, but spent it on clothes and pools for neighbor kids and Omaha steaks for her neighbor and friend. She would call us when she needed help with the fuse box or when the dog ran out, and we'd go help. Her house was trashed. She asked us to come over to find kittens as she was sure one of the cats had a litter somewhere. I found them under one of the beds, but my knee was all cut up from broken glass that I didn't see because of all the trash. I have pictures of maggots coming up from the carpeting. She had no food, and the sink and tub had cat feces in them. The heat vent covers were missing, and the cats kept bobbing up and down from them all through the house. It was like Whack-a-Mole. She just didn't see any of this. She didn't see the mess, the filth; she didn't see that her animals were not well and were feral from no interaction. She kept a 50-pound bag of cat food on the kitchen floor and just cut it open for them. The litter boxes were loaded about three feet high. The most horrifying thing I saw in Kay's house was her bed. Now, I don't know for sure if she was even sleeping in there or not, but when we checked the master bedroom, her bed had a cloud of flies swarming in the formation of a tornado over the bed. I just gasped and yelled and cried. I still cry thinking about it. How can anyone live with this? I grew up on a dairy farm and never saw anything like this EVER. I'm just glad we were able to get her out of the house, though it took some doing.

We did our best to get her family involved . . . no such luck. At this time, she had her dad (a past president of the Michigan support group) and two sisters and a brother. She had lost a brother to HD many years before, as well as her mother and grandfather. Her brother and father were the ones who had cared for Kay's mother, so they were familiar with Huntington's disease, but with Kay, they would actually just get angry because she wouldn't listen to them. Made me wonder how they were so "expert" with HD. At this point, she wasn't Kay any more, just the disease. And that's what the disease does. We did our best to reach out to adult protective services, animal cruelty places, and no one would help. Kay had stopped making payments of mortgage and taxes and was about to lose her house. We didn't know what else to do. I even called a national HD organization to ask for help, and they told me to do what I had been doing. I can honestly say that we have never received any help from any HD organization; I guess they just fund research and don't "do" family. Any help we have ever received has been from our extended online HD family. We got lots of encouragement and advice from our HD family, and I could call them any time. For that, I thank them ALL and love them.

Finally, we heard that our governor was going to be at the park down the street, so we quickly wrote an essay entitled, "What Would You Do If It Was Your Mother, Sister or Friend?" and printed it out with pictures taken inside the home of cat feces, maggots, and trash, and gave it to our governor. Within DAYS, the very people we had called, and who had done nothing, took action. Kay was removed from the home and taken to the mental hospital, where she stayed for months until she got a guardian and a place to go. Her house was sold, and we all went to clean it out and save what we could. Sadly, the township removed 50 cats, and we also found some dead kittens. It was just miserable. The person who bought the house soaked the floors with industrial sized bleach and put in new everything, painted, and turned it into a showcase!

From the hospital, Kay went into an adult foster care home, which she hated. The people that ran it meant well, but they treated everyone there the same. That cannot be with Phds (People with Huntington's disease). We often got phone calls from her, crying, and then we'd go pick her up and bring her home for the day, and later, it turned into an overnight visit. She came and spent a couple of nights with us during Christmas and also at New Year's. Finally, one night she called me, crying that they were holding her door closed and wouldn't let her out as she wouldn't turn her TV down. In the past, they had also removed her light bulbs as she liked to keep a light on when she slept, and they were very concerned about the cost of the electricity. With this last call, I told her to pack as she was coming home with me and not going back.

We called her guardian and told him she hated the foster home, and we wanted her to live with us. He actually tried to talk us out of it, but then he agreed, and we went to court, and the judge approved it. Steve was all for this idea, absolutely he was. It was kind of ironic, because one of her sisters went to the court hearing, and she disagreed and said it would never work. The judge asked her where else Kay could go, and she had to say she didn't know. When the judge asked Kay about her wishes, Kay said, "Well, it's the lesser of three evils." It broke up the courtroom. Steve loves to tell this story and frequently says, "I'm the lesser of three evils!!"

Since it was spur of the moment, Kay had to sleep on a blow-up mattress, but eventually, we were able to get her a good bedroom set. We asked my former husband to live with us, too, but he said his mom wouldn't let him. Before I'd moved to Michigan, we had talked about it, and he said he would come. If I were to be brutally honest, I guess before Kay moved in, even though it was kind of my idea, I felt a little insecure about Kay living here, wondering if Steve would feel sorry for her and become more attached to her. But I then got my confidence back and knew nothing would take him away from me. Only ONE time was it awkward . . . we were in bed for the night . . . and she just walked in. Now, nothing was going on, but we WERE in bed together . . . from that night forward, our door was LOCKED.

I'd like to say we all lived happily ever after together, and for the most part, that is true, but not always. We all had our moments. Kay insisted on a McDonald's diet pop every day, which was fine, as Steve had to have one every day also. The problem was that when she gripped the cup, the lid would pop off, and it would splash all over everything . . . floor, furniture, her computer. (Yes, she had her own computer and played solitaire every waking moment!) Her keyboards were always getting all gunked up with spills and food, so Steve kept buying extra keyboards at yard sales for a couple of bucks, and he changed them out periodically. Very frugal, huh? Yet WE didn't mind if she kept a light on, not only all night, but all day. If she wanted her light on, that was fine with us. I always used a mug with a lid, so I got one for her. BOY, OH, BOY, did she hate that! She thought we were treating her like a baby. Pointing out that I also had one didn't help.

This is when we decided we had to have unbreakable rules . . . follow our rules or out . . . We called them "deal-breakers." So she used the mug. Another rule was to always take her meds, no refusing. A third rule was to always take a shower at least three days a week. We had to make that rule as she would pick times to NOT shower for weeks at a time. She also would walk around the house in the middle of night, naked. Her son, who was also living with us, was scared to death he was going to see that, but I talked to her first and explained that she HAD to leave her room with

SOMETHING on her body, or I didn't think her son would survive the experience.

As with Jay's family, Kay's family was pretty useless. Although they lived nearby and were told to stop in anytime, not only did they not come see her, but they didn't call, either. Some holidays, they would pick Kay up to bring her to a dinner at their father's house, but after he died, that ended. Even after Kay moved into a nursing home, three of them went to see her one time at Christmas for about ten minutes. That's another group of people I cannot forgive.

Kay lived with us for about five years, and her falls became more and more frequent. The day we decided we just couldn't keep her safe anymore, she had fallen at least three times by late morning. Steve was out doing a McDonald's run, and I heard a thud in the bathroom. Kim was using or starting to use the toilet, which was directly in front of the tub. She fell and had actually turtled herself into the tub, and try as hard as I could, I could NOT get her up. I had to call Steve to come home right away, and between the two of us, we were finally able to get her up. She fell two more times and pretty badly, too. We emailed her doctor, and he agreed to see her and tell her that he wanted to do x-rays and then tell her that he no longer felt she could live with us anymore. She didn't like it, but she finally gave in. If WE had been the ones to tell her that, we'd probably STILL be arguing about it.

We consider ourselves fortunate that she was placed in a nursing home five minutes from our home, so we were able to bring her her McDonald's fountain pop every morning. I have to say that the nursing home was not always on the ball, but for the most part, they did try to do their best. Kay was a very stubborn woman . . . nothing was going to hold her down. No one was going to tell HER she couldn't walk. Alarms on her bed and wheelchair made no difference to her. She got up and walked whenever the mood hit her. Several times, she had to be taken to the emergency room for stitches, which had also happened when she lived at our house.

Finally, she took a fall when her regular nurse was off for several days. They had just started Kay on a new medication, and we knew from experience that the first day or so on a new med usually made her sleep very deeply. Well, I guess they thought that was what was happening, because she slept through three meals, and that was NOT Kay. She not only didn't miss a meal, but each meal was usually triple the normal amount or more. We insisted that they call an ambulance, and they did. Turns out she had a brain bleed, and they did do surgery, but she never really came back. She died a couple of weeks later. Although it was very, very sad, we like to say that Kay went out her way.

While Kay was living with us, their son decided to test for the gene without telling us. He had been having problems since high school with paranoid thoughts and delusions. His delusions had been getting worse, though, and affected all of us. He was probably in the middle of a panic attack when he accused me of trying to poison him with his dinner. He called an ambulance and was sent to the local hospital, which ended up with him in a mental hospital. We asked that they put him on the same antipsychotic medication that his mom and my ex were on, as that seemed to help them so much. It did help him. There were other delusions, but since he has been on this med, that seems to have gone by the wayside.

Their daughter has been having many problems for what seems like forever. She's never kept a job, she lies about the most mundane things, and she's stolen from family, friends, and businesses. She's been picked up with drugs in the car she was driving and also had no license. She's been in jail for short periods of time and, this last time, for over three months. Nine years ago, she had a child, a boy, who we have been raising now for almost three years. Before that, we had him every summer and weekends. Her son has had three men in his life that he was encouraged to call "Daddy," and when they broke up with his mom, she would not allow them to be in his life anymore. We love him like he's our own, and now have custody. She willingly went to court to allow us to have guardianship, as she had no job and no place to live without staying with "friends."

After two years of guardianship, we applied for custody. She never showed up for hearings or for interviews by Friend of the Court. We try to get her to visit her son about once a week, but she usually cancels or just doesn't show up. He loves his mom and is very disappointed with his situation, but we are trying to give him a good life, and he sees counselors and is thriving in school. His mom is, of course, at risk, but she will not test, so are her problems HD related? We just don't know.

How has HD affected our lives? Well, I can say it hasn't all been bad; there has been good. We have met the strongest, most loving people in the world, and this never would have happened had it not been for HD. It brought me a wonderful husband and a new, additional family and the most precious grandson I could ever ask for. I miss my kids with a flying purple passion, and THANKFULLY I see no symptoms in them. They choose not to test so far. They have had problems in life, like anyone else has, but have handled them very responsibly.

Along with the good, though, comes the bad. Most of the people we first met in our first online support group have lost spouses and children due to HD and Juvenile Huntington's disease, and that is horrible. I now buy sympathy cards about four or five at a time to keep on hand. Going to a child's funeral is gut-wrenching, but we've done it for our dear friends, and we will probably have to do it again. We continue to keep our friendships with our HD family and probably always will.

As I sit here writing this, I am watching my grandson eat his breakfast and watch his cartoons, and all seems good. I try to not think about his at-risk factor, but of course, I cannot keep those thoughts away always. He's a snuggler, and that helps wipe away any sadness I may have. I will see my kids and Jay in May, and I'm focusing on that, also. Steve is a wonderful husband and grandfather, and life with my stepson is all good!

I think this disease has definitely changed me, not always in a great way. I have lost faith in doctors, I have lost hope in the researchers, and I am sad a lot. I also have no interest in religion anymore. I see how it gives so much comfort to others and wish I could feel the same, but I don't think I ever will. I've never believed in miracles, for one thing. I'll believe in them when an HD-positive gene goes spontaneously negative. In the very beginning, I used to have a dream about my boys being on a very large hill, playing, and I was way on the bottom of the hill. Turns out they were playing on railroad tracks, and a train was coming, and they couldn't hear it. I screamed and yelled and tried to run, but it was like my legs were in quicksand, and my voice could not be heard. I turned my head away so I couldn't watch them get hit, and it felt like the hand of GOD turned my head toward the train and said, "WATCH"...... I watched, and the train stopped in time. I actually told that story only one time, and that was at the Guthrie Center. I do hang on to that dream, but I just don't have the same faith I used to have.

On the other hand, I think I have more compassion for people, especially if they face their problems. I have a really hard time getting involved now. I cannot handle AT ALL the snake oil salesmen who claim to have found the cure, and then see that some of my HD family actually believe them. It just sends me into an anger I cannot explain, and it makes me cry. I think it's probably about my worries over my kids and my grandson.

I hope my boys never have to worry about HD ever again. Same for E, my grandson. He knows about it. He knew his Grandma Kay had it and died from it. He has seen me cry over lost friends that died of HD and has comforted me. He doesn't really know about his at-risk status as we don't know if his mom has it or not, although he does know she should test for it. I don't really want to tell him he's at risk till I know about his mom. This is where I disagree with NOT testing children under 18. Kids don't have to wait till they are 18 to test for HIV or

Diabetes and other diseases. Symptomatic or not, I feel the parents or guardian should make that decision, so the children can be guided in life. If I knew he had the bad gene, I certainly would not tell him now, but I would know when to tell him. As it is, I will express strongly how important it is to NOT get anyone pregnant, lol. He's 9, but it's something to think about. He does bring it up at times, asking if he can get it. Right now, I'm not sure what to say, so I just tell him, "We will know more if Mommy tests, and E, I don't think you have anything to worry about." He has ADHD, and sometimes, he confuses things by saying HDAD . . . but then he corrects himself and laughs.

Through this journey I've come to admire the Guthrie family so much. Of course, I love hearing the stories about Woody. I remember reading that his mother, who had HD, gave her furniture away . . . well, that must be a symptom . . . Kay's mom did the same thing, and Kay's dad had to go to Goodwill to get it back. My close friend's wife, who has HD, wanted me to take THEIR furniture when she learned I was moving to Michigan.

I've met Arlo (Woody's son) a few times, and for a long time he would not talk about HD, but he does now, and I admire that. Every year, he opens his church up (Alice's Restaurant, now the Guthrie Center) for a Thanksgiving dinner. He invites all the researchers that can make it and also some HD families. His whole family is very warm and inviting.

Knowing what I do now about Huntington's disease, and learning more and more about Woody, I can understand why he didn't want his fans to see him that way all those years ago, although that makes me sad. I don't like our Phds (people with Huntington's disease) to be hidden; they should enjoy their lives as long as they can, and we should love them as long we have them with us. I just hope Woody knew how loved he was, and how loved his music is to this day.

—m—

Please consider making a donation to Help 4 HD International, Inc., a nonprofit organization.

Donations can be made via their secure web site, www.help4hd-international.org, or by mailing a check to:

Help 4 HD International, Inc.
436 Playa Blanca Street
Santa Maria, CA 93455

You can also contact Help 4 HD International at 805-441-5618.

About Margaret D'aiuto

Margaret D'aiuto was born in California, USA, in 1924, 91 years ago. She grew up in the United States, went to high school and part of junior college, and then studied nursing at the Queen of Angels Hospital in Los Angeles, where she interned for three years until she graduated. Margaret met Luis Gallardo, a doctor from Mexico, while she was studying to be a nurse and later married him. Together, they had seven children. A little over 22 years ago, Margaret established the Mexican Association of Huntington's Disease. Today, she serves as president. She says she believes she inherited her determination and persistence from her father, a very busy, hardworking man who "always had five things going at a time." She says she is always doing something, and that she cannot stop. It is her dream to see an end to Huntington's disease.

You can see and hear Margaret speak at https://www.youtube.com/watch?v=vGdmazsR2KI.

CHAPTER 9

~~~~~~

Turning Tears Into Hope
By Margaret D'aiuto

This is about Huntington's disease, the destruction, the sadness, the horror, the absolute control it possesses as it takes over the lives of all those destined to have been born with the HD gene. It also demands the time and effort of a healthy family member or a caretaker for the patient suffering Huntington's disease. I will tell you this: this is the worst disease that could possibly exist. There's AIDS, there's cancer, there's Parkinson's, there's Alzheimer's, there are all kinds of horrible, horrible diseases, but Huntington's lasts 15, 20, 25 years. What happens to the family with this illness? If you abandon them, can you live with that on your conscience? I could not. Some people do, but I could not.

If you don't abandon them, then you are there for them 24 hours a day. They get up at the wrong hour, they go to sleep at the wrong hour, they eat at the wrong hour. They eat like chickens. When they eat, they scatter the food all over the table, all over the floor, but they don't realize that. They don't know that. They're eating, and they're enjoying their food, and they don't know that they're bothering you. It is very expensive, the cost of their medicine, their treatment, and their medical care.

Huntington's disease is not a well-known disease; the diagnosis often is not correctly made, or is made too late. But HD (as it is often called) is coming to the forefront. You will be hearing more and more about it as it slowly comes out of the closet. I, myself, before knowing about HD, certainly would have crossed the street to avoid coming face to face with such a strange looking person as one who has HD.

I know many of them now, ugly and twisting, ragged and unkempt. But now I know their hearts, their suffering, their loss of love and home and decent care and, worst of all, the loss of their independence. I know how noble they are and how they must accept the fact that, through no cause of their own, they have inherited a disease that has no cure, no helpful treatment, only the sureness of slowly wasting away until death rescues them. Their knowledge and intelligence may or may not last throughout their illness.

Each child born to an HD parent has a 50 percent probability of inheritance. In most cases, symptoms begin to be noticeable between 35 and 50 years of age, after they are probably married and have had children. But there are cases in children (about 1.2 percent, who may live to be 5 years old), juveniles (12 to 15 years), and in older ages (10 to 25 or more years). No two cases are alike; all are tragic and ugly and frightful, with suicide in first place of 7 to 1 in relation to other causes of death among people with HD.

I do not have Huntington's disease; I could never inherit the gene, even if I try. I cannot get that "pinche" (an excellent Mex-Spanish adjective) disease, and yet, my adult life has been dominated by Huntington's disease, every day, every instant, every moment, leaving no time for myself. It has been over 50 years. Yes, I am 91 years old, and this started when I was 50 years old. Or was it even before that when I was young and in love, with seven wonderful children and an active life of sports and interesting traveling?

It was in the year of 1940, when I was 15 years old, that three important happenings opened up to me the path of what was to be my future. The first one put tears in my eyes forever, my mother having died in a tragic way. The second one was the illness of my father and his six years of hospitalization, and the third was the entering of the United States into World War II.

Suddenly we were six sisters on our own (the oldest was 27 years old, and the youngest 13). My older sisters became guardians of my younger sister and me. Because of the Italian strictness of my father, my beautiful sisters had not been allowed to do much dating, so of course, with this sudden parentless freedom, within six months, three of the older sisters were married (marriages that lasted for the next 70 or so years).

My sister Pauline, the second oldest sister of 25 years old, had studied law, graduating from the University of Southern California, with very high honors (actually, she was a born genius, and in those days it was not very common to see a woman lawyer). She did not marry so soon, taking care of my younger sister and me as we moved into our own future.

During World War II, a family friend who was a registered graduate nurse of the Queen of Angels Hospital nursing school was flying back and forth to Europe to bring back the wounded soldiers. That inspired me to want to do something to help our soldiers, so I began to look for where I could also help. Amazingly, the answer was being born exactly as my need. I would become a nurse.

The U.S. government was in need of more nurses, and so a new Army nurses' corps was started, offering snazzy uniforms, plus the usual white uniforms that nurses use, and the tuition paid for classes at the Queen of Angels Hospital in Los Angeles where the nurses would be interned. The offer also included tuition payment to Chaffey Junior College in my hometown of Ontario (upland) California in order to first take the science courses that would be needed (anatomy, physiology, etc.). There would be an allowance of $15 a month. We had one day a week off and orders to be in by the curfew hour of 10:00 p.m. Breakfast at seven, then four hours of classes, one hour for lunch, followed by six hours of floor duty, where one really learns nursing.

A school friend, Alice, decided to join me, so together we started at the Chaffey Junior College. We went for six months. It was a strange experience—there were no male students, just the male anatomy teacher. Evidently, the boys of Ontario and of Upland had all gone to war. I had a cousin, David, who was very handsome. He was in the Navy, so when on leave, he would come to visit me. He would take me to school in his jalopy, and I became very popular as the girls gathered around, being nice so that I would introduce them to my cousin.

Soon, we were a group of ten girls starting together to enter in the Army nurses' corps and becoming good friends. Only six of us graduated three years later. Alice and I entered the Queen of Angels Hospital, largest hospital west of the Mississippi, as it was known. We became good friends and learned to work hard together. My friend Alice was from Michigan, where her mother lived. Unfortunately, her mother missed her and constantly asked her to come home. One day, she came to visit Alice at the hospital and took her out to lunch at a very elegant restaurant. Alice looked great in her new Army nurse's uniform. During the lunch, her mother began to choke on a piece of meat. Alice jumped up and down, screaming, "Help! Help! My mother is choking!" A waiter rushed over and helped her. That must have been some scene of the choking mother and the hysterical, uniformed nurse. After a year and a half of training, Alice did give up being a nurse and rejoined her mother.

I had wondered if I wanted to be interned three years at the Catholic Hospital with the strict German refugee nuns. I jumped at the chance, and I loved it. I loved the Queen of Angels Hospital, the schooling, the nuns. The German nuns were strict, hardworking, and marvelous; my favorite nun was Sister Geraldine, the night director. You could hear her during her nightly rounds, the soft sound of the long strings of wooden rosary beads hanging from her waistline. One evening, as I was shaking down a thermometer, it slipped from my fingers and skidded to the end of the hall, shattered. I went to Sister Geraldine for a new one; it cost me one dollar. She asked: "Would you like to help me?"

"I would be glad to, Sister," I replied.

"I have a patient who is well. They cannot come to pick her up until morning. But, as I cannot leave her alone, I need someone to stay with her tonight. Will you do that?" she asked.

My answer was "yes." Wow, surprise! She paid me five dollars. Great! So every now and then she would call me, and I would help her.

One night, the patient was a man; he was unconscious because of a car accident. There were many doctors bustling around and running tests, and then there were none, just me. I kept calling the interns on duty, asking, "What shall I do if he doesn't wake up?"

One intern said to me, "Talk to him soft and low, and relax. He is never going to wake up." Noooooooooooooooo!

At the hospital, I began to hear whispers and rumors about a new intern at the hospital from Mexico. I could have cared less; I had just one more day in surgery training and would have to leave the next day for two months as part of our training in a psychiatric hospital.

Luis Gallardo, who was from Guadalajara, Mexico, was the new intern. He had just graduated from medical school there. He had come to the U.S. during World War II in order to offer his services to a group that would help in the war effort. A friend presented him to the head doctor of the Queen of Angels Hospital, where they were pleased to accept him for a one-year internship. After that, he would go for one year to the Santa Monica Hospital.

Is it possible that ONE DAY can be responsible for the result of how things turn out for the rest of your life? Was this that day?

First, I had to scrub in for surgery, cover my hair and my face so only my eyes showed, and help the doctor operating. He had an assistant to whom I had to pass the instruments needed, and he then would pass them on to the doctor that was operating.

I would pass an instrument to the assistant, but he would not take hold of it; I would look at him to try again, and he would be there making eyes at me. It was the new intern, Luis. Then he would take the instrument. When he was to return the instrument, he would not let go of it until again I looked at him when again he made eyes at me. I was in shock. Thank goodness the operation ended, and I rushed to do the cleaning up necessary after an operation.

When I left the operating room, he was there waiting with a doctor I knew who was married to a friend of mine. He introduced me to the new intern, the doctor from Mexico. I was too shy to say anything about the google eye business and said I was in a rush, then hurried away in order to pack and leave the Queens for new adventures that at times I wished I could have avoided.

Day one, good start: I was to help the head nurse to receive a new patient at the psychiatric hospital. She was such a beautiful woman, very elegant and so lady-like you could see that she was very rich. The head nurse said, "We will work together to start a treatment; then you will stay with the patient until someone comes to relieve you. Listen carefully; you must not for a moment leave her alone!"

On one of those carts with big wheels, we undressed her and began to wrap her complete body in wet sheets, all the while in conversation with this charming person. As the head nurse left us, she turned to me and repeated, "Do not leave her alone!"

The room was empty of furniture, not even a chair, so I stood close to the patient as she talked of her family and children. She seemed to be getting a little nervous and asked me to unwrap the sheets, but I told her I couldn't do that until the head nurse returned. Within an hour, I began to worry as the lady became angry and began screaming at me. She threatened as I stepped further away from her. I was beginning to get frightened. I was sure that she was going to tear off the sheets and attack me, but she couldn't move the sheets as she was strapped to the cart. The screaming, the curse words, the description of what she was going to do to me had me pressed against the wall in the furthest corner possible. "Do not leave the room; do not leave the room," I kept repeating to myself.

It was getting dark when the head nurse returned and said, "You may leave now." You bet I did; I wasn't going to be there when they unwrapped her.

A few evenings later, it was my job to help six patients soak in separate tubs of warm water. I was to make sure that I kept the water at a certain temperature for at least an hour. No one else was on duty, and this seemed easy enough. One of the patients said to me, "My water is getting cooler," so I tried to raise the water temperature. I could not, so I tried to find another tub for her. The water there was too cool. Then another patient complained about the cooling water. I had them get dressed when another patient complained. I tried to call the main office, but no one was on duty. I tried to find a janitor, but there was none. I could not leave them in cooling water, so now all the patients had to leave the tubs.

In the morning, I made my report. I was scolded for my ignorance… "Why didn't you go down to the basement and change the gas tank?"

"Ye gads," I thought, "how do you do that?" With my luck, I would probably have set those tanks on fire and blown up the whole hospital.

My third joyful day was with a nutty patient. She wanted to go to a store about two blocks from the hospital and buy some donuts. They gave her permission, but they told me to go with her and not to leave her as she might try to escape. So we started out through a vacant lot, a short cut. Then she began to complain that she didn't feel well and that I should go for help.

"Better I help you; take my arm," I said.

"I need to pee," she said.

"Then let us hurry."

She spread her legs, and I could see the wetness leaking down the leg of her slacks and out into her shoes. It was beginning to get dark. She lay down on the ground, so I sat with her. Finally, she realized that I was not going to leave her alone, so we returned empty handed.

"Darn it," I thought, "I was getting hungry for a doNUT and here, there are only NUTS!" Ha, ha, ha. As the saying goes, "Laugh, and the world laughs with you; weep, and you weep alone."

I began to get comfortable at the hospital, different from the normal ambience; the patients were more intimate as they pulled you into their problems. One had to judge what is "make believe" without getting involved, being always honest and patient and understanding.

Every two or three weeks, I would make a visit to the Queens when my friends had time off, and we would all get together and have hamburgers someplace. This time, my doctor friend and his wife joined us and, surprise, so did the intern from Mexico. We were all comfortable together, the burgers delicious (as a matter of fact, I could eat that right now, but lately cannot find one that I really like).

Soon, it was time for me to catch my bus and return to the psychiatric hospital in Compton, California. The doctor and his wife insisted that they take me back. Are you surprised that the intern from Mexico joined us? (Hmmmm, was this DAY TWO responsible for the results of the rest of my life?)

Both he and I were very busy with our hospital duties. He started calling me whenever he had a couple of hours free. Getting to know Dr. Luis Gallardo opened a new world for me. He really knew how to enjoy life; there was always something new to see, to do, concerts to attend, oceans to swim in, friends wanting to invite him. He enjoyed it when we visited with my sisters and his many friends that were always so glad to see him. It was always run, run, run to get me back to the hospital before curfew time. I began to wonder if there was anything he didn't know.

Once, there was something I should have had doubts about. After our visits, he would leave me at the door of the nurses' home, and I would usually go upstairs to my room. Once, I decided to visit my friends that were off duty; they would be in the nurses' entertainment room, reading or listening to music, etc. We chatted awhile before I went to bed.

The next morning Luis called me and asked, "Where did you go last night?"

"What do you mean?" I asked.

"You did not turn on your room lights."

HAD HE BEEN SPYING ON ME?

Ladies, ladies, all over the world, that is not a compliment. That is jealousy!

At that time, I did not know that. Maybe my thought was that he cares! And he really did, but still, it was a sign of the future that neither he nor I could ever have expected. It came in the form of a disease, HUNTINGTON'S DISEASE.

The war ended shortly before I had finished my nurse's training, so I continued my studies at the Queens until I graduated, and then I worked as a registered nurse at the Queens for three months, earning a salary of $200 a month. Luis, in the meantime, would finish his studies at the Santa Monica Hospital three months later than I would finish at Queens.

LUIS AND I HAD FALLEN IN LOVE. HE PROPOSED. We took a quick trip to Mexico so I could meet his mother and a sister who lived with her. It was important to him that his mother approved, and she, too, wanted to meet me. That trip turned out to be a bit romantic, as my future sister-in-law saw to it that I went to bed early at night. Then the music started! There were Mariachis singing and playing on their guitars outside my window. I was only allowed to peek. So beautiful, so very impressive!

As the war had ended, each of my sisters was joining her husband in different parts of the world. One of my sisters was in Japan, where her daughter was born; three of them were in Hawaii. Another was traveling to meet her husband in the East. As all were away, Luis and I did return to Mexico to be married and in the Catholic Church, as his mother so desired. I don't really know what was said, as I didn't speak a word of

Spanish yet (hmm, maybe a few curse words that he had taught me), but I also learned to read the "google" look in his eyes. Yes. We had a special and interesting marriage for many years. I was 23 years old, and I have lived in Mexico since that time, in 1947.

My nice Mexican man was very intelligent, brilliant, and (I'll say it in Spanish because it's a beautiful word), "simpatico." He was very "simpatico." We had seven children. When he was around 50 years old, his personality began to change. He became very aggressive and confused because something was happening to all this beautiful health that he had always had. He was very athletic, energetic, full of ideas: "let's do this, let's do that, let's do the other." It was a whirlwind life with him. We were living with a little money but with big adventures. He didn't know that he had the disease, though, because by the time we got a diagnosis, he was almost 55 or 60 years old. We didn't get a diagnosis for a long time, so we didn't know what was happening to him. He didn't know that he had Huntington's disease, which is fine. But he lived 22 years ill, and I took care of him for 22 years. It was very painful to see this man decline, this man that did exercise every day, that climbed mountains, that was heroic many, many times. If we went to Acapulco, or Puerto Vallarta, or any place we went, if anybody was drowning (which seemed to happen very often), he was always the first one to notice, and he would be saving people's lives. He would run off, and I would say, "What's the matter? Where is he going swimming all of the sudden?" He wouldn't even take his pants off. No, somebody was drowning, and he saw it. He was quick to act. Quick.

Luis worked as a doctor. He would occasionally have a business lunch with friends, but mostly he preferred his routine of coming home to do an hour of exercise, shower, and then have lunch, after which he would do as they did in his hometown of Guadalajara; he would take a nap. Yes, in those days, most of the businesses of Guadalajara would close down for one hour, and it was nap time for many. Luckily, Luis started being ill at an advanced age. Although his character became more difficult, he was still working until 48 or 50 years old, which is a small advantage, considering the horror of having and living with HD. I cared for him until he was 73 years old, when he finally could rest and slipped into eternal sleep.

But life just leads you on, and I'm not sorry that I had my children. Not now. They're wonderful, they are wonderful. And I take care of them. My first son that got ill, I took care of him for 18 years because he came home to live with me. And my two daughters got very ill, and have had good husbands and children who take care of them. And my baby, he's 52 years old now. He's living with me. It's very hard. But we had those marvelous years together. Their youth was filled with adventures. All other kids, friends, everybody wanted to go where Dr. Gallardo went with his children. They were climbing mountains, and they were doing all kinds of adventurous things. He was taking friends to underground rivers with terrible risks, and everybody wanted to go with him. His friends were young; his friends were old. People liked to be with him. He was an adventurous person. I didn't like him all the time, because husbands and wives don't like each other all the time, but I wouldn't have left him for anything in the world.

Most everything we did was activities with the children, often taking their friends with us. The following four are those who inherited the Huntington's disease gene.

My first born, on May 25, 1949, was a baby boy. Named after his father, 'Luis' who was overjoyed, Luis, Jr. became a doctor as did his father. We had no worries then of HD, but he did get polio (the terror illness of those days) when he was four years old, as did his sister Diana a year later when she was four years old. So my husband was a doctor, and I a nurse…. we sure were kept busy. We treated them with hot compresses day and night, and they both won that battle. Luis, Jr. does not have the HD gene.

Diana (Dolly), my second child, born in 1950, has the HD gene and became ill as an adult after being married and having children. We had no knowledge of HD in the family until Luis was diagnosed when he was almost 60 years old.

I think of her very often, remembering how beautiful she was. I am going to take myself down Memory Lane and live some of our moments together from a tiny baby to a beautiful mother and all the happiness that she gave me. I can see her in her buggy with her round face, pink cheeks, and beautiful blue eyes; people would stop me on the street just to admire her.

Once, I got the scare of my life: one day, I went to buy bread, and I had two-year-old Luis by the hand and Dolly, 11 months old, in the buggy. Conveniently, the store in the front part was all opened, so I didn't have to go inside to choose or pay. As I paid, I let go of the buggy for a few seconds, and when I reached for it again, oh NO, it was gone. I could see, not too far away, a man and a young boy about eight years old running as they took the buggy with my baby in it. I picked up Luis and ran after them. God must have loaned me wings. When I grabbed the buggy, the man raised his hands and repeatedly said: "It's a joke, it's a joke!"

I could not speak, being petrified as I watched these miserable jokers walk away. Even if I had already paid for it, we'd have no bread that day.

I remember Dolly as she grew, later in the French school uniform, a little girl, brilliant, getting all A's and first place medals each year.

I even see her so happy on her wedding day with Alejandro, who turned out to be such a wonderful husband, caring for her so tenderly while she was ill, until he died. As a beautiful mother, she was so in control bringing up her children. She deserves the best, and she found that in her children.

Now she has Huntington's disease, and she carries it with great dignity. Yes, HD has taken over; I do not believe that she realizes that anymore. Her children tell me that she is very happy when her grandchildren are with her, eight of them.

Alejandra (Cookie), my third child, was born in 1951. Born with the HD gene, she started having symptoms as an adult, after marrying and having three children. She passed away in April 2015. With Cookie, it was the same as with her sister. We did not know about the HD illness until their father (Luis) became ill and was finally diagnosed when he was almost 60 years old.

Lovely, lovely Cookie. She also had blue eyes and rosy cheeks, but she was stronger and healthier than her sister. She was tall and lovely. She liked very much to help others. She liked to have many friends of different interests, was quick to make up her own mind and quick to find interest in books and the world of art around her. I could always count on her to confide with me. She was a bit adventurous and liked to play "hooky" from school. She told me about the day that she and two schoolmates were planning to escape when they heard the teacher coming, so they squeezed into a cupboard. "Shhhhhhhhh!"

"Ouch!" they wanted to yell. Luckily, they weren't caught.

"Ouch, me too!" I said, "Remember, mothers also are responsible for how children behave, so thank you for the confidence because they may kick you out of school, and you are too brilliant to want that."

"Okay, Ma," she said. "Don't worry."

I didn't worry; she was a very sensitive and sensible person. There was only one occasion that it was hard to reach her, and that was when I had to give her injections of medicine. After promising that, "Okay, now I will let you give me the shot," she would have me chasing her all over the room, up and over the beds, while squirting the medicine into the air. That made us laugh, let me win, giving her a big hug and the shot after so much exercise and fun.

After Cookie, Gabriel was born in 1953. He was not born with the HD gene. There is no greater blessing. He is the tallest of my five boys and somewhat of an individualist. I always feel that he knows best how to work out his problems, and surely there are times I take advantage of that for my own benefit.

Jorgé (Georgie Porgie, "Pudding and pie, kissed the girls and made them cry. When the boys came out to play, Georgie Porgie ran away [or something like that]) was born in 1956. He graduated as an engineer, was married, and had two beautiful sons. Born with the HD gene, he was the first of my four children to become ill with HD. He was only 29 years old when the first symptoms appeared. Married and living in Chiapas, he could not tolerate this change in himself. He lost all that he loved most, his home, his work, his family. He came home to live with me and tried three times to commit suicide. Maybe the first time he drank a little too much and could not load his pistol, spilling bullets all over the floor. He was unconscious, and I hid his gun forever. The next time, he emptied all his pills, swallowing them and throwing the boxes out the window. We found them in time and rushed him to the hospital where they emptied his stomach. He was unconscious for two days, but recovered.

Another time, I cannot explain it, maybe because I was the cause of why he could not live his life as he wanted, that he had to live with me—I understand that NO ONE wants to give up his independence; giving up your independence is one of the most horrible steps to take for a Huntington's disease patient. So one morning, as I opened my bedroom door into the hallway, I only saw blackness. Everything I touched turned my robe and my hands black. My son had piled up a stack of blankets outside my bedroom door and set them on fire. Then he had gone to bed. The hallway windows were closed, and as fire needs oxygen, when the oxygen was gone, so was the fire, leaving most of the indoors with black soot and in need of painting. I asked him why he had done that, but he denied it. I believe him! I love my son. He would not do such a thing; it was just a moment of HD, gone and forgotten.

For a time, he seemed to be adjusting, and as a civil engineer, he could get some jobs and was working. Jorgé was a born engineer. He could fix a watch or anything one needed; he made me a secret hiding place for my important papers and valuables. Football was his passion, and when he came home late at night, he would fix his own dinner as we chatted. He was a Galan with the girls, but I would hang up the phone when they called him. (Times have changed, eh?) One day, a beautiful girl with long, golden hair, big eyes (I called her a live Barbie) came to see me, asking questions about HD. She had heard about my son and asked to meet him. I took her to his room. "Someone to see you, Son," I said.

When he saw her, he must have thought that he had died and gone to heaven. He jumped up, and they immediately became friends. As his illness advanced, she was always there for him and would take him in a wheelchair to concerts and many places, bringing him gifts and goodies. She came to visit him almost daily until the end. He was only 48 years old when HD won its battle. The following words, I hate to say or even think of. This angel that had come to Jorgé so generously is beginning now to struggle with her own entrance into HD. I think I should take her some cookies today.

My son Eduardo (Equis to most everyone) was born in 1958. It took us a month to decide his name, so meanwhile it was the X baby (hence, pronounced *Equis*). He does not have the gene, although he has never taken the predictive test to prove that. I hope that that solution holds up. So many people find it impossible to be tested. I agree with them, unless they need to know in order to marry or have children.

Christopher (Cristobal, Bubus) was born in 1961. Chris became ill a few years after he was married and has three beautiful daughters. He is my baby, having turned 53 in September. DON'T TOUCH MY BABY, YOU FILTHY, STINKING HD! DON'T TOUCH MY CHILDREN! I have no power over HD; I can only be there for my children as long as God allows it. When Chris used to come home at night, we would sit on the kitchen counter and chat for hours. Sorry to say this, but besides HD, he has a witch in his life. He was just a naïve boy overtaken by Huntington's disease. It is rough going for him now. He is very ill, a little hard to know what he is feeling or needs. He demands nothing, always polite and thanking those that help him.

(A NOTE TO MY NIECE) Yes, Gaby, God gave us strength to deal with the problem, but the time is now, before it hits. Be intelligent, be ready, SO THAT THE CHILDREN OF NOW ... TODAY ... do not pass it on to another generation.

Forgive me for speaking; this was my job long ago. I failed, but I was told not to interfere unless I was given permission. From now on, this is my theme; it is time to save the future from what we have had to live through. So many years, so much time living with Huntington's disease. Very often, I feel that the days are too long. A profound sadness reminds me of what it is to live with HD. This time, it is my baby, my youngest child who is now 53 years old. I remember the day that he was born. As I held him in my arms, I felt so blessed, so grateful. Although he was my seventh, could it be possible that this perfect baby was really mine?

I remember walking with him to kindergarten, all dressed in white, just like a little prince, then later, the last day of first grade, when he came home so excited, saying, "Mama, the maestro said tomorrow you must arrive early, as we get our yearly prize, and that I will be the first one called upon."

"Of course, of course, I will not arrive late," and there I sat, very early, in the front row, while the teacher announced, "Cristobal Gallardo, first place in ACEO!" ACEO? CLEANLINESS! He was there looking at me, so happy, so content, with a big smile. I smiled back at him, full of pride as I saw his happiness and his innocence.

It was when he was four years old, and was to be operated on for the removal his tonsils, that I took ice cream and funny books for him to enjoy. I began to notice that there were constant movements of his little fingers. For about four months we went from doctor to doctor as the movements continued. Finally, one doctor told me: "This is the Chorea of Sydenham; it is a chorea that children get. It will go away, little by little, on its own."

And that's the way it was, or not??? Was it HD hiding in the shadows all those years, destroying not only one, but four of my children that I have, with so many dreams, held in my arms? Could this be the first notice of the horrid future in store for us? My sadness is overpowering. There is no doubt that suffering is a part of this life.

I could not change the world. Believe me, for the past thirty-plus years I have worked as a volunteer, trying to serve Huntington's sufferers and their families. I now feel that I have had my chance and have failed. Patients that have the disease are suffering without a hope for a cure. But family members continue to live normal lives, and many of them are unknowingly gene carriers. They fall in love, get married, and have children (who may or may not be future gene carriers). No one seems to be learning from experience. I need to know now, what shall I do, to whom shall I turn that will make a difference in what needs to be done to break this chain of horror, to master this monster? Sometimes I feel sad and need a shoulder to cry upon, not because I have Huntington's disease, but because my husband had to suffer it, and unfortunately so did two of my children, and still do two more of my children. And what about all the young ones that have been born at risk?

It has taken me a long time to learn how to live in this atmosphere of sorrow and suffering. But it has also taught me the value of life and what a precious gift it is. Do I, do you, appreciate this gift? It really pisses me off to see healthy persons who ruin their own lives by smoking or taking drugs. As you know, now-a-days even our "over-eating" habits are weighing heavily on our health.

I decided to help others through an association. I'm the president of the Mexican Association of Huntington's Disease. It's been a little over 22 years that we have worked with patients who have this disease. Patients who don't have possibilities of having much health. We run a day-center where they can go and stay all day. They have breakfast with us, lunch, and we give them therapies. We try to give them a better life. Huntington's disease is a fatal disease that has no cure. And so, from the moment they find out they have Huntington's disease, they know of what they're going to die, although they don't know how long they will live. So we try to give that part of their lives meaning, happiness, and love.

We help them as much as we can. For instance, we provide medicines, diapers, and we give them food baskets once a month, which is not enough (maybe they eat better for three days or something like that). But we never charge over 30 percent of what the medicine costs us, we never charge over 30 percent of what the diapers cost us, we never charge over 30 percent for whatever we give them. We only charge 30 pesos, which is what, two dollars? three dollars? for a basket that costs us almost a hundred pesos or more. So we try to help them, but we never have enough to do everything we want to do. And we work at getting money. That's a very important part of the work. To get donations. We have been lucky up to now to have enough to subsist well, but we could do a lot better. And we are going to try to do a lot better.

I want this association to succeed. I feel that it has done quite a bit, but I want it to succeed when I'm not here. I want the people to have this. We treat the poorest people in Mexico. Some of them only have breakfast and lunch because they come and stay with us during the day. Some of them don't have anyone to feed them, and they don't have food. Some of them are not so poor. But the majority are miserably, miserably poor.

I feel now that I have still too much to do to really get this stable enough to make it last longer. I have some marvelous people working, marvelous people interested, but I always feel that we need a little more union between us. So what I'm doing, somebody else will just take over and make the sacrifice of their lives for it. I really don't know. I don't know anything anymore.

The misery that we see is almost intolerable. It's hard not to cry with them all the time. You don't want anybody to see you crying because you don't want them to realize that they're suffering so much. It's the way I treat my family, also. I tell them: "C'mon, let's go walking; or c'mon, let's do this; or c'mon let's do that." I don't let them think that anybody's feeling sorry for them. They have to face up to things just as if they weren't sick. And then we have this luck that after so many years of being sick, they lose that notion that they're sick. They lose it. So they don't know they're sick anymore. They do so many things wrong, but they don't know they're sick anymore. They're not suffering. You are the one who's living your life for somebody else. And that's what happens when they get older.

I find that a great part of my strength comes from working with patients who have HD, and seeing their nobleness in the acceptance of their fate. Their strength becomes my strength. I find that turning my problems over to God does not always solve the problem, but it does enlighten me. It is not always the problem that is the problem, but the lack of acceptance of what we must face up to.

So my friends (old and new), thank you for lending me your shoulder these last few moments and, by being there, helping me turn tears into hope. I just hope that this goes into somebody else's heart, you know? We could trade hearts if anybody wants to, so I would just wish that people would take an interest in Huntington's disease because you don't know; tomorrow, you may fall in love with somebody who has Huntington's disease. It will change your life forever. Blessings to all!

Please consider making a donation to the Mexican Association of Huntington's Disease, a nonprofit organization.

Asociacion Mexicana De La Enfermedad De Huntington I.A.P.
Tesorelos 97, Toriello Guerra Del. Tlalpan, 14050 Mexico City, Mexico
tel: 52-5424 3325; fax: 52-5424 3189
Email: asocia@prodigy.net.mx
Website: www.huntingtonmexico.org

About Brenda A. Vega Fonseca

Brenda Vega Fonseca is the founder and President of Fundacion Huntington Mexico. She lives in Mexico City and is married to a wonderful man named Mauricio Espinoza. They have two beautiful children, Ximema and Mauricio. She gives presentations on radio and television in order to publicize information about this disease and will soon give talks and conferences to inform, educate, and raise awareness in society in general with leading specialists in the field of Huntington's. Brenda has become the voice of patients and their families and understands the needs and deficiencies of those who are afflicted by the disease. Through donations, she has made IVF-PGD available to couples who want to have children and was also able to receive the drug tetrabenazine, an extremely expensive drug that treats chorea, at a discounted rate. She was invited by Help4Hd International to participate in the 2014 Symposium in Santa Maria, California and has been invited to participate in the 2015 Symposium in Riverside, California. Brenda was awarded the Mexican National Award for WOMEN, 2013 and 2014. She works tirelessly to eradicate this disease, in collaboration with all the people who work in the Fundacion Huntington Mexico.

About Daniel Medina

Daniel Medina lives in the city of Moreno Valley, California, an hour from Los Angeles. He works for a school district and has actually been there for a while now, doing everything except be a teacher. He enjoys playing sports, running, traveling and socializing. He became an advocate for Huntington's disease because three years ago, he found out that his half-brother was at risk. This motivated him to attend walks, and little by little, he started getting more and more involved. Towards the end of 2013, he was introduced to Help 4 HD International and has been a part of it ever since, serving as the International Affairs Director and now vice president. About a year and a half ago, he started an HD support group in the city of Riverside, California. He's also coordinated a walk, been part of an HD Symposium, and has established ties and partnerships with various institutions here in the Inland Empire and abroad that are making it possible for Help 4 HD International to better serve our HD Community. He lives a normal life and finds time to do the things he loves, and that being said, being an advocate and making a difference for the HD Community fills his heart with joy. He sees and feels the pain and the struggles that are faced by our HD Community and that is why he hopes that his contribution will someday help eradicate this terrible disease.

CHAPTER 10

Love in Action
By Brenda A. Vega Fonseca

Translated from Spanish by Daniel Medina

My name is Brenda Vega, and this is how my journey began: I was raised by my grandma, Ma Luisa. She was like a mother to me. I spent every evening with her and with my wonderful grandfather, Miguel. They lived on the third floor of an apartment building. My grandma enjoyed going out and really liked taking us to the park to play. When she took us to the park, people used to stare at her in a weird way. That being the case, my sister and I used to insult them so they would look elsewhere and not stare at my grandma anymore. As a child, you don't measure your actions, but people tend to be cruel, and the only thing we didn't want was for them to look at Ma Luisa as if she were some sort of freak.

My grandma fell down the stairs many times, but the only thing we could do is help her get up and help clean up her blood and run to alert Grandpa that she had fallen. She continued deteriorating rapidly, and in November of 1995, she succumbed to pneumonia. My grandpa behaved like such a gentleman!! He never once thought of leaving her while she was so sick and was by her side and took care of her till her dying breath. He was always a great example of unconditional love. Oh, how I miss them, and how our hearts ache for their presence!!

So what was this ailment my grandma suffered from? Why did she move like that? Why did my grandma's brothers show the same symptoms? "What is Huntington's?" we asked ourselves.

Who could imagine that such a disease could unleash such destruction on the families that it affected? All we knew at this time was that it reached the third generation, and then the chain was broken, and no more passing it on, so with the death of my grandma, I thought this disease had ended. Long before her passing, I recall that as a child, before going to sleep, my sister and I prayed and cried out to God not to afflict our mother with this disease. We pleaded that it be given onto us and not to her.

There were occasions when my mother also cried because she didn't want to be affected by this disease that had destroyed her family. My mother, for the most part, possessed a very tranquil personality, but when we went to the market, she behaved rudely if she wasn't attended quickly. She was also very emotional and cried rather easily. Those are the only things I noticed that were a little off, and nothing else. We never spoke about Huntington's or the possibility of being at risk. I never really investigated anything until 1996, when my son was already two years old. I don't know why or for what reason, but I decided to ask my mom if she had already taken the HD genetic test. She responded by saying that she had, and that they had told her that she wouldn't have it.

Ahhhhhhhhh, sigh of relief.....
I didn't question anymore.....
I didn't ask anymore....
I didn't investigate anymore.....
I didn't do anything else....

My parents decided to move to Cancun, and at this time, I was already pregnant with my second child. Soon after they moved, my sister went to visit them and called me, frantic and crying. She told me that we had to take my mother with us because she was starting to get sick, and my father treated her badly…he screamed at her, insulted her by telling her to stop moving and saying to her, "You wanna dance, or what?" His tone was very aggressive, and it was obvious that this made my mom nervous. I understand that what happened to my dad is that he feared this disease. He couldn't handle it, and a long time had to pass before he could really thoroughly understand it.

When my mother returned from Cancun, I saw that she really was beginning to get sick. She still had the will to continue forward, to continue working, and she didn't feel any different. She used to ask us if we noticed anything, and I used to just ask her if she felt anything. Her denial was obvious, and so I used to go along with it and tell her that I couldn't notice anything and that she was well. At this time, we still didn't have any scientific diagnosis that led us towards HD. We took her to the only place in Mexico where a diagnosis could be made. It took them three months to give us the results, and yes, they give you the results as if they're giving you someone's phone number. In a very cold way, they told us, "Yes, she has Huntington's. She has 55 repetitions. Any doubts or questions?" We replied, "Doubts, no doubts….We know what Huntington's is because we lived it with my grandma."

……UFFFF! I started contemplating the possibility that I was at risk for HD, and in turn, my two children were also at risk. After thinking about it, my sister and I decided to get tested. I thought that I could handle any diagnosis; I thought I was prepared for any result. I never really thought about my husband's reaction or that of my brother-in-law. I never really considered whether my sister was prepared for a diagnosis of this magnitude. But who could really ever be prepared? To be honest, I never really thought about what would occur with all this. The only thing on my mind was to come out of the obscurity of doubt and find out whether or not I had the HD gene.

And my children???? No!!! Please!!! That was what tore me apart, to think about what I was condemning them to, to think that there was the possibility that they would have to care for me if I was sick. Other thoughts also came to mind...would my husband at some time not see me as his wife, but as a person that he must care for? What if I allowed him to leave in order for him to find someone that is healthy? What if I found a good woman for him? How should I tell my kids about what is happening? I also contemplated not saying anything and playing it off until the symptoms would start appearing. But I couldn't stay quiet!!! I wouldn't be doing the correct thing for myself and for them!!!!

I searched for a thousand answers. Some told me that it was a curse, that it was karma, that it was because of what I'd done in my past lives. Some others went as far as to say it was a family curse because of murders, rapes, and abortions that were deep, dark, hidden family secrets. So many theories just confused me more and more.

Now, with the passing of time, I have found answers in many places and have found this to be the best medicine for the mind. Now I don't search for an answer to, "Why me?"; I search for an answer to, "What is the purpose of my having HD?" Every time I meet someone with the disease or with the HD-positive diagnosis, I understand the reason it's me.

Somehow, I am grateful now with Huntington's disease because, thanks to Huntington's, my life has changed a lot, and it has been for the better. I'm trying to be a better human being every day, a better wife, a better daughter, a better sister, and a better friend. Although I have a lot to work on, I know I'm on the road not of perfection, but to being a better human being, to understanding people who are going through this experience, and all I can say to them is not to be afraid, that this is a disease, but there are some worse ones. You can prepare yourself and occupy yourself in order to be prepared when the time comes, but in the meantime, you are alive and there is no time to lose; every minute, every second counts. Every day that I wake up, all I can say is thank God that I'm well today. I don't know how I will be tomorrow because nobody knows what tomorrow will bring, but today I am well. Today I am happy with what I have, and I cannot waste a moment!!!! Happy to love, live, feel, smell, walk, talk, think, woowwwww, many gifts that many others cannot see and take for granted!!! I LOVE LIFE as it is; it is perfect!!!!

Of course, I wouldn't choose to get sick, but if that's the case, be it by genetics, karma, or any other reason this occurs, let it be; my essence will not change. Perhaps I'll be in a useless body, but as for my being, my light, I will never lose what I am or who I am, no matter what.

I have worked hard so that my children and my beloved husband do not see this disease in fear or anger, so that they see it without judgement, because that's the way life is. My family has been touched by Huntington's ... then let us work, and let's take care of Huntington's. There will be others afflicted by Parkinson's, cancer, etc. I had to talk to my children, who were 18 and 11 years old at the time, and tell them that they are now at risk and should not have babies while a diagnosis has not been made, and if they come out positive, it is better not to have babies, or to have them responsibly, or to adopt. HD Awareness starts first with my family and then society in general. Educating people about Huntington's disease is the first step, and teaching them that it's preventable is the next step.

Making a conscious effort to understand that there needs to be a change is the first step. If we all put some sort of interest into making a difference, we could start having conversations about eradicating this disease in very high percentages. Knowing that you are HD-positive and wanting to continue having children is a crime, in my opinion. There are ways to have children, through adoption or through IVF (in-vitro fertilization), without passing along the gene.

I don't know any human being that doesn't seek happiness, and we have to understand that happiness consists of those instances in which you decide to be happy. It doesn't matter what is happening around you; you decide to be happy or not. In everything there is a positive and negative side; which side will you choose for your life?

You know that those people who survived Hitler's Holocaust did so because they knew that someday what they were experiencing would end, that when they left the concentration camps, they would be reunited with family members. Even though many of them did not find anyone when they were released, the meaning of life helped them survive. It gave them hope that everything would be all right once all this was over. That's what gave meaning to their life. In my situation, knowing that we are closer to a cure or treatment because researchers and doctors are working hard gives me hope. I trust in them wholeheartedly that someday there will be a treatment or a cure, and that gives meaning to my life.

At one time, I asked myself what I could do for others. How could I do something to help people like myself that seek help? Then I came across something that for many might seem like mere words, but when I heard them, it was something that moved my heart. We all need love, we want love, but love without action is useless! That's why today, "Love in Action" is my motto. I decided to start an organization where everything we do is based on putting Love in Action. We walk in other people's shoes and see how we could improve their quality of life.

I created **Fundacion Huntington Mexico** in 2011, in order to assist and help people with Huntington's disease and their relatives. It is calculated that in Mexico there are more than 12,000 cases of people suffering from Huntington's, and there are 36,000 who are at risk of inheriting the HD gene. It is estimated that the number of those who are sick could increase to 90,000 people if we don't work on prevention. The primary functions of the foundation are to disseminate information about Huntington's, to support and help those affected by Huntington's and their families, to find different ways to prevent the disease, and to generate clinical investigations and help find the cure.

The lack of information about Huntington's in general and the lack of information specifically in the diagnosis represent a great challenge for the Foundation that demands many aspects that must be understood. With a good strategic plan, it is possible for us to reach our objective of educating people about prevention and rendering support and help to improve the quality of life to those who have been already diagnosed.

Our mission is to work for emotional, physical, and mental health of the human being by helping patients and their families improve their quality of life. We work on raising awareness and informing people about what Huntington's disease is and that even being diagnosed with HD is a great opportunity to transform and bring out the best of yourself. We are working to be the leading organization in the Mexican Republic in broadcasting, care, prevention and treatment of Huntington's disease. Our values are love, commitment, honesty, loyalty, and gratitude.

I am currently working on a campaign called STOP HUNTINGTON'S where the goal is to gather all the possible countries to join this movement in order to work together to prevent Huntington's. I created an initiative in which March 12th is celebrated as THE INTERNATIONAL DAY FOR THE PREVENTION OF HUNTINGTON'S and persuaded the National Lottery to print more than 10 million lottery tickets with the image and information of the STOP HUNTINGTON'S initiative as part of the dissemination in order to reach as many people as possible in Mexico.

A genetics laboratory has given us In-Vitro treatments with pre-implantation diagnosis (IVF-PGD) in order to work on prevention and also to fulfill the dream of having children for many couples who decided NOT to have children for fear of passing the disease to their babies. The IVF-PGD treatment was not previously known in Mexico, and it is extremely expensive, but through my foundation, it is now possible for families to prevent passing HD to the next generation by taking advantage of IVF-PGD. I've had talks with the Ministry of Health, achieving an important partnership that focuses on working on prevention and on improving the quality of life of HD patients.

Don't ever forget that the patient, be it your mom, dad, brother, sister, or any other person that is going through this experience, is still a human being that feels, that needs a lot of love. That is Love in Action! Whatever happens, you have to continue going forward, and if you do it from the bottom of your heart and with a smile on your face, that will make it easier on everyone!!

Life continues with Huntington's, without Huntington's and in spite of Huntington's!!

Thank you, life, for giving me so much!!!!

—∿—

Please consider making a donation to Fundacion de Huntington, a nonprofit organization. If you want to help us with a donation, the account number is:

Banamex 3467290, Branch 7007
Bank Code: 002180700734672906 (for bank transfers)

Web page: www.fundacionhuntington.org
Facebook: https://www.facebook.com/FHuntingtonMX?fref=ts
(By clicking "LIKE" you are helping us tremendously!)
Twitter: #FhuntingtonMX

About Sharon McClellan Thomason

Sharon McClellan Thomason was born in Georgia in October, 1952. She has lived in south Florida and in Louisiana, and currently lives in Tallahassee, Florida, with her son, a dog, and two cats. She earned her B.S. in English Education and M.A. in English from Florida State University. After teaching English, journalism, and hospital homebound classes in the public schools for 38 years, Sharon retired in June, 2013. During her tenure as a teacher, she also worked for the *Tallahassee Democrat* as a copy editor and as a Newspaper in Education consultant. She has also done freelance writing, editing, and page design. Sharon first learned about Huntington's disease over 30 years ago and has been hoping and praying for a cure ever since. In June of 2011, Sharon started a Huntington's disease support group in Tallahassee that serves northwest Florida and southwest Georgia. She is the managing editor and a contributing writer for Help 4 HD International's online newspaper, *The Huntington's Post*, and serves as a regional advocate for "We Have a Face." Sharon is also the Community Education Manager for Help 4 HD International and was the point person for an effort to educate law enforcement officers about HD at the International Association of Chiefs of Police conference in 2013. Sharon loves animals, traveling, music, books, cooking, and gardening. She is passionate about raising awareness for Huntington's disease and believes that regenerative medicine holds the key to a cure for both HD and Juvenile Huntington's Disease. Her greatest joy is her son.

CHAPTER 11

Into the Storm

By Sharon McClellan Thomason

A loud clap of thunder literally shook the church as Paul and I walked arm-in-arm up the aisle to the tune of "Mendelssohn's Wedding March." Family and friends laughed nervously, while Paul grinned at me and whispered, "Don't worry, Shug. It's just a little thunder bumper." I smiled back at him and held his arm a little tighter, not knowing just how ominous that July thunderstorm really was.

I was so in love, and Paul was everything I had dreamed of in a husband. He was smart and funny and friendly and handsome and charming and generous to a fault. When I first met him, I thought he was the cutest, sweetest thing I'd ever laid eyes on. His sparkling green eyes and big smile could just make me melt. He'd grown up on a farm and had such good, solid values—a strong work ethic, a love for family and children and animals, and a respect for nature. He'd fought for our country as a door gunner in Vietnam. He'd jokingly said that those guys didn't wear their helmets; they sat on them to protect other things. He'd been drafted and went to Vietnam because that was what was expected of him, not because he wanted to go. He came back with a bunch of medals that he gave to his little brother, who was twelve years younger than Paul, but never talked about 'Nam. He loved to read, and he wrote beautiful poetry. He was a man's man, too, a master hunter and fisherman, and he could fix just about anything. We loved the same music, the same books, the same styles, the same everything. Being with Paul was fun! We went fishing and went to concerts and went horseback riding and read the same books. We watched college football games. He took me hunting with him and was surprised when he learned I could shoot. We never ran out of things to talk about. We enjoyed playing games. We visited family and friends, which always turned into a party of sorts. The only complaint I had was that he wouldn't dance—said he couldn't, that he had two left feet. Those were the halcyon years.

When Paul asked me to marry him (on a phone call because he couldn't wait till he saw me in person), he was working as a "company man" for an oil and gas company on an offshore oil rig. He ran the operations on the rig, made a good salary, and had good benefits, including a company car. When he came home from the oil fields, he'd buy a bunch of steaks and take them to his cousin's house in Pleasant Home and grill them there. He'd bring a toy to his cousin's little girl, and she'd always say that when she grew up, she was going to marry him. We spent a lot of time with his cousins, and I learned that he'd been the catcher on the Pleasant Home High School baseball team. People told me he'd been an exceptional athlete, absolutely fearless, with a warrior spirit. Everyone loved him, and he was probably the most unselfish person I'd ever known. He told me that after we got married, I could go back to college and become a lawyer, or I could just stay at home, or I could keep teaching—whatever I wanted to do was fine by him, as long as it made me happy.

By the time Paul and I got married, we'd known each other for years. He'd grown up in the same small farming community where my uncle owned a farm, and my first cousin, Elizabeth, and Paul's first cousin had been sweethearts since she was fourteen. By the time we started dating, he'd just recently come home from Vietnam and moved into his daddy's house with a couple of other guys, one of them Elizabeth's boyfriend. They eventually got married, and Paul and I went our separate ways, living about 200 miles apart. Then Elizabeth and her husband moved back to the Pleasant Home area, and she set Paul and me up on a date. By this time, we lived even further apart—Paul was working in Louisiana, and I was working in Florida, but we talked on the phone every day, met as often as possible in Alabama, and when he'd get a good chunk of time off, he'd come see me in Florida.

About a month before we got married in 1983, Paul lost his job. The oil company had fired him because of "people and paperwork" problems. Nobody could understand that. Paul got along with *everybody*; in fact, he never met a stranger, and he'd give the shirt off his back to anyone who needed anything. As one of his cousins said, Paul ruled the roost because everybody liked him, and looked up to him, and wanted his approval. I remember him telling me that people couldn't resist Paul's smile, that he had a smile like Jack Kennedy, and that he'd been blessed with a personality that just attracted folks. Another cousin had told me that in almost every situation in life, Paul strove to do the right thing, and that he was rock solid under pressure or stress. Losing a job because of "people problems" just made no sense at all. Paperwork problems, maybe, but how bad could that be? Certain that Paul would land another job quickly, we went ahead with the wedding. I got a job teaching in Louisiana, where Paul was living, although the job was in a different parish. We moved from Lafayette, where Paul lived, to Church Point, where I'd be teaching; after all, if he was going to be working on oil rigs, he'd have to drive to jobs anyway.

Before we got married, Paul had told me he was at risk for Huntington's disease. I'd met everyone in his family—mother, stepdad, brothers, in-laws, cousins, aunts, uncles, nieces, nephews—but none of them had the disease, and no one talked about it. The only thing I knew was that it caused chorea, and I thought I could deal with that. After all, I reasoned, if I loved someone who had cancer, I wouldn't NOT marry that person just because he was sick. We agreed, though, that we wouldn't have children because of the risk of passing the disease on to any kids we might have. I knew that Paul's father had died in a nursing home, that he'd been one of 16 kids, and that 12 of them had had HD. I'd even been with him to a funeral for one of his uncles who had died from HD. No one talked about the disease, though, just about good times and good memories of his uncle.

Soon after we married, Paul found another job in the oil industry, this time as a mud logger, which was a few steps down from being a company man, but he was happy to have the job, happy to be back out on the rigs. The only downside was the work schedule. He was supposed to work two weeks on and one week off, but that would often change at the drop of a hat. He put me in charge of the finances, telling me that he just couldn't keep track of money. I knew how generous he was and that money flowed through his hands like water, so that was fine with me, until he started getting angry if there wasn't enough money for him to spend on whatever impulse he might have.

Paul also drank heavily and sloppily, to the point of passing out and having blackouts. It wasn't daily, and he didn't drink when he was out on the rigs or in bars, but it was soon evident that alcohol was a really big problem. His favorite thing to do when he was home was to watch "Monday Night Football" and drink a bottle of Crown Royal. I'd be trying to sleep, having to get up early and teach the next day, and I'd hear him going back and forth to the kitchen, getting ice out of the freezer, fixing drinks, and I'd hear the TV and his whooping and hollering over the plays being made. One night, it finally got real quiet, and I thought he'd finally passed out. Once that happened, I'd go turn off the TV. This night, though, he'd passed out with his knees on the floor, his head on the sofa, and a cigarette cupped underneath him. The sofa underneath him, where the cigarette was touching it, was on fire. I started yelling, "Paul, the sofa's on fire! Wake up! You could've burned the house down!" That woke him up. He looked at me with crazed eyes and started attacking me. He broke my glasses, tore my nightgown, and ripped pieces of hair from my head. I got away from him and ran next door to our landlady's house. I knew if I waited long enough, he'd pass out again, so I eventually went back to our house, peeked in the windows to make sure he was asleep, and crept back in. We'd only been married a month, and all I could think was, "What have I gotten myself into?" The next day, though, he had no memory of anything that had happened and was *so* apologetic. He said he wouldn't drink so much anymore.

That promise didn't last long.

I started going to Al-Anon, learning the principles of "Let go and let God," "One day at a time," "How important is it?" and "Let it begin with me." I learned the Serenity Prayer—"God, grant me the serenity to accept the things I cannot change, the courage to change the things I can, and the wisdom to know the difference." These became words that would guide me through the journey of more than just an alcoholic's wife. I just didn't know yet what that other journey would be.

A couple of months later, I was in the bedroom, talking to a friend on the phone. Paul was drinking heavily again, and he became very angry at me for being on the phone. He threw a heavy ashtray at my head and missed. I ran from the house to the next door neighbor's and called the police, who came and picked him up. After they had left, with Paul in the back of the police car, I went back home, put my cat Charlie in his carrier, packed some clothes and toiletries for the night, and went to spend the night with an Al-Anon friend. I called the police department to ask what they were going to do with Paul. They said they'd give him a bunch of black coffee, sober him up, and send him home so he could drive to his offshore job early the next morning. He had to be on the road by 4:00 a.m. The next morning, I went back home to get ready for work. When I walked in the house, it looked like a bomb had exploded in our living room. Potted plants had been thrown against the wall and broken, and shards and dirt were everywhere. Pictures had been pulled from the wall and smashed against the floor, adding shattered glass to the destruction. Knickknacks lay in broken pieces. Photographs of Charlie were ripped to shreds and lay on the floor amidst all the debris.

I was so distraught, trembling and crying and wondering where to turn. I called in sick to work and called a friend who lived in a town about 30 miles from us. Her husband had worked offshore with Paul, and they'd become good friends, and so had we. She came immediately, cleaned up the mess, and took Charlie and me back to her house, where I stayed for the next three days. After that respite, I felt strong enough to return home and go back to work. In the meantime, I'd consulted an attorney about laws governing separations and divorces in Louisiana. I went home and had been there about five minutes when Paul called. He told me he'd been sent home early from the job, and said, "I'm in New Orleans and need to know whether to turn right and go to Mother's or turn left and come home." I told him he could come home, and we'd talk. That night, he agreed to go into treatment for alcoholism.

The next day, we went to a rehab center about an hour away from where we lived, and we signed up for a couples' outpatient program. They were so willing to work with us and with Paul's schedule, allowing us to come to meetings on nights when Paul was home from work rather than the regular weekly schedule. We completed the program six months later, and Paul never drank again—except once, years later. He continued working offshore, though jobs were getting few and far between. There continued to be occasional violent outbursts of anger, but I was told those were "dry drunks"—when an alcoholic exhibits alcoholic behavior, without having had anything to drink. I kept applying the principles I'd learned in Al-Anon and continued to go to weekly meetings and focused on remembering that alcoholism was a *disease*, not a *choice*. I reminded myself often that I'd taken vows: in sickness or in health, for better or worse. I was determined to keep those vows and focused on the good times—and there were so many! We laughed, we played, we traveled, we entertained, we fished, and we talked about our dreams for the future. Little did I know that those dreams would all be stolen away from us.

While Paul was working offshore in the fall of 1984, he read the Ochsner Clinic Report in the *New Orleans Times Picayune,* which said an exciting new discovery had made it possible to detect whether a fetus had Huntington's disease. We both wanted children, but had agreed not to have any until we knew whether Paul had HD. This opened up a whole new possibility but also carried serious implications: if the fetus had HD, that meant Paul (who hadn't been diagnosed) had HD. Were we ready to handle that news if it came? If the fetus had HD, were we prepared to abort? We thoroughly discussed everything and decided to go ahead and try to get pregnant.

Within less than a month, I was pregnant! I took the home pregnancy test and came out of the bathroom with the stick, beaming. I made a doctor's appointment and had to wait a whole weekend to get the results of my pregnancy test there! I thought I'd never waited so long for anything in my life—it felt longer than a child waiting for Santa Claus! I called the Ochsner Clinic as soon as I had my pregnancy test results confirmed by the doctor, only to be told that the information that had appeared in the paper was erroneous; while some conditions could now be detected through this new procedure called chorionic villus sampling, HD was not one of them. Now we faced a whole different set of decisions.

When I told my mother-in-law I was pregnant, she said, "Oh, I wish y'all wouldn't do that."

Our friends in AA and Al-Anon encouraged us to have faith in God and have the baby, and we both wanted a child so much—many, if possible—so we decided to take a leap of faith. We were both so excited and had so much fun fixing up a nursery and buying baby stuff. One of the Cajun women did the "nail-on-a-string" test and predicted I was having a boy. An ultrasound confirmed it. Our beautiful, perfectly healthy son was born in August 1985. Paul was in love with that boy from the moment he was born. He was *so* proud of him, reveling in every new and wonderful thing he did, bathing and dressing and feeding him, even changing dirty diapers—something not many men did back then! He thought the sun rose and set on our baby boy and bragged about him to anyone who would listen. Paul loved to talk, and talk he did. He always had a story to tell about our boy and his amazing achievements.

Then the oil industry took a big hit in 1985, and Paul ended up being out of work most of the time. I was on maternity leave, which was leave without pay for six weeks. We were broke with no help in sight. One day, I drove to the parish seat to apply for food stamps. We were turned down because we owned a one-year-old truck. I went to a Catholic food bank and was able to get some staples (milk, bread, cheese) that I brought home, only to discover that Paul had just bought $100 worth of garbage bags while I was gone practically begging for food! I just about had a stroke when he grinned rather sheepishly and told me that a kid had been selling them door-to-door as a fundraiser, and he'd just wanted to help the boy. That was the first of many extravagant purchases, though certainly not the last.

Finally, with no work for Paul in sight, we decided to move back to Florida and live with my parents until we got on our feet. When our son was 10 months old, we made the big move. I got a teaching job, and Paul immediately found work, driving for Wells Fargo, a 200-mile round trip twice a day. He had such a strong work ethic and was so proud to be providing for his family that he couldn't see that he was actually losing money rather than making money—until it came time to do our taxes six months later. When Paul saw in black and white what I'd been trying to tell him, he quit that job and started applying for other jobs. In the meantime, he'd had several wrecks in the truck while making that long drive twice each day. Soon, he had another job with a pest control company. That lasted a few months—I can't remember why he lost that job—and then he went to work with a boat manufacturing company.

I had withdrawn all the money from my retirement account in Louisiana, and after living with Mamma and Daddy for six months and saving up more money, we used that to put a down payment on a house financed with Paul's VA loan. We moved into our house just in time for Christmas of 1986, and set about making it a home. I started noticing that Paul's toes were twitching oddly and that he was dropping and spilling a lot of things.

One day, I was reading the local paper and saw a notice for an HD support group meeting in Thomasville, a small Georgia town about 30 miles away. Paul and I decided to go and were instantly welcomed by a very warm and loving group of people that included two men with HD (one about Paul's age), a young lady who was at risk, several caregivers, and a few friends who were there simply to support those of us dealing with HD. The instant connection and the warm welcome I felt there reminded me of the feeling I'd gotten from my Al-Anon group in Louisiana. Here were people who GOT it. We could talk about Paul's family history and his behavior and our fears. We took our son with us to the monthly meetings, and we'd all go out to eat afterwards. I started hearing about Bob's behavior (the man who was Paul's age), and it sounded a lot like Paul's. I saw that neither Bob nor Joe (the elderly man with HD) had the chorea that I'd always thought was the hallmark of the disease. I began to get really scared.

In 1988, the woman who'd started our support group helped us set up an appointment at a Center of Excellence in Atlanta and even drove us to the appointment. We met with a social worker, a psychiatrist, and a neurologist. The neurologist did a standard clinical exam and an MRI on Paul. The social worker and psychiatrist took a family history and talked to me about Paul's behaviors. I told them that he'd just lost his job with the boat manufacturing company because he kept falling off the boats he was helping to build. I told them about his problems with managing money and his anger outbursts. I told them about the history of alcoholism. There was no genetic test yet, but at the end of the day, Paul was diagnosed with Huntington's disease, based on family history, the MRI, and symptoms I'd described. Paul had a mood disturbance with anger issues, a few odd twitches and a bit of clumsiness, but he didn't have full-blown chorea. Nevertheless, he had HD.

The next day, I went back to work, and in the planning room at school, confiding to my department head what had happened, I broke down in sobs. She sent me home for the rest of the day. Paul had started a job as a hall monitor at the same school where I taught, and his legs would just about give out at the end of a day of walking the halls. The kids loved him. I remember one of my girls telling me, "Mrs. Thomason, he's a fox!" Two weeks later, Social Security approved him for disability, and he was able to quit. I thought that without the stress of working, things at home would get better. Paul would be able to care for our son at home instead of paying for daycare. He wouldn't do that, though, and insisted that we keep him in daycare, despite the strain on our budget. He decided, responsibly, to have a vasectomy so that we wouldn't have any more children who'd be at risk for HD.

Over the next two years, Paul, still a recovering alcoholic, became harder and harder to live with. There were many episodes of angry outbursts and violence that I attributed to dry drunks. HD never entered my mind because no one had ever said anything about symptoms other than chorea. Finally, some of that anger and violence turned against our son. Paul got mad at him for not picking up his toys and grabbed him around the neck and picked him up. Our son was left with a mark around his neck, so I took him to the doctor, who reported the incident to child protective services. They came to our house and investigated, but closed the case file.

Another time, I came home from school to find that Paul had sent our son off somewhere with a woman he'd met in AA. He didn't know where they'd gone, when they'd be back, or the woman's last name. This was before the days of cell phones, and he had no phone number or address for her. He'd also given her some of my clothes. I was frantic. Eventually, though, the woman returned, and I had my baby safe in my arms again. I didn't know what to do. Paul was sick; how could I leave him? Life at home had become dangerous; how could I stay with him? I kept thinking of my marriage vows, especially "in sickness and in health."

I struggled to find an answer. We went to marriage counseling, and the counselor tried to help us develop some strategies to defuse situations instead of getting angry. One day, I shared something with the counselor, and he looked at me with the most startled expression and said, "My God. I've been telling you to be flexible and bend over backwards, and you're already bending so far backwards, the back of your head's touching the floor!"

The last Christmas we were together, Paul brought home a bottle of Crown Royal, drank it, and fell into the Christmas tree and on top of all the packages, crushing them. I called my sister to come and get our son so that he wouldn't see his daddy in that condition. I kept going back again and again to what I'd learned in Al-Anon, but I didn't know how much more I could take. I had started working two and three jobs, in addition to teaching, to try and make ends meet, as well as taking on all of the household responsibilities and the care and responsibility for our son. Paul and I went to church regularly, and I prayed for God to show me what I was supposed to do. One night, I dreamed that we were all in a boat on a river, and the boat sank. I floated to the bottom of the riverbed, thinking how peaceful it felt to just lie there. Then, in my dream, I saw our son sinking down through the water, and I realized that he couldn't swim and that I had to get up off that riverbed and save him from drowning. When I woke up, I knew that I had to get the two of us out of that situation.

Little did I know that Paul had already started looking for an apartment and had found a lawyer friend in AA to help him get a divorce and gain custody of our son. I found a lawyer, too, a wonderful woman who was so compassionate and would make sure that Paul was going to be okay after the divorce. We divorced in 1990. I made payments on a mobile home we bought for Paul to live in, paid him alimony, and I got a monthly disability check for our son. We had shared custody. There were many times when I feared that our son wasn't safe with his daddy, but I had nothing definitive, just a gut feeling. When our son was with his daddy, I'd call Paul's home to talk to our son and tell him good night, and Paul would say things like, "He's dead." He'd show up at our house right at bedtime and get our son all keyed up, roughhousing with him. He'd neglect to bring him home when he was supposed to. He'd take him hunting and fishing, and guns and boats and Paul's driving just absolutely scared me to death.

One night, I got a phone call from Paul. He and our five-year-old son had been fishing that day, and Paul said our son had been injured. He had a bad gash on his forehead, across his nose, and Paul didn't know what to do. I told Paul to take him to the emergency room, and I'd meet them there. When I got there, Paul walked across the parking lot, carrying our child in his arms. My baby was bleeding, pale, and he stretched his little arms out toward me. I grabbed him and rushed into the hospital. He was in shock, and he'd been cut so badly that they had to call in a plastic surgeon to repair the damage to his face. Paul told me that he'd let him, a five-year-old child, start the outboard motor. He'd given it so much gas that the force had thrown him out of the seat against a jagged-edged aluminum rod holder in the boat.

After that, I went back to court and got an order for supervised visitation. Either Paul's brother (two years younger than Paul) or mother would supervise Paul's visits with our son; that way, our son could still spend nights and weekends and vacations with his daddy, as long as the brother or mother was there. Paul was no longer supposed to drive with our son in the car, nor was he allowed to have guns around him. My mother told me not to ever say anything bad about Paul to or in front of our son because Paul would always be a part of who he was. That was advice I heeded, although sometimes I had to bite my tongue so hard I thought it would bleed.

The next several years were rough. Paul was very angry at me and told our son horrible things that just weren't true. He would tell him, "I'm going to *kill* your mother."

Paul would show up at our son's elementary school and try to take him. Of course, they knew not to allow him to leave with Paul, but that just made Paul angry. At our son's first grade Christmas party, Paul—ever so generous—embarrassed everyone but himself by bringing a sexy teddy for our son's teacher. She was mortified when she told me about opening the lingerie in front of the kids and the parents who were there. I didn't know that this behavior was part of HD, too.

I wasn't allowed to set foot on his or his mother's property. He deliberately bashed in the trunk of a new car I'd bought. Paul told our son, when he was eight, that he needed to be nice to his daddy because one day, he (our son) might have this disease, too. He kidnapped him one Christmas Eve day, and I kept sewing and crying, hoping and praying that Paul would come to his senses and bring our son home. Finally, he did. Our son started having nightmares, and I stopped advising the school newspaper so that I could spend more time with our son and take him to counseling. Then one day, Paul just took off, and for about a year, he wandered the country, staying with friends and family and living in his car. Friends would call me and say, "We love Paul, but we can't get him to leave. What do we do?" We never knew where he would turn up next.

Meanwhile, I kept up payments on the mobile home and gave the alimony checks to his brother, who would deposit them in Paul's account. Finally, Paul moved in with his mother, Gwen. She was also taking care of his youngest brother, who appeared to have the juvenile onset of HD. Eventually, Paul stopped being so angry at me, and I was able to stay at his mother's house. The three of us were able to do things together again, as a family. We'd go to a movie or the beach or the video arcade, out to eat or to get ice cream. We celebrated birthdays and holidays together. Finally, we could be a semblance of the family we'd started out wanting to be.

In 1999, we got word that Paul had been placed in a psychiatric hospital in Pensacola. Gwen told me that he'd started wandering at night and had been picked up by the police in the middle of the highway and had also been reported for "stalking" around neighbors' houses at night. He'd also stopped eating and was losing a lot of weight. From the psychiatric hospital, he was discharged to a nursing home in Panama City, where a feeding tube was inserted. We would make the 100-mile trip as often as possible to visit him there. Over the next five years, he was moved to a nursing home in Destin and then in Milton, FL, closer to his mother, who visited him every week in Panama City and in Destin, and then every day in Milton, but each move put him farther from us. Still, we visited him regularly, celebrated birthdays and holidays together, either in the nursing home or at his mother's home, and I remained involved in his care as much as I could from that distance.

In January 2003, Paul's younger brother, the same age as me, was fired from his state job. He'd been diagnosed with HD a few years earlier, and his symptoms were interfering with his ability to work. His boss assured him that they'd help him get on disability. He came over to our house and asked if he could stay with us, and then he asked if he could sleep in my bed with me. I told him no!!! He wasn't thinking or talking rationally, and I called his oldest brother, the only one of the four siblings without HD, to tell him what was going on and that I was worried. The brother told him he should go to his mother's for a few days, so he did. The next day, while she was taking their stepdad to the doctor, he went into the bathroom, climbed into the bathtub, wrapped himself in the shower curtain, and shot himself. We were all devastated.

My son and I drove to the nursing home and picked Paul up to take him to the funeral. By then, he was incontinent, was in a wheelchair, and was having a lot of trouble speaking. During the funeral, he began shaking so badly that we were afraid he was going to fall out of his wheelchair. Our son and I each got on one side of the wheelchair to hold him in there. After the funeral, I left our son with his grandmother and uncle in Alabama and took Paul back to Destin. On the way back to the nursing home, we were driving down a country road in Alabama, farmland on both sides of us.

Paul said he needed to go to the bathroom. I stopped in a field and pulled down his pants and his diaper. Right at that moment, a farmer came along in his truck, driving across the field and pulling two horses behind the truck. I was mortified because there was Paul in all his glory, peeing in the man's field! The farmer just waved at us and kept going, though. We got back in the car and continued toward Destin.

About 15 miles later, Paul said to me, "I used to pick cotton there."

By then, there was no farmland in sight, so I had no idea what he was talking about. When I shared the comment with his older brother later, though, I learned that he'd been talking about the field we'd stopped in so that Paul could pee—Paul had picked cotton for that farmer, the one who'd driven by and waved at us. It had just taken 15 miles for Paul to be able to formulate the thought and put it into words and tell me about it.

Later that year, in June 2003, our son graduated from high school. It was Paul's proudest moment, and there was no way he was going to miss that ceremony! Paul's older brother brought him over here for graduation, Paul lying in the back of his SUV for the trip. Once he was here, I fed Paul through his feeding tube, and then we headed to the Civic Center for graduation. As a senior homeroom teacher, I was on stage and was allowed to call our son's name and hand him his diploma. I'd had Paul wheeled to the foot of the stage so that he could see everything, and when our son walked down the stairs after getting his diploma, he ran to his daddy and gave him a huge hug. There wasn't a dry eye on that stage. Even the stoic history teacher seated next to me welled up. After the ceremony, our son wheeled his dad through the crowd and proudly introduced him to all his friends and teachers.

Throughout high school, our son had struggled with depression and with problems with testing. When he'd started having so much trouble with tests his junior year, I'd had him evaluated at the Florida State University psychiatric testing and evaluation center. His IQ still tested in the gifted range, but tests showed he was having trouble transferring information from short term to long term memory. He'd missed much of his senior year, too sick to go to school, and inexplicable problems with sleeping (sometimes insomnia, sometimes oversleeping), but no one could figure out what was wrong with him. He kept up with his classwork only because his amazing teachers were willing to send his work home and allow me to bring it back to them when it was completed. Still, he managed to graduate with honors and earned a Bright Futures Scholarship. We were so proud of him, our wonderful son who was bright and artistic and compassionate and giving and musically talented. For the Senior Showcase, he'd surprised me by directing the school's symphonic band in playing an arrangement he'd written for Queen's "Bohemian Rhapsody." Little did I know at the time that his future would not be so bright.

After graduation, our son turned 18. In counseling for depression, he decided that he wanted to have the genetic test for Huntington's. I did not want to know and wasn't sure it was such a good idea, but I promised him I'd support him in whatever he ultimately decided to do. In January 2004, we made the trip to the Center of Excellence in Atlanta. He met with the same psychiatrist his daddy had seen all those years earlier and convinced her that he was fully prepared to find out his genetic status, either way. She ordered the blood draw that same day, and afterwards, he and I went out for a nice dinner. A month later, we got his results: positive for HD, with a CAG of 45. My world shattered. Three of my friends had gone with us to get the results. Upon hearing the news, I collapsed into the arms of one of our friends. All of us cried, including the psychiatrist. All except my beautiful boy. He started calling his close friends and sharing the news with them, insisting that he was okay. Our family doctor knew about the appointment, and she called me as we were leaving the Center of Excellence to find out what we'd learned. I sobbed as I gave her the devastating news. I will always be grateful for her thoughtfulness and compassion.

After our son was given his test results, we rocked along without any big changes for several months. He insisted that no one tell his daddy that he'd had the genetic test, much less tested positive; he was emphatic about not letting Paul know. Such a gift, not inflicting this pain on his daddy.

He started college that fall. Then, on September 16, Hurricane Ivan decimated northwest Florida as a Category 3 storm, having been downgraded from a Cat 5. By then, Paul was in the nursing home in Milton, along with his youngest brother, and they had been evacuated further inland because of the impending storm. Paul's mother, stepdad, and older brother and his family had evacuated as well. The 20-foot storm surge covered Gwen's home, destroying everything. The shelter to which Paul and his brother had been evacuated lost power when the storm hit further inland than expected, and Paul developed pneumonia. He was taken by ambulance to an emergency room in a nearby town, given antibiotics, and sent back to the temporary shelter. There, he quickly worsened, and was sent back to the hospital. We went to see him, were somewhat reassured about his condition, and returned home the next day. I talked to his mother daily, and she told me he was going to be okay.

Then, about a week later, I heard from his aunt. She told me that Gwen didn't want to admit it, but Paul was probably not going to make it. I took our son back over there, and he stayed with his daddy until he passed away on October 1. With our son sitting right next to him, Paul fought so hard not to leave his precious son; he coded twice and came back, and then the third time, he just couldn't fight his way back. Our son planned and paid for his daddy's funeral, and he was so happy that Paul had passed without finding out that his only child carried the toxic protein in his brain. The only time my son cried was when he called me to break the news. Such a strong young man, yet I knew his heart was broken.

After the funeral, my son went back to working full time. He dropped out of college because he'd missed so many days. Then he bought a house with insurance money he'd gotten when his daddy died. I was so proud of his steps toward independence and happy that he seemed determined to make a life for himself despite his devastating diagnosis. The next semester, he enrolled in college again, only to drop out when he developed a heart condition, neurocardiogenic syncope, which caused him to pass out in one of his classes and be taken by ambulance to the emergency room.

I had remarried in June of 2005, and was spending a lot of time in Panama City with my new husband, who lived there, and my son was living on his own, so I didn't see him a lot. Then I came back to Tallahassee in the fall to resume teaching and, as I saw my son more frequently, I started noticing that things didn't seem quite right. He wasn't getting his bills paid; he was drinking a lot; he was spending tons of money; he suddenly quit his job; he started using drugs; he accidentally set his house on fire; he started having paranoid delusions that included things like me trying to poison him and hiring a contract killer to kill him. A lot of his delusions had to do with sex, usually with him being a victim of sexual abuse. Finally, right before Thanksgiving, he had a psychotic break so severe that I took him to the emergency room. They admitted him to the psychiatric unit for observation and evaluation, then transferred him to the Behavioral Health Center. The psychiatrist who evaluated him had treated him for depression as a child and remembered him; she was quite puzzled by the changes she saw in him and wasn't sure what was causing these changes. She suspected that it might be from drug and alcohol abuse or possibly schizophrenia. I didn't know *what* to think, and navigating the mental health system, especially with an *adult* child was frustrating and confusing.

My sister found several articles that talked about the psychiatric symptoms of HD, and I started doing more research on the psychiatric and behavioral symptoms. I remembered the things that Paul had gone through, and how he'd gotten real suspicious of many people, just downright paranoid, and I remembered what his two brothers had gone through, and I saw distinct parallels. I remembered the inappropriate hypersexuality. Slowly, reluctantly, I started realizing that this was probably all HD. I told the doctors about this, but they said it couldn't be HD because he didn't have chorea.

After about a week, my son was released from the hospital with a prescription for Abilify. It just about made him jump out of his skin, so the doctor switched him to another atypical antipsychotic, Zyprexa. In the meantime, I'd joined some online caregivers groups, and everything people said underscored the fact that these were psychiatric symptoms of HD. I knew he had tested positive for the gene, but it was just too soon for symptoms to be starting, wasn't it? He was only 21!

When I took my son to his first outpatient appointment with the psychiatrist, I was told that if it was HD, we needed to see a neurologist. I made an appointment for him with a neurologist, who said he needed to see a psychiatrist. I felt like a ping-pong ball being bounced back and forth. This continued for several years, with trips to the psychiatric hospital about every two or three months via a Baker Act or a Marchman Act. I sent my son to several inpatient and outpatient drug and alcohol rehab programs, but he'd start drinking and/or using as soon as he got out. Then he'd stop taking his meds, and pretty soon, he'd be back in the psych ward. It was like a revolving door. Still, NO ONE would address that all of this was HD-related, until I took him to a neurologist here in town who said that he suspected my son had the juvenile form of HD, like his youngest uncle. Then I took him to the Center of Excellence in Atlanta; they wouldn't diagnose without chorea. More rehab, more psych appointments, more Baker Acts, more psychiatric hospitals, a few months in the county jail for violation of probation, several wrecks.

Quite honestly, we went through so much in those first few years that I've lost track of when things happened; it's only by looking back at copies of medical records that I can reconstruct a reasonably accurate timeline. Eventually, I took my son to the Center of Excellence in central Florida, and there, he was diagnosed with HD, with the psychiatric symptoms being an early manifestation of the disease. This was in 2009, five years after the nightmare had begun, but by no means was a diagnosis the end of the nightmare.

The trip there was a nightmare in itself. My son's girlfriend had come with us, and about midnight, she woke me up to tell me that my son had mixed alcohol and sleeping pills and had passed out and vomited, and she could not wake him up. I called the front desk of our hotel, and they called for an ambulance, which took my son to the nearest hospital. After making sure that he was going to be okay, I convinced them to keep him until I could pick him up at 8:00 a.m. to take him to his appointment. When we arrived at the Center of Excellence, neither the neurologist nor the social worker had read any of the information I'd sent weeks in advance. The doctor told him to smoke pot instead of drinking. When the doctor finally stopped to take a breath, I told him that smoking pot made my son hear voices, and that he'd know that if he'd bothered to read the records I'd sent! Then he started talking about using voices to your advantage and told us that as a young man, he'd traveled through South America, doing hallucinogens, hearing voices, and that was how he'd decided to become a neurologist. I was FURIOUS and ended up reporting him. In the end, he wrote a letter diagnosing my son with HD.

A firm diagnosis meant I could finally file for disability on my son's behalf, and I hoped it would make a difference in the treatment of his symptoms. The disability claim was denied, and the doctors here changed nothing about how they were treating my son. We appealed the disability denial and won, and finally, with one of my son's hospitalizations, he got a psychiatrist who was interested in the HD aspect and would read articles I brought him. He added Depakote and Namenda to the Zyprexa my son was taking, and for the first time, we began to see some improvement, but he still had breakthrough delusions, so the doctor added first Seroquel and then perphenazine for the breakthrough delusions.

Then came another slip into alcohol and drugs, and noncompliance with his meds. One night, he asked me to take him to the hospital. On the way there, he changed his mind, grabbed the steering wheel and tried to run the car off the side of the interstate. I told him that I would get off at the next exit and did so, but I didn't turn in the direction he thought I should, so he once again grabbed the steering wheel and ran the car into the median of the road. I tried to call for help, but in a rage, he climbed across the console, grabbed my cell phone and threw it across the car. He started pushing me out of the car and slamming the door on me when I'd try to get back in and finally succeeded in pushing me completely away and taking off in the car. There I was, in the middle of a six-lane highway at midnight, no purse and no phone, miles from home. I eventually made my way home, and at 2:00 p.m. discovered my car sitting at the end of the driveway. The windshield and the windows on the driver's side had been shattered. Just as the deputies were arriving, my son came walking up the street with his bicycle, covered in dirt and leaves, and said he'd been hiding in the ditches. My heart broke for him as I saw the terror and confusion on his face.

This time, my son went to a year-long dual diagnosis program in Georgia. It was the only rehab program he went through that actually seemed to make a difference. For the 11 months he was there and for a year afterwards, he stayed clean and sober, took his meds, but still had the paranoid delusions and the cognitive problems, especially with executive functioning. By this time, I was convinced that the problems weren't caused by substance abuse; otherwise, they would have gone away. We asked his psychiatrist about switching him to Risperdal, after hearing at a national conference that it seemed to help some people with the psychiatric symptoms of HD, and that change seemed to knock out the delusions completely—but only for a while.

Finally, I found a neurologist who specialized in HD at a teaching hospital in Gainesville, much closer to us than the Centers of Excellence we'd been to. I started taking my son to see the neurologist, who confirmed that his symptoms were from HD, although the doctor said he considered my son to be in the "prodromal" stage since he didn't show any of the movement disorder. Then my son became noncompliant with his meds again.

He attempted suicide in September 2012. He wrote a suicide note and took an overdose of a variety of meds he'd stockpiled. As the drugs started to take effect, he came into my bedroom, stumbling into furniture and slurring his words, and told me what he'd done, and said that as he was lying on his bed, saying goodbye to our pets, he'd changed his mind. I called 911, and an ambulance was dispatched. By the time I met him at the ER, he was unconscious. He spent two days in the ICU in a coma, followed by some time in the Behavioral Health Center.

For a few months, he was so happy to be alive. He started taking his meds again, and he stayed clean and sober. He started working with Vocational Rehab to try and find a job. Then, in January 2013, we went to his appointment in Gainesville. When told about the noncompliance with meds ending in a suicide attempt, the psychiatrist who works with the neurologist suggested that my son be put on an injectable antipsychotic. Thus began a three-month power struggle among doctors. The psychiatrist in Gainesville wouldn't prescribe the injections because he said a local psychiatrist needed to oversee administration of the injections. The local psychiatrist wouldn't prescribe it because he said his office wasn't set up to give injections. Our primary care physician, our wonderful family doctor, said SHE would administer the injections if someone would direct her on the dosage, but neither psychiatrist would do that.

By the time we'd gone round and round about this for three months, my son had stopped taking his meds altogether and had started abusing drugs and alcohol again, worse than ever before. More Baker Acts, more hospitalizations at the Behavioral Health Center and a community mental health center, with releases after just a short stay each time. We were back to the revolving door. One afternoon, my son took off in his car and disappeared for two days, ending up in Mississippi. He missed work and was fired from a job he'd worked really hard to get. He flipped his car on the interstate and walked away without a scratch. If only that had been his much-needed wakeup call.

In May of 2013, I had him Baker Acted again on a Tuesday. By Friday, the attending psychiatrist was calling me at work to tell me she was going to release him, even though there'd been an episode of verbal abuse toward me the day before, in front of the nurses' station. I refused to come get him, and she told me she would have a friend of his come pick him up. When she told me who the friend was, I begged her not to release him, telling her that he was a danger to himself and to others, and that this "friend" was one of the people he'd just gotten into trouble with. The doctor released him anyway. I called the hospital administrator and threatened a law suit; she suggested I contact a woman who is a social worker and has a private case management service. I called her; she agreed to help and referred me to a guardianship attorney, and I started the proceedings for getting emergency temporary guardianship.

That was a Friday. On the following Tuesday, May 14, 2013, I came home from work at 5:30 p.m. and found my son, the person I love more than anyone in this world, unconscious on the deck in the back yard, slumped in a chair, his guitar at his feet. At first I thought he'd passed out from drinking or doing drugs again, but then I realized he was barely breathing. I thought my heart would stop beating. Shaking, I called 911. This time, he was in the ICU for four days, unconscious, on a respirator. When he came to, it was like he had full-blown HD, with jerky movements, an inability to hold on to things, slurred speech, and violent outbursts. He cursed at me and tried to hit me and kicked one of his nurses. As time passed, everything but the violent outbursts went away. The court granted me emergency temporary guardianship, and I initiated proceedings for full guardianship. My son was moved to a regular room, where he was under guard 24/7. From there, he was moved to the community mental health hospital; I didn't want him going back to the Behavioral Health Center that had released him when I'd begged them not to, ending with the near-fatal suicide attempt.

The mental health center released him to the dual-diagnosis program in Georgia that had been so successful before. The program didn't want to take him because he was under a guardianship order, but finally agreed to, only to kick him out two days later for smoking on campus. Back at home, he called 911 and told the dispatcher I was abusing him. The deputies, very familiar with our house, with him, and with HD by now, showed up. Before they arrived, I was talking to the case manager I'd hired, and she tried to talk to my son and calm him down, but he was wild. He ran across the yard, screaming into the phone that I was trying to attack him, screaming at me to stop beating him and kicking him. He threw the phone down, and I picked it back up. The case manager stayed on the phone with me until the deputies got there, and then she talked to them and asked them to take my son back to the Behavioral Health Center.

Because of what had happened the last time they'd released him, and because of pressure from the case manager and the guardianship attorney, they kept him this time and petitioned the court for involuntary commitment to the state mental hospital. I was scared because of the reputation the hospital had had when I was growing up and because my next-door neighbor had been sent home from there on a weekend pass and had committed suicide. I was the one who had found him. After visiting the hospital with my mom, though, I felt much better about the place, and I reassured my son that this would be a safe place for him and that they would help him to get well. The reality was that there was nowhere else left for him to go where he would be safe. The irony was that he wouldn't be safe, even there.

The state hospital was a nightmare of incompetence, lies, abuse, and cover-ups. After a month, they wanted to release my son, despite the fact that he was still delusional and had been so in front of staff. They hadn't done anything with him, other than keep him on a locked ward—no medication, no therapy. He had gradually earned day visits, which meant I could take him off the hospital campus to shop or to eat, and when I'd brought him back from a visit, he'd refused to go back upstairs to his room. They'd had to call security to take him upstairs. He'd told the staff that God and Jesus and the Holy Spirit were in the room talking to him, and didn't anyone else see them or hear them? After that, the doctor started him on the minimum dose of Risperdal injections, but they didn't touch the delusions, and the doctor wasn't trying anything else. "Art therapy" consisted of coloring pages copied out of a coloring book. There was no individual or group therapy. More than once, his clothes and shoes and books were stolen, and no one would do anything about it, other than give him raggedy clothes to wear out of a donation pile. Each time it happened, he reported the theft, and I reported it, yet every time he asked about his things that had been stolen, they would tell him, "Well, this is the first I'm hearing of it." The psychiatrist and medical doctor told me he didn't have HD. I'd requested from the time he was admitted in August that he be seen by a neurologist; that finally happened in February, and it took four more months to get a report from that visit. When the injections weren't working, but they wanted to release my son, I met with the treatment team and requested an increased dosage of Risperdal, so they started that. That wasn't the answer either.

After three months, there had been no change, and there was a new psychiatrist that I was meeting for the first time at a treatment team meeting. He walked into the room and asked me, "Do you know what chorea is? C-H-O-R-E-A," spelling it out and acting it out for me. He told me my son didn't have HD because he didn't have chorea, and he didn't have dementia. His proof? He called my son into the room and asked him what day it was, who the various staff members were, and who I was. I used it as an opportunity to give him a quick education on Huntington's, but he didn't listen. My son agreed to start taking oral medication if he could stop taking shots, so after talking with other caregivers who'd gone through similar behaviors with their loved ones, I asked the doctor to put him back on Zyprexa, Namenda, and Depakote and to stop the Risperdal injections.

The psychology resident, who was new and was appointed as my contact person, wrote to me in an email that my philosophy of HD was different from their doctors', and I would be better served finding a doctor whose philosophy was the same as mine. She also told me that if my son had HD, that was a medical illness, not a mental illness, and he shouldn't even be there. I felt like my son was lost to me forever, and no one was willing to help me try to get him back.

With the change in meds, though, my son started to improve. The delusions remained, but the angry outbursts decreased dramatically. With Namenda, he was able again to keep the normal rhythm of a conversation and seemed to be thinking more clearly. The hospital helped him file a petition to get his rights restored and remove the guardianship order, and they decided it was time to get him out of there. I'd told them from the beginning that they would have to find a secure, locked facility to discharge him to because I still wasn't convinced that I could keep him safe at home. We had another team meeting, along with the case manager I'd hired, a court-appointed psychiatrist, and members of the FACT (Florida Assertive Community Training) team, part of a community mental health program that helps patients transition to living back in the community. FACT refused to accept my son into their program, deeming him too high risk at that time.

We came up with a plan to develop a behavior contract for my son's home visits, give him progressively extended leaves of absence to come home, up to a month, and FACT agreed to reassess him after that, if he was successful. Everyone left feeling like we'd gotten a lot accomplished, and this was a plan we could work with, and my son could be successful. Two days later, we got a scathing email from the psychology resident stating that this was NOT agreed on, and this was NOT something they were set up to do. Over the next few weeks, her emails got more heated and more aggressive in tone. Then the hospital social worker found a placement for my son in an assisted living facility in Panama City. The case manager and I called and talked with the owner about the facility and learned that it was neither locked nor supervised. After the case manager told the owner about my son's record, she withdrew consent for placement. We were right back where we'd started.

July rolled around, and I flew to Houston to visit an HD caregiver friend and then on to Santa Maria, California, to attend an HD symposium hosted by Help 4 HD International. I was worried about being so far away for so long. My last day there, Sunday, July 20, my son called and told me he'd had a verbal altercation with someone on staff because the guy wouldn't give him any soap for a shower, and he was afraid he'd be punished for it. He said the shift supervisor had taken him downstairs and told him he wouldn't get in trouble as long as it didn't happen again. Monday morning, I got off the plane in Tallahassee about 11:30 a.m. and had two voice mail messages from my son when I turned my phone back on. In the first one, he said he'd met with the treatment team, and they'd told him he wasn't in trouble. The second one, about 30 minutes later, said that they'd lied and had thrown him on the closed ward and taken away all his privileges. I called him back and told him to stay calm and that I'd come see him the next day. He wanted to know why I couldn't come right then, and I explained to him that I'd been on planes and in airports since 6:30 the previous evening and could hardly hold my eyes open. I went home and went to bed, only to be awakened by a phone call about 9:30 that night. My son told me he'd been beaten by a security guard.

I immediately called an abuse hotline, which directed me to call 911. I called 911, and the dispatcher told me to call the sheriff's department in the county where the hospital is located. I called them, and they told me to call the city's police department. The cop I talked to told me the hospital had its own security force, and he'd call them to go check on things. I told him they were the ones who had supposedly beaten my son, so someone else needed to investigate. He told me he'd check into things and call me back, but never did. The next day, Tuesday, still jet-lagged and not having slept well because of my anxiety over my son, I got a social worker who works for the case manager to drive me over to the hospital to see my son. He had bruises and marks on his face and arms, so I took pictures of them with my cell phone. When I got back to Tallahassee, I took the pictures to my guardianship attorney's office. Department of Children and Families (DCF), which runs the hospital, showed up at the hospital the day after that to start an investigation. At least, they called it an investigation.

Thursday, I went back to see my son, and this time, they sent a staff member downstairs with him to watch us while we visited, something that had never happened before. My son had discovered additional bruises on his back, so I took photos of those bruises with my cell phone camera. The unit supervisor came downstairs and told me I couldn't have a camera in there. This was the first time in almost a year of visiting my son there that anyone had said anything about having a camera or taking pictures. I had brought my cell phone with me to every visit and had used it to take pictures of him and to show him pictures. No one had ever said a word—till now.

I went outside and called the hospital administrator's office. She wasn't in the office, and neither was the next in line, so the secretary told me she was sending the medical director over to talk to me. I waited outside until the medical director got there. She told me we were going to meet with the entire treatment team, something I was not prepared to do and did not expect, and told me to wait in the lobby. I sat there with my son, and we called my mother, who had just had a stroke and a heart attack while visiting my sister in Indiana and was still in the hospital. The unit supervisor came back down and told me we couldn't talk on the phone and that I would have to put my cell phone in my car. Again, this was the first time anyone had ever said anything about having or using my phone there. I was getting a real uneasy feeling about everything.

The medical director reappeared to escort me upstairs and wouldn't allow my son to meet with us. As soon as we got in the conference room, she had me sign a receipt form for a list of "contraband" items. Upon looking over it later, I could see that it was obviously a list meant for patients rather than visitors, as it included things such as a driver's license, which you have to present at the front desk as a visitor. Of course, camera and phone were on the list, too. The "meeting" consisted of the psychology resident claiming that there had been no abuse. The meeting was cut short, and I was escorted back downstairs, where I was met by two security guards who told me that I had to delete my pictures, or they would call the cops on me. I smiled at the guards and deleted the pictures, knowing the photos had already synced to my iPad at home, and knowing that my attorney had a copy of the pictures I'd taken Tuesday.

The DCF investigator called me the following week and asked me to send her the photos I'd taken, which I did. As it turned out, she ended up dismissing the case, saying there was no evidence to substantiate the claim. I asked her about the photos, and she said they could be of anyone, any place, any time; I told her if she'd asked for clarification, I could have included photos that clearly showed my son's whole face, not just a close-up of the bruise, and that you could recognize the ones of his arms and back by certain distinguishing marks, a watchband, and his clothing. I told her that the photos had a time and date stamp as well. She said it was too late, that the investigation was closed and couldn't be reopened. I called my state senator and tried to get some help from him, but after an initial conversation, he turned things over to his assistant, and she bought everything the psychology resident told her, hook, line, and sinker. There would be no help there.

I contacted the director of the FACT program and updated her on all that had happened since our meeting with the treatment team. She agreed to re-evaluate my son for the FACT program. The next day, she called the psychology resident to ask about my son, and the resident told her it would be a violation of HIPAA to talk about him and wrote a nasty email to my case manager, my attorney, and me, telling us not to contact FACT.

I called and made an appointment with the hospital administrator. She followed up by telling me we would meet with the entire treatment team. I told her that I wanted to meet with her alone first, and I took a witness with me. The hospital administrator listened carefully to my concerns, and then we met with the treatment team. She told them to get busy and make the placement with FACT happen. By the end of the next day, FACT had evaluated and accepted my son, and by the next week, he was home with me, under the supervision of FACT. At the hearing, the doctor testified that there had been no behavior problems with my son, no incidents, no concerns—yet they had thrown him on a closed ward and taken away his freedom of movement! He said there was no other medical condition that might be affecting my son. As one lie after another came out of this man's mouth, I sat there and kept my mouth shut, knowing that I had to get my son out of there, out of the place I'd trusted to keep him safe, even though I was anxious and uncertain about what the outcome might be.

Despite my trepidations, my son has done really well since he's been home. He takes his meds, sees someone from FACT three times a week, sees their psychiatrist (first weekly, then bi-weekly, now monthly), and attends a group once a week. They're there for support in any crisis, just a phone call away. The doctor has increased his Zyprexa and checked his Depakote level—something that the hospital NEVER checked. Outbursts of anger are rare and end quickly. He believes that he's been healed by God and that the Holy Trinity talks to him all the time, guiding him in everything that he does. He's happy, laughs loudly and frequently, and seems very content—but he also isn't doing as well as he was initially. Medicare Part D insurance suddenly denied one of the medications he was taking, Namenda (or memantine). We've appealed their denial twice and have lost both times. Finally, the pharmaceutical company that manufactures the drug has agreed to supply the medication for a year. My once outgoing, "never met a stranger" son no longer wants to leave the house because it makes him too anxious, and it takes him longer to process information.

He's more forgetful and a little more irritable. Is it because he's no longer taking the Namenda? I don't know. It's the only thing that's changed in the months that he's been home.

I count my blessings daily. My son is clean and sober, and he says he has no desire to drink or use drugs. He's happy just doing things around the house, and he's so loving and thoughtful. He loves to pick flowers from the yard and put them in vases around the house to surprise me. He's started playing a little music on his guitar again. He takes his meds and goes to medical appointments without any problems—but he won't go out to eat, to a movie, to a store, or anywhere else without a fight, so I don't push him to do those things. Anything that indicates that I think he still has HD makes him angry, so we don't talk about it. I hope and pray that stem cell research and/or RNA-interference are going to give us a cure, SOON! That cure they promised we'd have within ten years of discovery of the huntingtin gene is long, long overdue; it's now been 22 years since the gene was discovered.

The journey with my son is certainly easier than it was with Paul because there are now meds to treat the cognitive, behavioral, and psychiatric symptoms—if you can get insurance to cover it—and *some* doctors are beginning to acknowledge that there's a lot more to this disease than chorea. The official diagnostic criteria needs to change, though, so that the people with HD who *don't* have chorea don't just fall through the cracks. We need FDA-approved drugs to treat the psychiatric and cognitive effects of HD. Right now, the *only* FDA-approved drug is Xenazine (tetrabenazine), and that is strictly for chorea and carries a warning label that it can increase the chances of depression and suicide. No one should have to fight the battles I've fought for my son. And what do people do if they don't have advocates who *can* fight on their behalf?

Living with HD is an ever-changing, ever-challenging journey. It's ripped my family apart, destroying people along the way, and has stolen every dream any of us had about the future, but it's also brought into my life some of the most amazing, most caring people I've ever known. It's given me a strength I didn't know I had. It's given me opportunities to help others, something that makes me feel like I'm at least doing *something* to make a difference, even if I can't "fix" this monstrous disease for my son. I can only hope and pray that a cure is found in time to save my strong, loving, intelligent, talented, beautiful son from the ravages of what has been called "the cruelest disease known to man."

This has, without a doubt, been a journey straight into the storm, a journey that was foreshadowed 32 years ago by the church-rattling clap of thunder that marked the beginning of my life with Paul and the end of life as I dreamed it would be.

—⁓—

Please consider making a donation to Dr. Jan Nolta, stem cell research scientist, via Help 4 HD International, Inc., a nonprofit organization.

Donations can be made via their secure web site, http://www.research4hd.org/Researchers.html, or by mailing a check to:

Help 4 HD International, Inc.
436 Playa Blanca Street
Santa Maria, CA 93455

In the "memo" section of the check, please specify "Dr. Jan Nolta."

You can also contact Help 4 HD International at 805-441-5618.

About Katie Jackson

Katie Jackson lives in Sacramento, California, with her husband, Mike, and three beautiful children. Katie is the president and CEO of Help 4 HD International, a nonprofit organization serving the Huntington's community. Some of the programs Katie is most proud of are: The HD View radio show with over 87,000 listeners, the Clinical Trial Support Platform, *The Huntington's Post* newspaper, *Help 4 HD Magazine*, H4HDiRegister (a Patient Registry), Research 4 HD, and Help 4 JHD. Katie has played a key role in creating and implementing many of Help 4 HD International's programs and platforms. She speaks at government events and many symposia, conventions, and summits about HD. She has also spoken on funding grants for HD research. As a former Huntington's Disease Ambassador for Lundbeck Pharmaceuticals, Katie was able to travel to many different support groups and educational events all over the country to speak about numerous subjects like safe-proofing a house for one who lives with a movement disorder, caregiver support, research, and many other important topics. Katie is the published author of a novel entitled *Ferris Wheel*. Although Katie's novel is fiction, it mirrors much of her life as a patient advocate. The book helped launch and propel Katie's advocate journey.

Katie's writing has also been featured in numerous medical blogs, publications, and media outlets. Katie sits on many directing boards, advisory boards, and committees for different institutions and organizations. She has received humanitarian and leadership awards recognizing her dedication as a patient advocate for the HD community.

CHAPTER 12

When Strength and Resilience Are Your Only Option

By Katie Jackson

I was in the middle of my first year of college when one night, one conversation was going to take me on a journey that would forever change my life. If you had asked me back then if I were strong enough to handle this journey, I would have told you there was no way. The one thing this journey has taught me is that you don't know how strong and resilient you are until strong and resilient is the only choice you have.

My roommate and I lived in a house on a very busy street full of small houses filled with college students. It was a street full of excitement, the perfect street to live on for the social aspect of college life. I had met my best friend in kindergarten. We always said as children that we would be roommates and go to the same college. Sticking to our word, we ended up living on a street one block away from the college we attended. We were excited to get a house on this street because not only was it the prime location, but also my roommate's cousin had rented a townhouse a couple of houses down with two of his longtime friends. We all had known each other for years, so it seemed to be a great living situation for us girls.

One night, a couple of weeks into school, my roommate's cousin called to tell us they were throwing a party. We decided that we would stop in real quickly and see everyone before we headed to another friend's place. When we got to the guys' house, it was crazy. There were tons of people hanging out, like a typical Saturday night party at Chico State. We made our way through the kitchen to get something to drink. That's where it all started. We were all standing there when Mike walked up to our group. I had known Mike for many years. I saw him here and there when I would visit my best friend at her cousin's house. I had heard that Mike was moving up to Chico to take over one of the spare rooms the guys had. From what I understood, Mike wasn't going to attend any classes but was just moving up to Chico to work and hang out with his friends.

Mike walked up to us, and we all said our hellos. When Mike's eyes met mine, they locked on me. He held his stare long enough that everyone, including me, could see something was there between the two of us that had never been there before. I started to breathe heavily and noticed that Mike's eyes were green, something I had never noticed in all the years I had known him. I guess I had never looked at him that closely before. The way that my whole body became hot, and I felt like my face was sweltering with heat, I must have been attracted to him, another thing I had never noticed before. I smiled and then made my way outside to get some air.

By that time, all of my friends had scattered, and everyone went their own way. I decided I was going to make my way back inside to check on one of my friends that was in the house. I thought my body temperature was back to a normal level, and I hoped that my face was once again white instead of beet red with embarrassment.

Right before I got to the door, Mike was walking out. I almost ran right into him. Once again, our eyes locked, and there went my body temperature again. I could not understand what was wrong with me or what he was doing to me. After a long moment of awkward silence and a dead stare at each other, I told Mike I was heading inside. He told me that he had been looking everywhere for me. I can only imagine what my face must have looked like. I was confused about why Mike would be looking for me. He asked me if I would go for a walk with him so we could talk. Out of curiosity, I agreed to go with him. We walked around to the back of the street, away from everyone. He stopped, and I turned around, and just like that, we were face to face. Standing right there, looking in his eyes, I realized something I had never noticed before. "Oh, man! Mike is actually really good looking, and I really hope he feels the same about me!"

Then I started to feel a little reserved because I'd just noticed how attracted I was to him. My head started to spin. I went into panic mode about what I was supposed to do. I'd never had this problem with him before. This was just some guy I saw here and there. A guy I would say a quick hello to and go on my way. I was always so cool and nonchalant around him. Oh, how I wished for those feelings to come back. Now I was a nervous wreck, full of anxiety. I was breathing heavily and wondering what he was thinking.

Finally, he broke the silence and interrupted the thoughts running through my head when he shifted me and leaned me up against the wall of the back of the townhouse. He asked me if I had ever thought of him and me together. I looked at him bemused because the reality was I had never thought of us in any way other than what we were, acquaintances. He leaned in really close to me. There I was, confined between a wall and Mike's body. Then I noticed that he was responding the same way I was. He was trying to seem confident, but I could see the tension in his move-ments as well. This made me feel a little better because I quickly learned that I wasn't the only one feeling what I was feeling. Mike stumbled over his words about how beautiful I looked tonight and how he had been thinking about me for weeks but didn't know how he should approach me about how he was feeling. Right then, I felt his one hand touch my cheek. As he was moving in towards me, I was thinking, "What is going on?"

Before I could think another thought, I felt his lips on mine, and I in-stantly melted into him. That was it: the beginning of my story with Mike. That was my first night with Mike, and here I am writing this 15 years later, and I have only spent a couple of nights away from him since then.

The next couple of months were amazing. We quickly got to know each other, and I rapidly learned that I wanted to be with this man forever. I remember lying in bed with Mike in the beginning of our relationship and feeling like I couldn't get close enough to him. I would lie there and let him hold me as he slept, trying to push into him as close as I possibly could. I had never felt like this with anyone before. I fell deeply in love with Mike like I had never fallen before.

Mike and I were married a couple of years later. We had two beautiful children. I was doing well in my career, and Mike was working as a sheriff's deputy. We had just bought our first house, and life couldn't have been more perfect. I couldn't believe that I was 25 years old and literally had everything I had ever wanted. Looking back on that time, I would do anything to go back to that. We of course had worries, but they were all so superficial. We were healthy and happy; life was perfect. Little did I know that this was all about to change. My carefree life was getting ready to be turned upside down.

The last time Mike had seen his biological father, he was six years old. Mike told me that his biological father was sick with something called Huntington's disease. He really never talked about his father. I asked questions here and there over the years. Mike was always so good about telling me what he knew, but the conversations were typically very short. I could tell it made my husband uncomfortable to talk about his biological father. I would ask him about his father's illness, but he really didn't know much about it. His mom and dad had divorced, his mom had moved to Northern California from Central California, and he hadn't seen his father since. He did talk about how he had tried to contact his father a couple of times, but the conversations didn't go well, so he left it alone. Mike's mother had married a remarkable man who had stepped up and was everything Mike needed in a dad. He loved Mike as his own, and Mike had and still to this day has an amazing relationship with him. I believe that Mike is the man he is because of his stepfather. Mike was a hard worker that always put his family first and foremost, and that is what his stepdad has always done. Although Mike knew his biological father was sick, I think he was "out of sight, out of mind," and Mike was protected from what his reality was soon going to become as well.

We had been married for almost three years when we received a phone call that Mike's father had passed away. Mike was told that he had to go sign some paperwork at the mortuary. That night, Mike and I had the deepest conversation we had ever had about Huntington's disease. When Mike fell asleep, I got out of bed and headed to our computer. I was in bed, tossing and turning with so many unanswered questions about what Huntington's disease was, that I decided I would do some research of my own. I just ran a quick web search on Huntington's disease. I couldn't believe what I was reading. It almost seemed like the words were popping out of my computer at me. Cognitive impairment, psychosis, hallucinations, dementia, involuntary movements, choking, loss of one's ability to take care of oneself, dystonia, depression, suicidal thoughts, the list went on and on. I felt the tears start to flow down my face. I felt so bad for Mike's dad and the pain and suffering he must have had to endure with this horrific disease. Then I read the single most terrifying thing I have ever read in my life: each child born to an individual with Huntington's disease has a 50 percent chance of inheriting the disease. As I read that sentence, I literally felt like someone had just punched me in the stomach. I couldn't breathe, and I felt like all the oxygen was sucked out of my lungs, and I was suffocating. Panic was setting in. I must be having a nightmare, and I just wanted to wake up. This terrifying fate could *not* be my new reality. This couldn't be happening to me and my family. "Wake up!" I kept thinking. "This can't be really happening!"

This was a horrifying awakening for me. This meant that my husband, this amazing father and brave, strong sheriff, my one and only partner in this world, had a 50 percent chance of inheriting his father's same fate. If that weren't enough, another reality hit me like a ton of bricks, crushing my soul. If my husband ended up testing positive for Huntington's disease, that meant my two babies, my little girl and baby boy, also would have a 50 percent chance of getting Huntington's disease. The room started to spin, and I knew I had to close the computer and go to bed. Mike hadn't been diagnosed yet. There was a 50 percent chance that Mike wouldn't get Huntington's disease. I tried to tell myself that over and over in my head. I crawled into bed that night and cried silently all night so I wouldn't wake my husband. I decided in that moment that I wouldn't push my husband. He would make the decision if he wanted to be tested for Huntington's disease. It was his body, and I told myself I would support him in whatever his choice was as far as being tested. Little did I know it wasn't going to be long before a decision would be made about testing.

We drove out the next day to the mortuary where my husband had to sign paperwork. I tried to gauge how my husband was feeling on the way there, but there really was no emotion coming from him. To this day, I am not sure how he was really feeling throughout that day because he didn't want to talk much about it. On the way, I asked Mike how he was doing. He said, "Katie, I have decided I am going to go to the doctor and get tested to see if I have Huntington's disease."

At first, I didn't say anything. I didn't know what to say. Was ignorance bliss? What was this simple blood draw going to do to our lives? I didn't know how I felt about my husband making this very huge, life-changing decision. I did know it was not my decision to make. It was his decision, and it was clear to me his mind was made up. He wanted to know if he was positive or negative, a decision that must have been so hard for him to make, but he was strong and said he had to know. I wanted to hold him and protect him from all of it. I wanted to go back in time and never answer the call we'd received about his father's passing. I wanted it all to go away for me, for our children, but most of all for him. For once, my strong husband who had cared and protected me for so long from so many things needed me to protect him. I wanted to protect him, but I soon learned there was nothing I could do to shield him from the genetic fate of Huntington's disease.

We made an appointment to see our primary care doctor, figuring we could start there. When we went to see him, we told him that Mike's father had just passed away and had Huntington's disease. Mike asked the doctor if he could test him for it. The doctor looked at us, kind of perplexed. He walked over to his computer and started looking something up. I asked him if he had ever seen a patient with Huntington's disease. He admitted he hadn't and was looking up how to put the orders in to the lab. He told us he hadn't had a patient that had come to him before to be tested. He said that typically we would see a neurologist for testing of this type. He found the lab code and said Mike could go to their lab and get his blood drawn and that he would call us with the results when they came in. I asked him how long it would take, and he said he really didn't know, but it would probably take around seven days. We then walked down the hall to the lab. I remember that walk because I felt like this one simple blood test would change everything. Mike didn't say a word as we walked down the hall. He didn't have to; I sometimes knew Mike better, I think, than he knew himself. I knew that he was scared of what this simple test would tell. I knew that he wanted to be brave and act like it wasn't a big deal in order to protect me.

When we got about halfway down the hall, I reached out and grabbed his hand. He didn't look over at me or say anything, although he held my hand a little tighter than he normally did, and right then, I knew that we were in this together, no matter what. We had made a vow to each other "in sickness and in health." So many people take those vows, really not thinking what that promise actually means. In health, life is easy, and you really don't understand how easy "in health" is until that health may be taken away. I also thought of another vow I'd taken, and that was "for better or worse." Could I endure the "worse"? As we got to the lab, and Mike was called back, I couldn't help but wonder whether Mike was doing the right thing by being tested. I remember feeling like we were getting ready to open Pandora's Box.

It had been eight days since Mike had given his blood sample. Every day we would wonder, "Is today the day?" On day eight, though, we didn't really think about Mike's test results coming in because we had other things on our mind. Mike was attending a funeral that day for an officer who had died in the line of duty. When an officer dies in the line of duty, the whole department comes together to honor that person. It really is like a family, especially the department my husband worked for. I remember that day like it was yesterday. Mike had waked up early and was all dressed in uniform to go to the funeral. I knew this would be a hard day for him, but at that time, I didn't realize how much more devastating this day was going to become. I kissed him goodbye and told him I loved him.

An hour or so had passed, and I was taking care of our son, who was a couple of months old. My phone rang, and it was Mike calling to tell me he was going to turn his phone off, but he would call me after the funeral. A couple of minutes later, my phone rang again, and I thought it was probably Mike and that he'd forgotten to tell me something. When I answered, there was a man's voice that I didn't recognize. The man told me his name and said that Mike's doctor was away, but he had received Mike's test results. I explained to him that Mike was at a funeral and that I could have him call back when he got home. He told me that Mike had signed a release that said he could give me Mike's results. I could tell by his voice that something wasn't right. I quickly became aware that I was about to receive the single worst news I had ever heard in my life. I told him that I could tell by his voice that it didn't sound good. He told me that he was so sorry, but Mike had tested positive for Huntington's disease.

My legs started to shake, and I fell to the floor. The doctor on the phone kept talking, although I had no clue what he was saying. I was in shock. He said my name when he realized I wasn't responding to his question. I couldn't listen or hear anymore. I didn't *want* to hear anymore. I had heard what Mike's results were, and all I wanted at that moment was my husband. I wanted to grab him and run away and hide him from all of this. I wanted to protect him, and I could not believe that this was our new reality. As all of this was running through my head, all I remembered was the doctor asking if I would like the number for the neurologist to whom they were referring Mike. I told him I couldn't talk about it right now, and I hung up the phone. I sat what seemed like forever on the floor. Then it hit me; I still had to tell Mike that he had tested positive for Huntington's disease. The feeling of having to tell my husband this news was overwhelming. I had no clue how I was going to do it. I wished he were home, and the doctor could have told him. Then I realized that this had happened for a reason. I was the one that was meant to tell my husband his test results, and I had to be strong for him and think of the right way, if there was a right way, to tell him.

I waited for Mike to call me. I arranged for my mom to take the baby and pick up our daughter from school. I kept calling Mike's phone over and over, but his phone was still off. I paced around the house and had moments of falling apart and then had to pull myself together. I had to be strong for him and for our family. I couldn't let our family fall apart. This was our new reality, and we were going to deal with it and get through it together. After an hour or so, my phone rang, and it was Mike, telling me he was heading back to work. I asked him if I could come get him, and we could go get something to eat. I felt bad not telling him right away, but this was something I was not willing to tell him over the phone. Mike said that would be fine and to come pick him up. I somehow in the sea of people was able to find Mike. When Mike got in the car, it took everything in me not to fall apart. As we started to head towards home, Mike asked me if I thought that it was strange that the doctor hadn't called him yet with his test results. I didn't answer him because I couldn't lie to him, but I also didn't want to tell him as we were driving. He then told me that he didn't want me to worry. He thought everything was going to be fine. He told me he had a feeling he was going to test negative, and we could put this whole nightmare behind us. I found a street to pull off the road because I felt my eyes well up with tears. Mike stared at me with shock and confusion. He asked me what I was doing. I leaned over and grabbed his hand. I told him that his doctor had called with his test results. He looked at me and told me, "Well, I guess that is that. I have Huntington's disease."

I leaned over and put my head on his shoulder. I told him we were going to get through this. I was there, and I was going to be there. I told him he was not alone, and we were going to go to a neurologist and see what they could do. There had to be something they could do, right? I remember looking though website after website to see what type of treatments they were doing for people with Huntington's disease. I couldn't find anything on the computer. I figured the neurologist would know what to do. He or she would be the expert and would help Mike. We would fight this, and he would survive. Looking back on these thoughts I had, I realize now how much we didn't know about Huntington's disease. We were ignorant, and I was holding onto the hope that the neurologist would have the answers, and we would be okay. I knew that there was going to be a lot that Mike would have to go through, but the doctors would help. It is amazing, looking back and reflecting on these thoughts I had, just how little I knew about Huntington's disease. Oh, how quickly I was getting ready to learn how wrong I truly was.

We were both nervous walking into that first appointment to meet Mike's new neurologist. We were also anxious to finally get some answers to so many questions we had. Mike had done a lot of research on his own and started taking many vitamins and supplements. He had brought all of these vitamins and supplements to his appointment. He was excited to talk in further detail about other things he should be doing as well. I was wondering what they were going to do for Mike. The answer to that question was coming, and I didn't realize how devastating the answer was going to be. The neurologist finally entered the room after running over an hour late. He was very disengaged and acted like it was a bother that we were in his office. He was looking over Mike's records, and then he looked at us and asked, "What can I do for you?"

Mike told him that he had just gotten his results, and he had tested positive for Huntington's disease. Mike said, "I was just wondering what medication I should be on and if there is anything I should be doing."

The neurologist looked at Mike and me with a blank, cold stare and said, "Well, there is nothing you *can* do. It is Huntington's disease. There is nothing I can do for you." He said maybe in the future, if symptoms started to appear, there might be some medications he could prescribe that could help with the symptoms like his moods, but that was really it. He added, "Maybe you can find a support group, or I am sure they have a society or something."

That was it. He stood up to walk out of the room. He had given us five minutes of his time with no compassion and absolutely no direction whatsoever. I looked over at Mike, and I saw him put his head down. This horrible neurologist had just broken my husband's spirit. My husband put his head down, and I put my head up. No one was going to treat us like this. I am a very reasonable person, but I am strong, and I was not going to let this man make my husband feel the way he was feeling. I stood up and asked him right as he was exiting the room how many people he had seen with Huntington's disease. He admitted he had only seen a handful. I asked him if he had any patients at that time with Huntington's disease. He told me he didn't. I looked him straight in the eye and told him, "Thank God for that." I told him he was a terrible person for the way he had treated us.

He actually had the nerve to say to me, "Well, you can call if you need another appointment." I started laughing and told him that we would never see him again. I grabbed my purse and stomped out of the office, making comments my whole way out. When I got outside, I felt bad for acting that way in front of Mike. I told him I was sorry for totally losing it. He started laughing and told me that I had just said everything he was thinking.

Then Mike said, "Well, what do we do now?"

I called information right there in the parking lot. I knew I had to act right away. I had to find Mike a good, compassionate doctor that was willing to help us. I knew that there were no therapies, no treatment, and no cure for Huntington's disease, but there were other things out there. I wasn't going to give up till I found the right doctor for Mike.

I reached out and called a Huntington's disease organization. The neurologist in the office had said he was sure there was a society or something like that out there. I figured I would start there. I called information and just asked for anything Huntington's disease. I had no clue where or whom I was calling, but I figured I had to start somewhere. A lady picked up the phone, and I asked her if she knew of any Huntington's disease experts around the Sacramento, California area. She said she didn't handle the whole medical thing, but she had a number for someone who might be able to help me. I hung up and called the number the lady gave me right away. Little did I know I was making the single most important phone call I have ever made in my life.

A lady answered that second phone call, and I instantly started flooding her with what had happened to us over the last couple of days. The lady on the phone was so kind and gave me 100 percent of her attention. She asked me where we lived, and I told her in the Sacramento area, but I admitted I had no clue where I had just called. She laughed a little and said that I had just called the UC Davis Huntington's Disease Center of Excellence. I was shocked and relieved to hear that there were experts in Huntington's disease right in our own backyard. The lady on the phone asked me if I would like to schedule an appointment to see the neurologist and the team at the HD clinic. I couldn't get an appointment fast enough. I had so many questions, and I could tell just by talking to this lady on the phone for ten minutes, if I was going to get any answers, that was going to be the place. I didn't know how important the lady I was speaking with on the phone was going to become to my husband and me.

Terry Tempkin, nurse practitioner at the Huntington's Disease Center of Excellence, was the lady who answered the phone that day. She is one of the most intelligent, compassionate, and kindest women I have ever met, even to this day. Terry has done more for Mike than she will ever know. Terry has a way with Mike. He respects and trusts Terry and listens to any and all advice that Terry gives him. I know that we could be in a whole different place if it weren't for Terry and the expert care she has always provided for Mike. She has helped us through so much over the years when it comes to Mike's care. I will forever be grateful for all Terry has done for Mike and me. I am so thankful to have an expert like Terry to turn to when it comes to Mike's care.

Our first appointment at the UC Davis Center of Excellence was more than I could have ever asked for. Did they have a magic answer to all of this? Of course the answer to that is no, they didn't. There was no treatment, no therapies, no cure. What they did have, though, was compassion, and they were a wealth of information for me when it came to Huntington's disease. The incredible Dr. Vicki Wheelock was like night and day compared to the other neurologist we'd had to deal with. She is very soft spoken and made us feel so comfortable right away. I felt comfortable asking her very hard questions, and nothing I asked seemed to shock her. She was remarkable from the very first meeting, and I knew that we had found our home when it came to caring for Mike. I have never met a medical doctor like Dr. Wheelock, and I doubt I ever will again. She is in a class of her own, and I am so thankful to have found her.

I also loved that there were so many clinical trials going on right there at UC Davis. From the very first visit, we started talking about clinical trials, a world about which I really had no clue. Our amazing medical care team at UC Davis started teaching us about clinical trials right from the first appointment. We knew from the start that if we ever wanted to see any new treatments or therapies for Huntington's disease, we would have to rely on research. Mike enrolled in his first one right away, which was looking at CoQ10 possibly being a potential treatment for Huntington's disease. That trial established, unfortunately, that CoQ10 was an ineffective treatment for HD. We didn't understand back then the importance of retaining a clinical trial. If we want to see new therapies and treatments for Huntington's disease, we have to retain the trial all the way through for good solid data for the Food and Drug Administration to review. Looking back, I feel bad that we didn't retain that CoQ10 trial and that we dropped out very early on. If someone asks me, "Why didn't you retain that very first trial you guys were in?" my answer to that is that Mike probably wasn't ready for it at that time. He was in a state of denial at first and wanted to act like HD simply wasn't there. We now, though, years later, have participated in four clinical studies since then and have followed them through. We now understand the important role we must play in bringing new treatments and therapies to our Huntington's disease community. When we first decided to participate, we had two beautiful children at risk, and we understood that our children or children's children and all generations to come depended on the change we've started today.

At that time, Mike was still in the very early stages of Huntington's disease, and we only had to go to the HD clinic once a year. Mike and I decided we would take an "out of sight, out of mind" approach to the whole situation. We decided we were going to go on living, and we would handle things as they came. We decided we were going to travel. There were so many places that Mike and I wanted to see. We knew that there was no better time than now to travel. Although the kids were young, Mike had minimal symptoms, and we decided to take advantage of the time we had while he was well and to live life to the fullest.

One night, about a year after Mike was diagnosed, he and I were in our living room, watching TV. Suddenly, out of the corner of my eye, I noticed that Mike's finger was twitching up and down. I walked over and sat next to him. I put his finger on my leg and watched it move up and down. I asked Mike if he could stop moving his finger. He put his head down and wouldn't look at me. He mumbled under his breath that he couldn't stop it. I asked him how long it had been going on. He admitted that it had been happening on and off for a while. He told me that he didn't want to tell me because he didn't want to worry me. That was the start of my husband's long journey of dealing with chorea, the involuntary movement that is often associated with Huntington's disease.

Once Mike's chorea got worse, it seemed like he couldn't handle what was happening to him. I think the diagnosis for him was one thing, but once the symptoms of Huntington's disease started to show, the reality that he was getting sicker was too much for him to handle. Mike started self-medicating with alcohol. At first, I thought that it would pass. I would make every excuse in the book for him. I would say that dealing with a very high stress job on top of knowing he was going to die was just so much on him. I thought, "He's just trying to get through it, and once he works it out, he will stop drinking."

This wasn't the case at all. Mike started drinking every night. It wasn't that as much as the amount he was drinking. He would get to the point that he would just pass out every night. It started to scare me for him to be around our small children. He would get so drunk that he couldn't walk, and he would be falling everywhere. He fell on many occasions and hurt himself. I couldn't stand what he was becoming, and I couldn't sit back and let my children witness how their father was acting. I had many serious talks with Mike. We tried to go to counseling, but nothing seemed to help. He was on a road of destruction, and I wasn't going to let our family go down with him. I tried to explain to him that he was our children's hero, and this thing he was going through was going to mess everything up. I told him I had tried to hide it from the kids, but at that point, it was out of control, and it was horrific that our children had to witness how their father was acting. I told him that our children were already forced to watch

Huntington's disease take everything away from them. I asked him, "Do you want the only memories our children to have of you to be of you being drunk?" I explained to him that this was our time to make everlasting memories with the kids that they could hold tight to if he lost his battle with Huntington's disease. This was not the time to mess everything up. After I exhausted everything I could as far as trying to help Mike, I decided it was time to leave him. That was the hardest thing I have ever done. I remember, as Mike packed up his stuff and moved out of our house, I felt like I was losing a part of myself.

The first night Mike moved out of our home, I had never cried so hard in my life. I remember getting in the shower and sobbing for the longest time. I was so worried about Mike. I wasn't there to watch over him. I wasn't there to help him if he fell and knocked himself out. I was terrified for him, and I felt like I was failing him as a wife. I had a decision put in front of me. I could stay and protect Mike forever as he continued to ruin himself and our family, or I could protect my children and get them away from their father, who was making very poor choices. I always told Mike, though, if he could clean up and really show me he was serious about changing his life, I would be there to support him. Thank goodness that was a choice he would make soon after he left.

The one thing about my husband is he loves his children more than anything in the world. It was killing him not being able to see me or his children every day. The days that I had the kids with me, he would call us nonstop. He missed his family, and we missed him. That is what it took for Mike to get help. Mike started to go to AA (Alcoholics Anonymous). He was so dedicated and would go every single night. We slowly started to go out to dinner and do things all together again as a family. When Mike had been sober for a couple of months, he moved back home. I can imagine it wasn't easy on my husband, but he has been sober now four years, and I am so proud of him for making that change for our children and fighting through it for our family to stay together.

Right when everything seemed to get on track, Mike's chorea started to get worse. We also started to deal with depression and anxiety. I couldn't believe that right when we had worked out one problem, multiple problems started flooding in with Mike's disease. We saw our neurologist, and she put Mike on some mood stabilizers that helped him so much. I think back to the days that people didn't have the anti-psychotic and mood stabilizer drugs. What an awful time that must have been. I am so thankful that we have ways now to treat depression and the different symptoms that occur when dealing with a mental illness.

We decided it was time for a family trip. Our family had just gone through hell, and it was time for us to escape and get away to somewhere tranquil and beautiful. We chose to go on a cruise and visit six of the Virgin Islands. We thought beaches and sun were exactly what we needed. We liked taking cruises because it was so convenient to take the children. I was a little concerned about going on this vacation. Our last cruise we had been on, Mike had had very little chorea, and he was still really good when it came to his balance and walking. This trip, a lot had changed. Mike's chorea was worse. He had a harder time with depth perception, and he would run into things and stumble all the time. I was concerned, but I wasn't going to let it stop us from spending vacation time together as a family.

The one thing that I learned about very quickly when living with a young husband with a movement disorder is people's lack of compassion and tact. I learned very quickly how judgmental people are and how people have no problem staring at you and making comments. My husband's chorea makes him appear to some people to be drunk or on narcotics. People have no problem whatsoever telling my husband how he looks to them in their eyes. I have always been so proud of my husband, how he just shakes his head and shrugs it off. When I asked him if it bothered him, he said of course it bothered him, but what was he supposed to do about it? He said he couldn't help how he appeared to people, so the best approach in his eyes was just to shrug it off. I, unfortunately, am not as mature as my husband. This leads me back to the cruise.

One night while we were on the ship, our children wanted to go to one of the night parties they were having at the kids' camp. Mike and I decided that we would go to the casino while our kids were off having a blast. We picked our kids up from camp at around 11 p.m. We were walking back to our cabin to go to bed. As we walked through the ship, we had to walk through a bar area that had a live band and a ton of people dancing around. People were definitely having a good time and were pretty intoxicated by the time we were making our way through that area. The kids were busy talking to us about how much fun they'd had, so they didn't notice what was going on around them. The kids were so excited to show their daddy all that they had done at camp that night. My son pulled out a tee shirt he had made and handed it to my husband. As my husband held it out in front of him to look at it, he lost his balance and stumbled. Because of his HD, Mike lost his balance and stumbled. Luckily, he caught himself, and he didn't fall to the ground. Unfortunately, though, that little stumble gave the security guard who was watching Mike from the second we were in his view permission now to come up to us. There was a ton of people around, and many of them had stopped dancing to look at what was going on. The security guard approached my husband. Right in front of our two kids, the security guard told my husband he had had too much, and it was time for him to go back to his room. My kids looked up at their dad as the security guard was pulling out his book to write down our room information. I told him, "My husband has a movement disorder, and he hasn't drunk any alcohol tonight."

That jerk looked at me like I was a complete liar. He told me he didn't want to hear it. I completely lost gravity right there in that moment. I started telling the security guard how ignorant he was and to make sure that he wrote our room number down correctly because I wanted his boss to have something to reference when I told his boss how he had treated a guest. I almost kept going till I pulled myself out of my rage towards this man and looked at Mike and my kids. All three of them had their heads down, and I could tell they all just wanted to go back to our room. Our perfect night had been ruined because of one person's ignorance and lack of compassion and understanding.

This is just one of so many situations Mike and I have had to endure. I wish I could put a permanent shirt on my husband that says, "I can't control the way you see me through your eyes, but maybe look a little harder, and you will see I am not drunk; I am sick." If people would look a little harder, they might see a man who is an amazing father and who is spending valuable quality time with his children. The reality is my husband may not be around to walk his daughters down the aisle when they get married. My husband may not be around to see his children graduate from college. Huntington's disease is going to rob my children and my husband of many great moments in my children's lives, moments that they will want their daddy to be there standing by their side, so every moment counts right now. I realize that life is short, and tomorrow isn't a promise to any of us. Although most people will get to watch and experience most of the great moments in their children's lives, my husband will miss most of those moments, so that time and those moments we have now being ruined by people's judgment and ignorance is a true disappointment. The one thing that has become very clear to me through this journey I am on is that the general population's lack of human compassion is very scary.

The next day on our trip, I knew that I had to make it the most memorable day ever for Mike and our children. With what we had experienced the night before, I decided that we needed a day of laughs and fun. I booked a tour to hike up a waterfall in Dominica. I figured this was a tour we could do on our own, at our own pace. We could escape the staring, judgmental eyes of the public and go on a little adventure of our own. When we arrived at the waterfall, it started to rain. One would think that this would ruin our little family adventure, but it ended up being perfect. The light rain was refreshing as we made our way up the waterfall. We saw that people up ahead were jumping off the waterfall into a freshwater pool below. Mike asked the kids if they wanted to go to the top and jump off. The kids were excited and jumped on the opportunity to go for a swim. I decided that I would stay behind, at the bottom of the falls, and take pictures of their jump. I sat and watched Mike walk the kids to the top of the hill. He was guiding them and watching their every move. When they got to the top, they all held each other's hands and jumped off. When they all surfaced, they were laughing and splashing each other. I thought as I watched this perfect moment with Mike and the kids, "This is what life is about." Life wasn't about the judgment and the constant defense mode I was always in, trying to protect Mike from the world. Life was about letting all that go and not caring what people thought. If I'd been spending time watching to make sure that no one was staring at my husband, I might have missed that perfect moment that I had just witnessed. Looking back, I wish we could have stayed in that moment forever.

When Mike was diagnosed with Huntington's disease, we decided that we wouldn't have any more children. Since each child born to someone with Huntington's disease has a 50 percent chance of inheriting this devastating disease, we decided to do the responsible thing and make sure we wouldn't have any more children. I know that Mike's decision to get a vasectomy was a very hard decision for him. Of course, no man likes the idea of having a vasectomy, but it was more for Mike than just the invasiveness of it. Mike would have had ten children if I had been willing. He loved being a dad. Mike is a true family man. He adores his children and would have loved having a huge family. Our reality had changed, though, and now we felt it was irresponsible to have any more children.

We spent the next few years enjoying the family we had. Five and a half years later, we received a surprise that we were not expecting. Mike and I went out to dinner one night with our children and one of our friends. I had noticed that I had started to gain weight, and no matter how hard I tried, I wasn't able to get it off. I also wasn't feeling myself. I was extremely tired and woke up in the morning feeling nauseated. At first, I thought I had a flu bug. I realized, though, that this flu bug wasn't going away. That night, when my food arrived, I instantly felt like I was going to be sick. I started to explain to Mike and my friend about how I had been feeling over the past couple of weeks. My friend just blurted out, "Katie, it sounds like you are pregnant!" I started to laugh and responded that there was no possible way I could be pregnant. Mike had a concerned on his face. I could tell he was worried.

When we left the restaurant, I asked Mike if he was okay. He shared that he was very concerned about me being sick for so long. He shared with me that he wouldn't know what to do if something was seriously wrong with me. That's the thing I love about Mike. He wants to always protect me from everything. He was in law enforcement, and it was in his nature to protect. He was especially protective of me and our children. I could tell that his head was going crazy, and I decided I needed to do something to help him. I explained to him that it was probably nothing but a virus, but maybe it would be a good idea for me to run into Target and grab a pregnancy test. Mike agreed that it would be a good idea to rule it out. I joked with Mike and told him, "Wouldn't that just be our luck?"

He responded, laughing, "You know a vasectomy is only 99.999 percent effective." Both of us had a good laugh as we walked down the family planning aisle and grabbed a test. When we returned home, I went in the restroom and took the test. Really not having any feeling at all, a couple of minutes later, I checked the stick for the results. My mouth dropped open, and my eyes welled up with tears when I looked down and saw two lines, plain as day, on the stick. I scrambled for the directions, although having taken this test on numerous occasions in the past, I knew what those lines meant. I called for Mike. Then I sat looking back and forth from the directions to the stick and then back to the directions. Mike ran into the bathroom and grabbed me and held me so tight and asked me what was wrong. I handed him the stick. He started to laugh and said he figured as much by my response. I sat and cried into his chest. After a couple of minutes of him holding me tight and rubbing my back, he pulled back and pulled my chin up so I was looking into his eyes. He asked me why I was crying. He went on to say that we had done this before, and we would be okay.

He said, "Katie, we are going to have a baby, and I am so excited!"

I looked at him, horrified, and wondered how he could be so happy, so excited about this situation. This was everything we were trying to avoid. Mike and I had a long talk that night. He was so excited about having a baby again. He loved babies, and he felt blessed that he was getting a chance to have one of his own once again. He acknowledged that the situation was much different than when we'd had our other children, but he was excited all the same, and he wondered how I could cry over a baby. He assured me it was going to be wonderful, and we once again would get through it together.

The one thing that I loved more than just the support and love that Mike was showing through this pregnancy was that he never once questioned me as to whether it was his baby or not. The thought of this baby not being his never crossed his mind. I was the one who brought up that we needed to go back to the doctor and see what had happened. I knew that something had happened with Mike's vasectomy, and I knew that Mike was going to have to go in and get it redone. When we went to the doctor, he was rude and insensitive. He made a joke, saying that the order of probability was: one, your wife cheated; two, your vasectomy reversed. This was a joke that Mike and I didn't find at all funny. Mike just asked for the test, and we left and never spoke of what the doctor said again. When Mike's result came back, of course he had a sperm count, and the doctor said that he would feel more comfortable with Mike going to a specialist to have his vasectomy redone. Mike was terrified about going through the procedure again. I now say that if you think it is hard to get your husband to go in for a vasectomy, try to get him to go in for the second time when he *really* knows what to expect!

Eventually, I got used to the idea of having another baby and started to get really excited about the new addition that was soon coming. Mike and I had a blast shopping once again for all the baby stuff that we had gotten rid of years ago. Our other children started to get really excited and couldn't wait till their new baby sister arrived. As I got close to my due date, I started to look into cord blood collection. Anyone who knows me knows I am a huge stem cell advocate, and I knew how rich the umbilical cord blood is with stem cells. I started looking into what I wanted to do with the cord blood from my baby.

I decided that I wanted to donate the cord blood to Huntington's disease research. I emailed Dr. Jan Nolta from UC Davis and asked if I could donate my cord blood to UC Davis for Huntington's disease research. Dr. Nolta is the most brilliant scientist I have ever had the pleasure of knowing. Dr. Nolta has dedicated her career and life to finding a therapy for Huntington's disease. She is absolutely amazing, and my Huntington's disease community is so blessed that Dr. Nolta and her brilliant team at the Institute of Regenerative Cures (IRC) at UC Davis are working on HD and JHD. We are forever grateful to Dr. Nolta and the HD team at the IRC for their dedication and countless hours of work that have gone into research for our HD community.

Dr. Nolta put me in contact with Dr. Susan Pontow, who helped me with the process. Dr. Pontow was incredible and right away had a cord blood collection kit ready for me to put in my hospital bag so it would be ready to go when I delivered my baby. A couple of weeks later, I delivered our beautiful, 9-pound, 11-ounce baby girl. The cord blood was collected for Huntington's disease research, and now our family was complete.

Our new baby brought life back to our family. She was exactly what Mike needed. I watched him hold her and just sit and stare at her for hours. He was completely in love with our little girl. We all watched in amazement when Mike would hold her. His movement would almost completely stop. I don't know if it was the endorphins or serotonins or what type of scientific chemical process was going on in my husband's brain, but when he had his baby in his arms, his chorea seemed to disappear. This baby girl was Mike's perfect medication.

As much as Mike and I have been through, as many devastating life-changing events that have happened to us since the term "Huntington's disease" was brought into our lives, I knew one day was coming that would be the single worst day of my husband's life. I knew this day was coming soon. How long could a sheriff's deputy that is now starting to show symptoms of Huntington's disease continue to serve and protect and stick to the oath he took the day he placed that badge on his chest? The answer to that, for us, was not very long.

I remember for as long as I have known Mike, he talked about being in law enforcement. He just knew that that was what he was meant to do. When we were in our early twenties, Mike started the testing process with the sheriff's department. I watched Mike's commitment to the whole process. I knew that he wanted to be a deputy more than anything he ever wanted in his life. Mike had a heart of gold, and he was always trying to protect the innocent.

I remember when we were living in Chico, a guy that lived on our street was yelling at his girlfriend in the middle of the street. I am sure they'd had too much to drink. Mike watched from a distance as the fight escalated. The second the guy raised his hand to hit the girl, Mike took off as fast as he could towards the guy. The girl ran away once the guy's attention focused on Mike instead of her. Mike and the guy got into it a little, and then Mike walked away while the guy continued yelling. Watching that event, I knew that this was what my boyfriend at the time was meant to do. He was meant to protect the innocent.

Mike worked so hard through the whole sheriff's academy. Here we were, a young family with a baby girl. He was amazing at balancing his life.

He loved me, he loved his baby girl, and he loved getting closer to the end of the academy to finally be doing something he had always wanted to do.

I remember through the academy the guys always being around our house. I think because they were all single, they liked coming to a house that had food in the refrigerator. I watched the brotherhood form between Mike and the guys he went through the academy with.

The day Mike came home on the last day of the academy to tell me he had passed and that he was finally done with the academy had to have been one of Mike's brightest days. The days that followed, we got ready for his graduation. We invited our whole family to watch that star be placed on Mike's chest. As we prepared for the big day, Mike talked about who was going to badge him. I sat and listened as he rattled off names and watched my eyes the whole time for my response. I sat there not showing any emotion. Although I wanted to be the one to badge Mike, I wasn't going to say anything. It was his decision, and I knew how important and symbolic it was to get your badge placed on your chest for the first time. As Mike continued to talk about the ceremony, I looked at him and said, "Whoever you decide will be great."

Mike, who was sitting on the floor, fell back, laughing. I looked at him shocked and asked him what he was laughing at. He told me, "Kate, you are crazy. You have supported me through this whole process, and you are my wife. Of course you are the one I want to put my badge on."

Mike is a jokester and loves to mess with me all the time. The one thing about him, though, is he always makes the right decision when it comes to what will make me "happy."

The night of the ceremony was very long. We watched video of the guys being tazered and put into the room to be gassed so they would know what it felt like. I couldn't believe what they put these trainees through, although being in law enforcement is a very important job. People trust you with their lives, and you put your life on the line every day, so it is important that they take the best of the best for these positions.

Then they got to the awards ceremony. I listened as they presented awards to the recruits that stood out for different things. One I remember clearly was the top gun for the deputy that had the highest shooting score throughout the course of their training.

Then they got to the final award. This award was for the "Best Recruit." I thought when they talked about what this award meant that it must be such an honor to receive this award. As they started to talk about the recruit that would be receiving this award, they didn't read the recruit's name at first. They started with "born in Santa Maria, California." I thought, "How funny! Mike was born there." As they went on, and I, by the third or fourth thing, thought, "Wow! That is also like Mike," I learned, oh my gosh, it *was* Mike! I realized that my husband was getting ready to receive the last award of the night, the Best Recruit award. He had no clue he was receiving this award either. I watched his face as it turned, I think when he also realized he was receiving this award. Tears flowed down my face when they read my husband's name. I was so proud of him. I had watched him throughout the course of the academy and had seen how dedicated and committed he was to the department and the training, and I knew also that he 100% deserved that award.

Then it was time for the recruits to be badged and to finally be official sheriff's deputies. I walked up the aisle when I heard Mikes name. He was standing on the stage with the sheriff at the time. I was shaking like crazy as I took the badge from the sheriff to place on my husband's chest. The sheriff leaned over and whispered in my ear, "You are shaking so bad you are going to end up stabbing your husband with the badge."

I started to laugh, and that calmed me down a little. I realized I wasn't shaking because I was nervous at all; I was shaking because I was so proud of Mike. I knew he was exactly right there, in that moment, exactly where he had always wanted to be.

For years, Mike worked for the sheriff's department. He loved his job, and I rarely heard him complain about any part of it, ever. He was working

12-hour shifts, switching back and forth from four days a week to three days a week.

I could tell a couple of years after Mike's first symptoms of Huntington's started to occur that Mike's job was just becoming too much for him. I never talked to him about leaving the department because I knew that even thinking that I thought he couldn't do his job would break his spirit. Because Mike's fatigue continued to become more frequent, though, I did suggest that he should ask the department to lighten his duties.

Mike did so, and the department he worked for was so amazing. They asked Mike where he wanted to be moved. Once Mike told them that he wanted to be moved to the kitchen of the main jail just to watch over the inmates that worked there, they moved him just like that. The next day he was in a new position with a ton of stress taken off his plate.

Mike did better for the next couple of months, but I watched as his symptoms started to become worse. It was always such a gradual progression with Mike, but for some reason, HD was rearing its evil head at much faster speeds towards the end of his career.

One Saturday, Mike came home from work and looked me straight in the eye and told me, "Katie, I am done with work, and I am not going back."

I sat there, shocked, and just looked at him, not knowing what to say. It was so sudden for me. I knew that Mike was getting to the point that he wouldn't be able to work anymore, but I thought we would have more conversations about it before the official end. Mike told me his chorea was becoming so obvious to everyone, and he couldn't hide it anymore. He said the last thing he wanted was to show the inmates any weakness he had because it could jeopardize his or his partner's safety. He also said that people were constantly asking him to repeat what he was saying. I understood Mike, even though he slurred almost all his words. I was used to it, and I had taught myself to understand Mike. Others couldn't understand him, though. He said that he thought he was talking clear as can be, but he said when everyone he talked to asked him to repeat what he had said, it became obvious to him he wasn't as articulate as he thought he was.

I could tell by my husband's eyes that he was crushed down to the core about having to make this decision. The next day, we were hosting a birthday party for our son. We had to keep it together for him to make sure that his birthday was fun, carefree, and that he didn't have an emotional wreck of a mother during his party.

When Mike's parents arrived at the party, I whispered to his mother that Mike had decided to stop working. I had always known that this time was coming, but I think the overwhelming sadness that we felt for Mike's decision to stop working wasn't because Mike decided to stop working; it was that he had fought the battle with Huntington's disease for so long, and this was one of many signs that we knew were coming that meant Mike was losing the battle. Reality hits really hard when you have been in denial and avoidance for so long.

Monday, I started calling different departments within the sheriff's department, trying to get some direction on what I should be doing. They were so helpful and literally took so much pressure off of me. One lady that worked in the human resources department was my lifeline through this whole process. I don't know what I would have done without her. She set up meetings with the county about Mike's retirement. She set up meetings with the benefits department to explain to me all the benefits that Mike had. The sheriff's union stepped in and helped me file and be aware of all of Mike's benefits he had, as far as long term disability.

It was a whirlwind of information that came in really fast. For months, I filled out paperwork and waited for decisions. In the end, the sheriff's department set Mike up so he was making 85 percent of his income. I am so thankful that the sheriff's department watches out for their own and makes sure that if any of their officers are injured or become fatally sick, they are taken care of. I know that the stress I think my husband would have put on himself if he didn't think his family was financially taken care of would be too much for him to bear. Knowing his family is taken care of financially takes one huge stress off my husband. He is already enduring so much that I am glad the sheriff's department has taken the financial stress off us.

Mike has never stepped foot back into his workplace. It isn't because he is resentful; he loves the department and all his brothers that work there. I believe he has never gone back because it is a reminder to him of where he wants to be but can't be for reasons beyond his control that he can't change. The day that some of his coworkers came out to our house to pick up his gun and radio was a very hard day for Mike. He gathered his stuff that he had to return to the department. His gun and radio that he had carried with him and had had for 11 years now had to go back home to the department. The deputies had cleared out Mike's locker for him at work, and they brought his belongings to him the day that they picked up the department's property.

The deputies told Mike they missed him at the jail. He told them he missed work, too, but he needed to now be home with his family, enjoying the time he has left with us. I know those words were hard for Mike to speak, but they rang true. We don't know how much time Mike has left, so it's important to take all that time he has and build memories for his children to always remember him by.

As I mentioned earlier, one thing that Mike and I got involved in very early on in Mike's diagnosis was clinical trials. We knew that if there is ever any hope of a treatment, therapy or cure for Huntington's disease, it lies in research. We knew that we had to play our part as well. We live in the United States of America, and if we ever want to see any of the promising, potential, new research become available to our Huntington's disease community, it would have to go through the clinical trial phases to satisfy the Food and Drug Administration. No clinical trial will be successful without brave individuals stepping up and taking part in the trials. Mike decided right from the beginning that he wanted to be involved in any clinical trials that he qualified for. We now had three children at risk, and we understood the importance that the clinical trials play in our children's future if any of them end up being diagnosed with Huntington's disease.

Mike has been involved in five clinical trials and studies. None of them have been more exciting and hopeful, in our opinion, than the one Mike recently enrolled in over a year ago. Mike enrolled in a clinical study called Pre Cell that will hopefully soon move into HD Cell. HD Cell is a clinical trial that will be using mesenchymal cells as the first potential therapy ever for Huntington's disease. Because Mike and I are both very active stem cell advocates, we couldn't wait to enroll in HD Pre Cell.

I remember eight years ago hearing about Dr. Jan Nolta's science for the first time. I sat at a Huntington's disease conference, completely intrigued and hanging on to every word this wonderful scientist was speaking. Back then, I didn't truly understand that what was being talked about in that moment was going to significantly impact my life so many years later. I watched Dr. Nolta's science very closely over the next couple of years. There was a fear I had, though, from the first day I heard her speak. How was this brilliant science going to be funded? I didn't know much back then about science and what it took to get science from dish to bedside, but what was plain as day to me as a lay person in the science world was that this was going to cost a lot of money. I wondered what we could do to help as a community. A couple of years later, that question was thankfully answered.

I remember when Proposition 71 was put on the ballot. Proposition 71 was the California Stem Cell Research and Cures Initiative. I couldn't wait to go to the polls and vote in favor of Proposition 71. The stem cell field seemed so exciting to me from the very beginning. The potential that the stem cell field holds to relieve the pain and suffering that people are living with when it comes to devastating diseases like Huntington's disease and so many others is amazing. I was a supporter from the day I started to learn about this science and was thrilled to see that California had started a movement as far as funding stem cell science. Of course, Proposition 71 passed, and the amazing CIRM (California Institute of Regenerative Medicine) was formed in 2004.

When I heard that Dr. Vicki Wheelock's project, Pre Cell and HD Cell, was going in front of the Independent Citizens' Oversight Committee (ICOC), the 29-member governing board at CIRM, I knew that I had to go and speak up in front of the ICOC board about the importance of this project to my HD community. I, along with around 30 of my fellow HD advocates, marched into the Burlingame Marriott that day to show how badly we all needed this project funded. This project, to all of us and to all of our HD community, meant one thing and one thing only: HOPE.

When we walked into the banquet room where the meeting was taking place, there was a huge screen on the wall. Diseases were listed on the screen, showing how the different projects had been scored by the scientific review board. When I looked at the screen, I felt goose bumps rise all over my body. There, in the number one spot, was Huntington's disease. Huntington's disease, Dr. Wheelock's project, had been scored number one by the scientific review board! The endless hours of work and dedication by the HD lab team and HD clinic at UC Davis that went into this project is unbelievable. My HD community is so thankful to everyone that has worked so hard on this project. They have given us hope, and I will forever be grateful to all of them for that.

When I walked up to the microphone to speak, I talked about my husband and how difficult it was to watch before my very eyes this horrific disease take everything away from him. I spoke of my children and my children's children and how we desperately need help for the generations to come. "Never underestimate a mother on a mission to save her children," I told them. "There is no greater force in the world." At the end of my talk, I looked up and saw a couple of the ICOC board members with tears in their eyes. I felt so good that they had heard my story and that they understood how important this project was.

Then the most powerful person, in my mind, spoke, although I may be a little biased on this one. My brave husband got up and spoke to the board. He teared up as he talked about his children and how important they are to him. At the end of his speech, he said something I had never heard him say before. As he choked up, he said, "I am dying." Here he was, a 33-year-old man, standing so open and so raw about his feelings about what this disease is doing to him. My eyes, along with many others in the room that day, filled up with tears. The next speaker got up and spoke of her children and how Huntington's disease has affected her life. She was an excellent speaker, and you could feel from the energy in the room that people had gotten a little glimpse into our lives.

Now it was time for business, and the voting began. When the last "yes" was said, we shot confetti wands off in the air. Nineteen million dollars to carry us through phase one, FUNDED! We will forever be grateful to CIRM for funding this historic, groundbreaking, First-In-Human trial for the first-ever potential therapy for Huntington's disease. For me, this day will go down in history as one of the most significant days in our Huntington's journey.

I feel honored to have attended that meeting that day and to have been able to watch history in the making. Now, being a part of this trial with my husband, I feel this has been one of the most important things we have participated in in our lives. We are fighting for a change for our children. That change has to start somewhere, so we are excited to be playing a role in the start of a possible shift in the fate with which we have all been living for so long.

When I was speaking to the police officers' union, I told them about Mike being in a clinical study. I told them how if this future trial using Mesenchymal Stem Cells works, we may have a chance. The sheriff's department has put Mike on an extended leave of absence. That way, if the surgery works, then he could come back to work without having to reapply and go through the crazy process again.

Will Mike ever step into that uniform again? The answer to that is simply unknown. I believe in and have seen scientific medical breakthroughs that have changed lives. Will we see that in Mike's lifetime? Some say there is no way; others think there may be some glimpses of hope. We live our lives real statically, but we are also optimistic. We will not give up the hope until Mike takes his final breath. We are thankful that the sheriff's department has been so supportive of us through the whole process.

One of my newfound missions is to support JHD research. The children suffering with Juvenile Huntington's disease endure so much pain and suffering. There is nothing anyone can do for these children. This is a fate that must change. Children with JHD suffer from seizures, tremors, cognitive loss, dystonia, and so many other terrible symptoms. They lose their ability to walk, they lose their ability to talk, they end up on feeding tubes, and they lose every bit of quality of life. What these innocent, sweet children have to endure is so unfair and unfathomable. I have three children, and all three of them, like all children born to a parent with HD, are at risk for JHD as well. I, of course, was there when each of my children was born and took his or her first breath. I will fight like hell with all my might to try to make sure I am *not* there when they take their last breath. I am a mother on a mission to save my family from the terrible fate that HD promises. I *know* research is the key in that fight. I do all I can do to support research and clinical trials. I fight to be the last generation to have to live with Huntington's disease the way my generation and past generations have been forced to live.

People often ask me how I deal with all of this. My answer to them is, "What other choice do I have?" I am a survivor because I have to be. I have to keep going for my husband and for my children. I have an incredible family and wonderful friends that have supported Mike and me through this journey so far. I have to say, though, that the people who have gotten me through the really tough times have been my HD caregiver friends. The group of women that I have had the honor to meet and be able to work beside are like no other. I can call on them anytime, day or night, and they are there. They understand me and what I am going through. I can get on the phone with them, and I don't have to say much before they know exactly what to say to get me through it. Some of these women have already lived this journey for many years, and I am so thankful to all of them for taking me under their wings and for always being there for me to pull me up and to let me know that I *can* do this.

What will the future hold for Mike and for our family? The answer to that is simply unknown. We just live one day at a time and enjoy the time we have together now.

I will fight till my last breath for new therapies, treatments, and hopefully one day for the cure for Huntington's disease. This is my life, a patient advocate for Huntington's disease, the mother of three beautiful children, and the wife of the strongest, bravest man I have ever known.

—✺—

Please consider making a donation to Dr. Jan Nolta, stem cell research scientist, via Help 4 HD International, Inc., a nonprofit organization.

Donations can be made via their secure web site, http://www.research4hd.org/Researchers.html, or by mailing a check to:

Help 4 HD International, Inc.
436 Playa Blanca Street
Santa Maria, CA 93455

In the "memo" section of the check, please specify "Dr. Jan Nolta."

You can also contact Help 4 HD International at 805-441-5618.

Afterword

About Jimmy Pollard

In 1986, unfamiliar with Huntington's disease, Jimmy Pollard rejected a young woman with it for admission to his nursing home. Her mom called and gently twisted his arm to reconsider the decision. He did. A special education teacher by training and former nursing home administrator, that mom's call set him on a career path in nursing home, assisted living and hospital settings specializing in caring for folks with HD. Over the following three decades, he has become a frequent speaker on many topics related to HD across North America, Europe, and Australia. He now works with the CHDI Foundation, traveling about the United States as a guest speaker at support groups, conferences, and other HD-related events. He is the author of *Hurry Up and Wait! A Cognitive Care Companion for Huntington's Disease,* which has been translated into eight languages by national HD associations around the world, *A Caregiver's Handbook for Advanced Stage Huntington's Disease*, and many other HD publications.

Appreciations and Lessons from a Fellow Traveller

By Jimmy Pollard

When Sharon suggested I write something for this project, I quickly agreed. Generally because I try to help anyone with a project related to advancing the HD cause; particularly because it was she who was asking. "What shall I write?" I asked.

"How about what you've learned from families?"

I hesitated for half a second, remembering that I never do well with deadlines. But then it occurred to me that, for all the times that I have said that I've learned so much from families touched by HD, I should probably think about it and put something on paper. If not, it's just a cliché, almost trite, and probably overused. Like so very many of my professional colleagues, I have learned many lessons from you, ranging from general life lessons to more practical tips related to care. Most of them are difficult to articulate because they are more "appreciations" than "lessons." Many of them have touched me deeply over the last 28 years and are hard to express in writing.

For nearly three decades now, fate has uniquely positioned me to watch several hundred families face all the worries, challenges, fears, and losses that HD has put in front of them. Over 200 have entrusted the extended care of their loved ones to my teammates and me in nursing homes, assisted living centers, and hospitals. My travels around the United States,

Canada, Europe, and Australia have introduced me to at least another 200 who I am glad to call friends, good friends. I've walked closely beside about 50 folks, most of whom have passed now, as they walked their HD roads, over the bumps, through the tough times, into and out of crises, often having to take detours and shortcuts along the way. There were also plenty of good times, poignant moments, small victories, and many belly laughs, too. This has been my "career." Sounds awkward to use that word, doesn't it? But it's been a humbling, gratifying walk down all these folks' roads. I've been one lucky guy.

Care has evolved for folks touched by HD over the years. No longer is the statement, "There's nothing that you can do!" accurate. There are many things you can do to live positively with HD today. Some of the leaders making this point for some time now are Drs. Sheila Simpson of Aberdeen, Scotland; Martha Nance from Minnesota; and Mary Edmondson from North Carolina. Sometimes it's hard to see the forest for the trees from one's road, but advances in medication, rehab and complementary therapies, and neuropsychology allow one to strategize, more than ever before, about how to face HD, how to take it on and live with it at the same time, as well as how caregivers can better go about their support in all its forms.

Recognizing and capitalizing on the advances for this generation, though, still hasn't replaced those feelings of desperation and loneliness in times of crisis and/or exhaustion. It's humbling to watch folks endure these moments. It's times like these that I realize, even using all the strategies and tools at hand, recommended or provided by us professionals, how relatively little we have to offer families. As the gospel song goes, it can be "a lonesome valley . . . that you gotta walk by yourself." That's one lesson.

There's a related lesson in the curriculum, though. One of those "appreciations." In my 63 years, I've never encountered a group of people who have the resilience of families touched by HD. It is something to behold. Now I suspect, as you read this, that you'll agree that your family, for all it has been through, is resilient. I'm also betting that you might think of one or two family members whom you wish were more resilient or who haven't been resilient at all! I'm not naïve about this. But I suspect that can be said about all families, whether or not they're living with HD. And, in some instances, HD can drive a wedge between family members. Overall, though, taking families as a group, your resilience is astonishing! Generation after generation, decade after decade, one challenge after another, it humbles those of us whose families have faced far fewer difficult days. My wish is that you may recognize it and take a degree of comfort, reassurance, and appreciation of it.

Another lesson: The depth of any one person's resilience is unfathomable. But HD's ongoing challenges, repeated losses and relentless nature have a unique way of revealing it. Yes, professionals and friends can "hold space" for folks along their road, but not without beholding a degree of resilience most of us don't nor will ever have.

Looking ahead, folks and families often wonder quietly and ask themselves, "How will we ever get through this?" I've been asked this many times, especially when they find themselves in scenarios that appear hopeless and helpless. I think to myself, "Why ask me? How could I ever know? I haven't walked a mile, or even taken a step, in their shoes." I try to quietly reassure them but refrain from what I really want to say, lest it sound curt, cocky, or overly confident. I want to say, "I don't know how, but I know you will." That's because, with a few exceptions, families do get through the gauntlet of crises and losses without a lot of help, if any. They do. They endure. Time after time, family after family, loved one after loved one, folks endure.

Their endurance is interwoven with their resilience. It's hard to separate one from the other. But when you walk the road alongside them, this endurance shines through. Truth be told, it comes to some folks more readily than others. Some folks, too, have to endure longer than others in their lives. For example, my friend Ruth (as well as my late friend Wanda and a few others) has been carer to her husband, her children, and her grandchildren, all living with HD. But whether one generation or three, this ability to endure, to "get through it," is present in nearly every family that I have come to know.

I suspect endurance doesn't make it feel any easier to carry on. But somehow you do, without ever yielding in your commitment to put one foot in front of the next, in devotion to walk the road with your son, daughter, mom, dad, husband, wife, sister, brother, niece, nephew, uncle, aunt, friend, or lover, no matter what the hardship, with or without help from others. I list all the relationships because I've seen them all, every one of them, more than once. Somehow, people endure and do "get through it." Certainly with profound losses, great sacrifices and hundreds of annoyances from others; but they do. I hope it's not aggravating to hear me say this, another thing to behold. I've been gifted to have seen it up close time and again. Not really a lesson, but another appreciation.

Over 25 years, I've spent two long stints in leadership and management roles in nursing homes that "specialized" in caring for residents with HD. At both facilities, I was fortunate to have worked with "All-Star Teams" of colleagues. Even with the financial constraints of American healthcare and the many challenges posed by nursing home culture, I thought we did a pretty good job. For periods we did an excellent job. We were always trying to improve our programs in real ways. We struggled with fellow managers and staff every day to change the status quo and to accommodate the unique preferences and needs of our atypically younger residents.

We steadily developed a daily day-long schedule of fun, age-appropriate, interesting activities that were well attended by residents. We supported their families, and they supported us. In fact, they actually enjoyed living in these settings! Their families attest to that. Based on family feedback, the level of resident involvement, and independent industry evaluators, we felt pretty good about our work. Many families worked very hard to have loved ones admitted when they needed care for them outside the home. Some even moved long distances to qualify!

But no matter how much fun we had, no matter what the service or how effective it was, no matter how positively their "quality of life" was viewed, nothing we ever did even came close to matching the importance of visits from family. Some families would visit two or three times a year and others two or three times a week. Sometimes, you hear people say that a nursing home's staff becomes the resident's family. Bullcrap! Yes, when you depend on others to feed and bathe you and take you to the bathroom, you do develop a close, unique relationship that sometimes transcends client/employee. But family is family. Family remains family. Family is even more forged by that endurance and resilience. Nothing we paid caregivers do will ever compete with that. Complement it? Sometimes. Supplant it? Never.

There are some things I've learned from families that I may have learned anyway. But I learned them quicker and better because of them. Living these lessons in my own life is no easier than it was for those who showed them to me. One day at a time with these. I hope I can pass them onto my adult children.

"Not a hill I want to die on." I understand this is an old military expression. I first saw it used by a cyberfriend, Maggie, who was caring for her husband. "Pick your battles!" may be another way of saying it. With all love and respect for those who live with or will live with HD, this is taken from a caregiver and may be more applicable to them. I've seen it related to difficulties arising from caring for a loved one, disagreements in interactions with medical and mental health professions, and one's internal struggles in their role as a caregiver. It's a long road. Rough patches, crises, and some longer periods of relatively smoother sailing don't show up on the map. It's unwise to fight every battle and perhaps wiser to live to fight another day. It's hard to give you a few examples because it's hard to predict exactly what HD will throw your way, but I suspect you get what I'm saying.

Most often as it progresses, folks and families face a decision about a feeding tube as swallowing becomes increasingly impaired, and it becomes increasingly difficult to eat safely. Most folks have made their wishes known long before the time is at hand. Some folks and their families decide, "No tube, no way, never!" Others opt for supplemental nutrition via tube or other ways. Both are equally firm and committed to their decisions. Then the time finally arrives.

Sadly, the decision day is predictable. But the manner in which it arrives, the clinical context in which it presents itself, is much harder to envision and can still surprise even in its inevitability. It rarely appears as clearly and simply as it did years before. No matter how firmly committed to tube or no tube, sometimes love, compassion, and practicality subversively creep in and move people to reconsider. Some families resist reconsideration, having consistently and firmly expressed their preference for years. Some are concerned that a new decision made in stress may not be the right decision. A few others are simply embarrassed to change their minds. Either way, it doesn't make it easier for them. From all those families I've learned a simple, but sometimes hard-to-practice, truth: You can always change your mind. I've never seen such a decision reconsidered that didn't work out for the better. Being a somewhat intransigent fellow myself, I've already had opportunities to apply this lesson in my own life.

I learned another lesson from my late friend Ken, father to three and caregiver to his wife. Many of us knew Ken online. He lived in my town, so I knew him in person, too. Rose and Ken were madly in love with each other, apparent to those of us who read his messages online. As he described it, "the most important promise I ever made to her" was to never place her in a nursing home. But as the years went by, HD insidiously ensnared his family in an inept, callous, local human service agency. His kids, helping Dad care for Mom, missed some school. With truant officers and social workers casting the specter of determining his an inadequate home, he broke his own heart by breaking that promise. Ken visited Rose daily thereafter in the nursing home. Their love endured. Both have now passed. I'm certainly not worthy to speak for Ken, but I'm certain that he wouldn't mind me telling you the lesson that he learned and passed on to me: sometimes you have to break a promise to keep a promise. Although it was "the hardest promise (he) ever had to break," his greater unspoken promise to her was to keep their family together and stable. It was tough for this very strong, humble fellow; but for the greater good of their family. I know he'd want you to know their story.

The last lesson is a much easier one to talk about. That is, connecting families touched by HD is a worthy endeavor, allowing them to recognize that their family is just one of a greater worldwide family. I first learned this from Jean Miller in Tampa, Florida, well over twenty years ago. In the subsequent years, she has used her computer to connect countless folks touched by HD around the world. If a corner of the world is wired, Jean has probably connected those local families globally. Countless projects, friendships, and resources can be traced to her love of her late daughter Kelly and her fingers dancing across her keyboard at all hours.

If you can't trace it to Jean, then you can trace it to Sue Wright in Kent in the UK. Because the number is too damn high, it's impossible to count the connections among families that can be traced back to her labors of love. And that's long before Facebook!

As you all already know, it can get pretty lonely walking an HD road. However, so many folks tell of how their global computer families are sources of camaraderie, support, friendship, information, good times shared, and love. Their basic lesson? Connect people! It helps . . . a lot . . . in very real ways that were unavailable to families just a generation ago.

Today, there are many folks who've carried on Jean's and Sue's pioneering connections in all kinds of ways with all kinds of projects too numerous to name here. That's a good thing, a great thing! A tip of the hat to you all!

There's little I can do, say, or write to adequately express my gratitude to all my teachers. I know that it's a rocky road at times for everyone. Just as you cannot escape the progression of HD, you cannot escape periods of exhaustion, discouragement, and loneliness. I wish you a second wind at those times. I hope it kicks in at the most opportune moments. I hope you'll recall all that you have collectively shown me. You have resilience and endurance, for whatever reason, in greater store than the rest of us who haven't been fated to face all that you have. Your own humility and all that's going on around you may obscure what's been so easy for me to see.

There's not a single observation, appreciation, or lesson here that can't help but make me a better husband, father, father-in-law, grandfather, brother, brother-in-law, uncle, friend, colleague, and employee. My family isn't touched directly by HD. If I'm a real student, though, it will continue to be touched indirectly.

Thank you, teachers all. Keep on hangin' in there.

16046876R00215

Printed in Poland
by Amazon Fulfillment
Poland Sp. z o.o., Wrocław